The
Paperless
Law Office

A Practical Guide to
Digitally Powering Your Firm

BENJAMIN F. YALE

AMERICAN BAR ASSOCIATION
Defending Liberty
Pursuing Justice

Cover design by Mary Anne Kulchawik/ABA Publishing

The materials contained herein represent the opinions of the authors and editors and should not be construed to be the views or opinions of the law firms or companies with whom such persons are in partnership with, associated with, or employed by, nor of the American Bar Association, or the General Practice, Solo & Small Firm Division, or the Law Practice Management Section, unless adopted pursuant to the bylaws of the Association.

Nothing contained in this book is to be considered as the rendering of legal advice for specific cases, and readers are responsible for obtaining such advice from their own legal counsel. This book and any forms and agreements herein are intended for educational and informational purposes only.

Printed in the United States of America.

16 15 14 13 12   5 4 3 2

Library of Congress Cataloging-in-Publication Data
Yale, Benjamin F.

Practicing law in the state of paperlessness : digitally empowering the lawyer / By Benjamin F. Yale.
    p. cm.
ISBN 978-1-61438-372-7
    1. Law offices—United States. 2. Practice of law—United States. 3. Trial practice—Technological innovations—United States. 4. Electronic records—Law and legislation—United States. 5. Practice of law—Moral and ethical aspects. 6. Computers—Law and legislation—United States—Trial practice. I. Title.
KF318.Y35 2012
651.5'042—dc23   2012004134

Discounts are available for books ordered in bulk. Special consideration is given to state bars, CLE programs, and other bar-related organizations. Inquire at Book Publishing, ABA Publishing, American Bar Association, 321 North Clark Street, Chicago, Illinois 60654.

www.ShopABA.org

CONTENTS

CHAPTER 5

Hiding the Invisible Digits from Prying Eyes and Purloining Fingers: Confidentiality and Security in the State of Paperlessness 51

CHAPTER 6

Organizing, Analyzing, and Distilling Documents and Information in the State of Paperlessness 59

CHAPTER 7

Communicating and Transmitting Documents in the State of Paperlessness 77

DEDICATION

Some women and men make it their life's work to change and improve the lives of others through the practice of law. These professionals bring intelligence, craft, courage, compassion, and stability to a world that exhibits too little of these qualities. Over the decades I have had the privilege to work with, in front of, and opposite lawyers from coast to coast and border to border. In the process I have met a group of wonderful professionals, many of whom I call friend today.

The tools that we use in our practice have changed dramatically over the last decade or so. What was once a paper chase is now a digital ride. Though the media we work in and the tools have changed, the practice of law—the "being a lawyer"—has not. Paper burdens lawyers needlessly. The mountains of paper mask what lawyers do, even from themselves. Released from paper, the real characteristics of a lawyer—courage, character, intelligence, and compassion—come to the forefront.

While this book is in one sense a "how-to" for the new tools, it is also a reminder of the need to be first and foremost lawyers, professionals making lives better for others.

Counselors and attorneys—here's to you!

ACKNOWLEDGMENTS

This book incorporates the lessons learned from a career of finding better ways to handle the practice of law. I did not apply these lessons alone. The final transitions took place with the help of colleagues. Kristine Reed and Ryan Miltner, law partners and friends, led the office in adopting many of the key transitions that resulted in the paperless office. Ryan also provided key insights in initial drafts, which led to a much better manuscript. As a result of their collaboration, when fortunate events for all of us—but unfortunate for our partnership—came and resulted in us going our separate ways, I was able to effectively and efficiently handle the practice as a sole practitioner.

I learned long ago that my forte was practicing law, not making the wireless work. I just wanted it to work every time when I turned it on. Eric McKinniss, who serves as my administrative assistant and IT guru, makes that possible by keeping all of my apps and electronics working and equipment and software up to date.

Over dinner one night, I shared with Peter Silverman, friend and fellow attorney, that I could alone handle the broad scope of my practice due to my paperless office approach. His reaction was for me to share my experiences with others, which started me on the journey to write this book. It was Pete who connected me with ABA Publishing to get the process started. Then, as the manuscript developed, he provided invaluable comments and suggestions.

The person Pete connected me with at ABA was Tim Brandhorst, whose enthusiasm and encouragement came at the right times as the process from thought to book proceeded.

My son, David, read the manuscript and provided frank comments that certain sections needed work, and they did. One of the results of this was to reorganize the entire book by almost completely reversing the order of the chapters.

My daughter, Jennifer, busy with young children, a husband, and a career, still found time to help. The grandchildren gave me those enjoyable diversions from work so needed in a busy practice.

Most important, this book came about because of my wife, Bonnie. She was the first to celebrate when the book was done. Much of the time spent to write this book came from not spending it with her. Nonetheless, she supported the effort and periodically pulled me away from the work to refresh and replenish the mind.

To all of these, I am grateful.

ABOUT THE AUTHOR

Benjamin F. Yale is a graduate of Yale College and received his JD from Ohio Northern University. He is a member of the Ohio, New Mexico, and Texas bars and has been admitted to practice in the United States Supreme Court, and the Fifth, Sixth, Seventh, Eighth, Ninth, Tenth, Eleventh, and D.C. Federal Circuit Courts of Appeals where he has argued cases. He is also admitted to federal district courts in Ohio, Michigan, Wisconsin, Texas, and New Mexico.

Though he continues to practice in his small hometown of Waynesfield, his practice has evolved into a national practice in agriculture and dairy law. Over the years he has been involved in legal matters in all but three of the 50 states and several matters overseas.

Ben Yale now serves as outside general counsel for two related milk marketing cooperatives, Select Milk Producers, Inc. and Continental Dairy Products, Inc., and their family of associated companies, with whom he has been associated since their formation in 1994. Combined, they are the fifth-largest milk cooperative in the country and a leader in product innovation, production, and sustainability. He has professionally worked with the dairy industry since 1973 in a wide range of regulatory, legislative, pricing, marketing, and management issues.

He is recognized nationally as an expert in dairy policy, law, and regulation. In that regard he has testified before Congress and participated in nearly a hundred milk market order hearings. He is a regular columnist for *Progressive Dairyman,* a national trade magazine.

Prior to practicing law as well as during the early years, he was a systems analyst and consultant for various companies and helped them transition into computers and computer systems.

He lives in Waynesfield with Bonnie, his wife of 38 years. They have two children and two grandchildren.

CHAPTER 1

FREEING THE LAWYER FROM THE PAPER ANCHOR

A form of cross-country is played with two groups of runners. The first (hares) take a head start to blaze a trail with paper shreds (scent). The remaining runners (harriers) follow the scent. Hares win if they reach the goal before they are caught by the harriers. Those who play the game call it "paper chase."

Lawyers play it differently. The first (known as party of the first part) leads off by dropping trails of sheets of paper, bound and unbound. The others (party of the second part) follow this paper trail. It differs from the original because the party of the second part will also leave its own trail of paper. The first party follows the second party's trail while still leaving its own. More complex versions bring in additional parties doing the same thing. Back and forth, round after round, paper here, paper there, until a team reaches a goal or everyone drops from exhaustion or resource depletion.

Law practice begins with paper—notes, case books, phone messages, memoranda, letters. It results in paper—pleadings, motions, wills, contracts, briefs, letters, transcripts, and legal memoranda. Paper moves in the middle—delivering, stacking, filing, storing, producing, and shredding. And in the end there is paper—notebooks, reporters, file cabinets, boxes, folios, shelves, rooms, more shredding, and buildings full of paper.

Paper creates enormous costs. Not just for the paper itself, but for the handling, storing, filing, moving, or shredding of the paper. So prevalent is paper that lawyers often define themselves by how well they move how much of the paper. Litigators become absorbed

1

in moving pleadings and paper. Discovery is defined not in terms of discovering anything, but of counting the pages. Transaction closings create mountains of paper as documents are revised and revised. Junior associates, or staff, are specifically assigned the very important task of keeping the good paper from the bad paper, preserving the first and shredding the boxloads of the second. (Hopefully they get it right.)

Lawyers move for leave to file—not more intelligent or cogent arguments, but more pages of paper.

Offices are located and designed around the movement of paper. Libraries and shelves store the paper in books. Briefcases carry the paper from office to office, building to building. Whole rooms provide space and equipment to print, copy, index, bind, and organize paper. The entire workday for some involves no more than receiving paper, opening envelopes and boxes to get to the paper, distributing paper throughout the firm, collecting other paper, putting that paper into paper, and shipping paper out. Hallways and offices walls are delineated by file cabinets to store paper.

Those papers in filing cabinets are the fortunate papers. They have a home with an address for someone to find them on the scant chance they would want to. Others are dropped on cabinet tops, shoved in shelves, thrown on tables and desks, piled on floors, windowsills, chairs, and couches. These forgotten or "in progress" pages become orphans and widows separated from their file or document. Forgotten and abandoned, they protect the surface below them from dust or light while waiting to be claimed and used. More likely, one day in a quick cleanup, the lawyer, or most likely her staff, will gather them for shredding, burning, or burial.

Ultimately all of the paper is gathered in boxes that are moved to basements, storage sheds, and barns to join other paper boxes, or are shredded, burned, or buried. The paper buried in a box in a shed differs from paper buried in a landfill by the illusion that the former will actually be retrieved and used again.

Amidst this paper shuffle, lawyers also practice law. Burdened, tethered, and diverted by paper, they consider facts, research the law, lay out options, communicate positions, make arguments, and resolve cases—all with the goal of saving or protecting the client.

Paper dominates to define the lawyer. It defines what she does, where she does it, how she does it, and how effectively she does it. It weighs on her, slows her down, and saps her energy and enthusiasm until it stops her from being the great attorney she can be.

Paper pulls the lawyer like gravity. Astronauts experience the absence of gravity. In this state of weightlessness, they move in directions and speeds unknown on earth. They let go of tools in mid-air, where they remain to be quickly retrieved when needed again. Without the resistance of gravity, moving from one place to another or lifting objects requires less effort. This state of weightlessness permits routines, experiments, and manufacturing that would be impossible in the presence of gravity.

Without paper, the practice creates a state similar to weightlessness—the State of Paperlessness. In that state the lawyer moves with less effort, greater speed, and more focus. Unlike the weightlessness of space, which is available to a privileged few, any lawyer, whether solo, in a small firm, or in a large firm, can enjoy the State of Paperlessness.

Without paper, the practice of law becomes more sustainable and profitable. The need for less paper (a gigabyte equals 50 trees converted to paper) reduces not only the need to cut down trees for paper, but also the costs associated with buying, handling, storing, using, and filing the paper.

Without the scent of paper and its chase, the landmarks and guides move, morph, or even disappear. Without paper's scent and structures to guide, lawyers become lost and befuddled. But they should not be. The true purpose of practicing law has never changed, but now that purpose is no longer avoided chasing paper or creating a lawyer's own trail. Nor can the lawyer hide behind the filing cabinet; she must step forward and be what she was trained to be—a lawyer. Even paperless, she still must represent the client. The removal of paper has not removed the requirements of confidentiality, zeal, competence, and candor that define lawyers as professionals.

This book does not promote some utopian state defined by the total lack of paper. Such a state could be reached quickly and easily without any technology. Just ban all paper now! Empty every filing cabinet, desk, and table of paper and ship them to the shredder. Shred those bills, invoices, and checks. Empty the library of all books. No paper is permitted, no excuses, except maybe for that special kind in the restrooms. Inspect all backpacks and briefcases as they enter the office. Search for and remove the paper. Set up a paper barrier at the delivery door. Shred all paper that enters. No paper allowed beyond that room. Provide a table and chair for those who want to have at least one read before destroying the court scheduling order or the payment for services. Train everyone to improve their memory. The result is a paperless office, but a "practiceless" one as well.

Paper provides the medium and means for the lawyer to practice law. Digital replaces paper as that medium. Becoming paperless is not ridding the office of paper but using a digital medium in its place.

Bring all of the file cabinets in a room. Then pile up all the banker's boxes, expandable files, solo file folders, and sheets of paper in the firm on top of the cabinet contents. Go from room to room, drawer to drawer, and gather up every slip of paper and add them to the mass. Clean off the tables, couches, desks, and windowsills laden with paper. Gather the note cards, phone message slips, and post-its. Empty the shelves in the library and bring all of that into the room. Have audiovisual bring in the tapes and films as well.

Feed all of this paper into the shrinking machine. Page by page, piece by piece, file by file, until every shred of paper is reduced to nothing. The paper ceases to exist, but everything it contained thrives. Now, in the center of the otherwise empty room, sits a small boxlike item that fits in the palm. Open this finger-sized object and it becomes a file cabinet drawer. All the material that had been in the room is sorted chronologically by the date of the matter opening. Turn the box to the side and that same material is alphabetized by client name—not just the first client on the matter, but every single one of them. Turn it another quarter turn and it is sorted alphabetically by people associated with the matter—clients, witnesses, attorneys, judges, stenographers. Turn it upside down and all of it is sorted by types of matters, then alphabetically by client—all of the estate planning, contract negotiations, title searches, bankruptcy cases, criminal cases, or whatever was done. Reach into the box and pull from the center and the material is sorted by type of document, such as wills, building contracts, title abstracts, bankruptcy schedules and petitions, motions to dismiss, or the like. With a filter to view, all of these can be combined to find a particular matter or document by, for example, judge, approximate year, and kind of trial. All of the documents, e-mails, pleadings, research, notes, and contacts associated with the case are there.

Do all of the above in the office, conference room, elevator, car, plane, coffee shop, home, porch, courtroom, beach, wherever—anytime, every time.

This digital media is not only more compact and more convenient, but is also more productive. The ability to move digital information from where it is stored to where it is needed happens at extraordinary speed compared with paper to paper. It is this productivity that counts.

The genesis of this book was to share the sense of awe and wonder I experienced in a State of Paperlessness. But with the drafting came thinking (writing is, after all, a thinking process), and the focus began to change. The technology that I use is readily available to any lawyer. How I combined the tools and used them to reach a State of Paperlessness is clearly a key element. But the other, more important element was that while a State of Paperlessness freed me from the burdens of the time, place, and paper of practice, it also presented new and daunting challenges to ethical conduct, professionalism, and even the very concept of being a lawyer in the first place.

Being in a State of Paperlessness is thrilling and powerful. Practicing law is fulfilling and wonderful. Being a lawyer in the State of Paperlessness is all of those things and more.

Every lawyer can practice in the State of Paperlessness. There are no bar exams or motions. It is a question of wanting to, not earning the right. Clearly, for solo and small firms, it is an easy, almost obvious transition. Properly employed, the paperless office makes these firms as effective as larger firms. But lawyers in all sizes of firms, as individuals, groups, or in total, can enjoy the benefits of being in a State of Paperlessness as well.

This book shares my journey from an office with a manual typewriter and a single analog phone as the only equipment to where I am today with computers, tablets, scanners, cell phones, and the web. It is written so that those who wish to maximize the digital tools available can also reach that place in their career and be better lawyers.

How the Book Is Laid Out

Each chapter stands alone as a self-defined topic. Other chapters add to your general knowledge of the subject, but one can pick a chapter of interest and go to it by skipping the other chapters without much loss of meaning.

This book contains several different structures. In addition to the main text, which describes and addresses the issues, there are four other styles.

> This box includes hints intended to highlight opportunities, traps, or benefits related to the discussion.

> Here I describe experiences of mine that are used to illuminate the current topic.

> **The State of Paperlessness has to have some rules, and these are laid out in this form.**

> This is not a comprehensive book on sources for equipment, programs, or other materials. Where valuable, resources will be listed here.

Finally, the thoughts are mine, not those of the editors or the publishers.

CHAPTER 2

THE STATE OF PAPERLESSNESS MAKES THE LAWYER'S TIME MORE VALUABLE

Abraham Lincoln is the sage for the State of Paperlessness. His quote, that "A lawyer's time and advice are his stock in trade,"[1] made two centuries ago, describes practicing law in the modern paperless state. Paper no longer determines the lawyer's value. Time becomes more relevant and more valuable, as it is not just time, but better-quality time, for the following reasons:

- Practicing without paper, the lawyer can more easily get into "the zone" of highly satisfying and productive work.
- Without paper, practice can be scheduled to maximize the productive hours available to the lawyer.
- Without paper, reduced clutter limits the distractions at the worksite as well as time wasted sifting through the stacks and piles for "that piece of paper."
- Without paper, on-hand/on-time access to the tools of the craft (documents, law, and communication) reduces time spent looking for them.
- Without paper, finding documents, searching for information, and gathering support documents no longer provide opportunities for distraction from the task, which results in greater and longer focus.
- Without paper, the lawyer can communicate with others more timely and with less time spent.

These time savings bring other benefits to the lawyer:

- The ability to become more competitive as a lawyer because he has more time to dedicate to the real needs for his talent.
- His life is better balanced, with more time for family, friends, and avocations.

The value of time increases as paper volume decreases.

DIGITAL PRACTICE PUTS THE LAWYER IN "THE ZONE."

Being in the zone means to be so immersed in the project at hand that all of the senses are focused on making that event happen. Athletes talk of this during heightened competition. Sometimes this is called "flow psychology."

The zone is that special time when the work flows smoothly and successfully from one step to the next. The mind is focused on the task at hand, and every challenge is met with sufficient skill to overcome. The feeling combines success, accomplishment, self-satisfaction, and joy. Those who experience it want to do so again.

Evidence of having been in the zone includes a sense of how easy and doable the task was, ignorance of how much time has passed, no sensitivity to needs for nutrition, an incredible sense of self-satisfaction to the point of joy at completion, and lack of awareness of other things going on. Because working in the zone also results in higher pulse and blood pressure, completion has a physical sensation akin to that felt after a good workout.

Mihaly Csikszentmihalyi is considered to be the pioneer researcher and writer on being in the zone, or flow psychology. Being in the flow, according to Csikszentmihalyi, means "being completely involved in an activity for its own sake. The ego falls away. Time flies. Every action, movement, and thought follows inevitably from the previous one, like playing jazz. Your whole being is involved, and you're using your skills to the utmost."[2] Although he was discussing websites in that interview, the concepts apply to other activities, including the practice of law.

According to Csikszentmihalyi, in order to get into the zone, the following elements must be present:[3]

- The lawyer must have a clear goal that demands his highest skills.

- The lawyer must concentrate on one thing; attention cannot be diverted.
- The lawyer becomes immersed and loses the sense of self-consciousness.
- The lawyer loses the sense of time.
- There is ongoing feedback as to what is working and what is not so that changes can be made as needed.
- The lawyer has the skill to meet the demand of the challenge.
- The lawyer is in control of the situation.
- The action is self-rewarding.
- The lawyer has no awareness of hunger, thirst, discomfort, or other physical needs.
- The lawyer is totally absorbed in the activity to the point of being unaware of anything else.

Lawyers who have experienced the moment know it produces their greatest work.

The lawyer should seek to work in "the zone."

In the pre-digital age, I was working on an appeal. As I traveled back from a hearing in another case, the key to my argument in the appeal came to mind. I felt in the zone. I stopped at a restaurant, took in a pad, and over the next several hours or so I ate, drank, and wrote the brief. There were no references available; when the need for those arose, I merely noted it and moved on. Alone at the table, I completed the whole brief. Later I typed it, inserted the citations and needed quotes, and finished it.

Over the years I have experienced other times of being in the moment. They have been bliss. At times, others have popped the bubble, and the crash was painful. When I get in the zone, I want to make sure nothing will break my concentration.

IN A PAPERLESS PRACTICE, THE LAWYER CAN FIND THE ZONE MORE EASILY AND FOR LONGER PERIODS.

Distractions waste lawyers' time, undermine their focus on the issue at hand, impair the work product, and add to their stress.

In a study of worker interruptions, Gloria Mark, of the University of California at Irvine, determined that subjects on average changed from one single event to another about every three events. The problem was that when a person was interrupted within a task, the two intervening tasks that took place before returning to the original task consumed an average of about 23 minutes. The combination of the time to do the task as well as being forced to think of other things changed the focus. It took time, once back at the task, to re-orient oneself to what was done and what was to be done.[4] This break and redirection of the flow of thought will slow down the process of brief writing or trial preparation, for example, and expose the lawyer to making mistakes. The mistakes could come from losing a thought that should have been included, forgetting to complete something, or losing track of where he was in the project.

In the drafting of documents, briefs, or the preparation for trial, thoughts come and go quickly. The sooner they are captured in the document, the better. Distractions come from diversions to physically retrieve a file, open a reporter, find a note made in the margin of a transcript, finding the transcript itself, and more. These distractions increase the time between thought and expression and reduce the chances that such even happens. Now slowed down and diverted from the task, other demands and calls move the lawyer further and further away from what he was doing, not necessarily physically but mentally. Completing a thought, with instant digital access to exhibits, testimony, or research, does not break down the concentration. Without losing the chain of thought, the relevant exhibit, portion of the transcript, or law can be quickly found, captured, and placed or cited. The thought that led to its necessity won't be lost or diverted in a pile of files, folders, binders, and legal pads down the hall in the office of the other attorney working on the case, or while waiting for support staff to retrieve and bring it to you.

The distractions come in these ways:

- Environmental distractions, such as lighting, temperature, background noise, traffic.
- Surroundings, including clutter on desk, piles of competing files, reminder notes, and other items that demand attention.
- External distractions, including phone calls, e-mails, and staff or other interruptions.
- Task-associated distractions, such as needing to retrieve a file, find a quote, check a case, etc.

- Personal transactions, such as the ability to sit or stand comfortably, the ability to maintain focus, and sensitivity to other things going on.

Practicing in the State of Paperlessness reduces, and in some cases eliminates, these distractions. As a result, the lawyer is able to accomplish more and better work product in less time.

Increase focus by removing or reducing environmental distractions, such as lighting, temperature, background noise, and traffic.

Some distractions have nothing to do with being paperless. Poor lighting, flickering lights, noisy environs, and traffic noise exist even in the paperless world. Being paperless allows the attorney the ability to change to a more peaceful location. Some tasks, such as checking e-mail, signing documents, or discussions with staff, may survive the poor surroundings. But when it comes to doing a job requiring concentration, moving with the laptop to a quiet area such as a nearby library or park can be the answer.

Other ways to increase opportunity for concentration include:

- Dressing comfortably for the temperature in the room;
- Using headphones that block out the noise and provide gentle background music to work by;
- Turning off overhead lights and using lighting from portable lamps to focus attention away from distractions;
- Adding a small fan to the workspace to move the air; and
- Scheduling work time in the office during quieter periods, such as early morning, evenings, and weekends.

Remove clutter on desk and other distractions.

Albert Einstein asked, "If a cluttered desk signs a cluttered mind, of what, then, is an empty desk a sign?" While his messy desk suggests that genius and clutter come together, that is not necessarily the case. For intelligent and creative people, lawyers being in that class, the mind moves so fast that it leaves no time to clean up the mess along the way. Digital storing and indexing is so quick that there is time, and, when genius is critical, there is no need to go on a hunting expedition.

Clutter adds stress, increases distractions, interferes with the flow of information, creates opportunities for lost documents and deadlines, and confuses arguments. The answer to Einstein's question is this: Fewer distractions and less time spent looking for things. It also means better appreciation of the original décor and furnishings in the room.

In the papered world, the lawyer's work site has all kinds of papers. There are the drafts, notes, and files for the task at hand. Below them are other unfinished tasks. Around the work site are sticky notes and other reminders of calls to make and letters to write. A stack of phone messages is near the telephone. Surrounding the area, no matter where one turns, are files, folders, and boxes, all calling and shouting to be chosen as the next project. Each and every one of these diverts attention needed elsewhere. Even if they do not call for action, they set off a mental cascade that leads to consideration of other tasks to be done.

All of that clutter distracts me. When I was looking for a source document, a note, a phone message among the pile of paper, each of those documents called me to another task. "Stop writing the brief!" "Call me!" "I am more important, do me now!" "Have you thought about me?" With clutter—and I had it—I could not cast my eye anywhere on my desk, the work table, or nearby spaces without another task calling for attention. These distracted me from the task at hand. So serious did that situation become that I created a "dry counter." From the left edge of my sight line to the phone on the right side, nothing was to be in that space unless it had to do with the project at hand. But to put something out of sight risked putting it out of mind and undone.

Over the years, I have found an airplane one of the best places to get work completed. It is not just that there are no phone calls or individuals making demands and diverting my thoughts to other topics, but the clutter of the desk was gone, and only what was on my laptop in front of me demanded attention.

Going digital removes clutter. Consider the following techniques to remove the clutter in the State of Paperlessness.

- Only work digitally. If there are documents, notes, or other printed items upon which the writing depends, scan and save them. Call them up on the screen.

- Digitally mark, annotate and note research, exhibits, testimony, and other documents rather than using sticky notes and paper with underlining. If hand notes were made earlier, scan them and rely on that digital image.
- Use Outlook or other task lists for all of your to-do's. Use the reminder capabilities of those programs.
- Have phone and other messages sent by e-mail rather than on paper.
- Develop the skills to take notes on the computer rather than on paper.
- If you must make notes at the desk, use a single composition book or steno pads (smaller than a legal pad) for all notes rather than random pieces of paper.

In a study of work interruptions, it was estimated that it took 15–20 minutes on the task to regain the focus at the time of the interruption. Additionally, the rate of errors increases fourfold after an interruption. In half of the cases, the interruption takes the lawyer completely away from the task. In the same study, it was estimated that if interruptions occurred at the rate of eight per hour at five minutes each, that would be two-thirds of the total time spent.[5]

Besides, the interruptions caused by the burdensome tools to do the job (i.e., paper) are not the only ones. In addition, the staff interrupts for help on a document or a colleague stops by to ask a question about a judge. These interruptions are often invited unintentionally when the lawyer is diverted from the main task to get this or that. When others notice the lawyer is not working on the task, they assume he is "free," and there is less prohibition. The one minute to retrieve a deposition becomes a 30-minute diversion as other interruptions occur.

What the paperless office does is remove the potential for interruptions by eliminating the need to physically interact with others to find files or other information or to leave the desk. Removing paper speeds up the process. This irreplaceable time resource once wasted on handling paper can now be employed to add merit to the argument, research another issue, better prepare a witness, or relax the brain so it is always at the top of the game when needed.

Using all of the paperless tools helps put the lawyer into the zone. My practice includes formal rulemaking, which means hearings with testimony and exhibits. At the end, the requirements are to file proposed findings of fact and proposed rules. In my first case in the State of Paperlessness, the hearing took 12 days and generated over 4,000 pages of transcript from more than 40 witnesses, hundreds of pages of exhibits (many in tabular form), numerous citations to official data online, and proposed regulatory language.

During the hearing, I took notes on my laptop using CaseMap. After the hearing, all of the transcripts and exhibits were put online. Using initial CaseMap input, I supplemented it with quotes from the transcript and, outside the frenzy of the hearing, added more detailed analysis to the exhibits. After organizing the issues that were linked to the facts and exhibits, and without paper, I drafted over 100 pages of brief.

The drafting went smoothly. Because I had populated CaseMap with key words and objects, I was able to quickly navigate the transcript and the exhibits. This eliminated all kinds of disruption opportunities. I was able to have periods of incredible flow, because what I needed was right there. The time spent drafting was considerably less than in the past.

Reduce external distractions, including phone calls, e-mails, and staff or others interrupting.

The clutter of the desk is distraction enough. Then there is the phone ring, the cell-phone vibration, the incoming e-mail ding, and the pop up reminding that the security checks are up to date or the subscription to some service will terminate in 315 days unless renewed. Finally, a colleague comes unannounced to ask a question about a distinctly different legal and factual issue, then moves on to talk about the ball game last night. As she walks out of the room, an administrative assistant wants to know about leaving early.

While the techniques to reduce these distractions are not in and of themselves exclusive to the State of Paperlessness, working paperlessly reduces these opportunities. Without task and other interruptions, more gets done.

- Complete the "busy work" associated with the task, such as identifying files, opening folders, confirming case names and styles, etc., before the actual concentrated task begins.

- Turn off the automatic fetching of e-mails. Manually receive them when ready to read and deal with them, not when they demand attention.
- Put the phones on mute. Notify staff and family that you are entering a quiet period and will not be answering phone calls.
- Close the door to your office and display a sign, serious or whimsical, telling all that you are not to be disturbed.
- Instruct all others that during this period the "do not disturb" zone is wherever you are, even outside of the office. This includes even when when nature calls or the need for nutrition demands a momentary move.
- If communication with another is necessary during the task, consider using e-mail rather than calling or visiting the office.

More by accident than plan, I had developed an early-morning quiet time. I would arrive at the office early and begin to work. Staff came in at different times from eight to nine. I would work through that. Sometime during mid-morning I would take a break, and that was a sign I was open for business. So productive was this time that often what I had done by 10:30 represented most of the work I was able to accomplish all day.

Reduce internally created distractions.

Every lawyer has experienced those work moments when time flies by as he completes task after task or moves smoothly through a brief. This state, sometimes referred to as being in the zone, represents the best situation for the lawyer. Generally, such experiences tend to simply occur without the lawyer seeming to create them. But the lawyer should strive to reach that zone as much as possible. There are positive things he can do by trying to replicate the environment. There are also distractions created by the lawyer himself that prevent him from working in the zone.

The Mark study found that the individual himself created almost half of the distractions.[6] This is not surprising, not only because there are plenty of things to demand attention, but also, in the stress of the practice of law, lawyers commonly tend to procrastinate at starting projects and give in to unproductive urges to put them off. This atmosphere results in a state of "busyness" accomplishing little except to attract distractions that further detour the lawyer from the real tasks at hand. Working in the paperless environment reduces many of those distractions through the speed of accomplishment. In addition, the lawyer can take the following steps to increase levels of concentration:

- Do one thing at a time. Multitasking appears to deliver a lot while really accomplishing little, and that superficially.
- Routinely get a complete night of good sleep. Nothing improves concentration better than sleep. A tired mind is hard to keep focused. If a good night's sleep does not come, seek medical advice. The practice of sleep medicine has come a long way.
- Remove known distractions, such as noise, uncomfortable seating, *or* interruptions. Put a "do not disturb" sign on your door, like those found in hotels.
- Train yourself to stay still and work on the project. There is no requirement for a response to every distraction. Deliberately practice avoiding them. Be in charge.
- Use larger cups for tea or coffee or bring in a decanter to eliminate the need for refills.
- Save those tasks requiring little concentration for times *when* distraction is at its highest.
- Pay attention to those times when concentration and desire are at th*eir* highest and schedule important work then.

> In the course of completing a project, there are steps that will disrupt the flow and expose the lawyer to distractions. When these steps come, note them and defer completion until later. For example, in an argument, a particular statute needs to be inserted. Rather than take time to find the language and drop it in with full citation, leave a marker and move on. Come back later and fill in. Also, as part of preparation for the concentrated stage, anticipate those cites and quotes that will be needed and place them in another opened document which can quickly be reached without breaking concentration.

WITHOUT PAPER, THE LAWYER CAN SCHEDULE HIS PRACTICE TO MAKE THE MOST OF HIS PRODUCTIVE HOURS.

Traditionally, the lawyer had to schedule work at a specific place. The work had to be done in an office with bookshelves holding case and statutory law, file cabinets nearby with files, files in progress stacked or piled near the desk, and a legal pad on the desk near the phone. Limiting tasks at a specific place costs the lawyer time. To work elsewhere required the collection of some of that paper and moving it. Depending on the case and the task, the load could be great. Lengthier trips often required bringing even more material, sometimes boxes and boxes. As a consequence, travel was limited or tasks had to be done at the desk. As a consequence, the time spent in the office was long.

Paper no longer ties the lawyer down to a specific location at a specific time. Work can be done wherever and whenever. Leaving the office early to see the children play soccer does not mean a trip back into the city to finish working on a project. The project can be finished at home or from some other place. Less time in the office is more time spent on other things.

> **The lawyer shall have the freedom to choose when and where to work unless dictated otherwise by a court or other authority.**

In my earliest years as an attorney, I had a land-line phone at the office and one at home. Answering machines were taboo. A major fear was that when "The Call" came, no one would be there to answer. This became abundantly clear when, to my surprise, my legal assistant was seated on a criminal jury panel. For over a week I not only had no one to do the typing, etc., but also no one to answer the phone when I was gone. Every time I left there was the gnawing feeling that The Call would be missed. Shortly after that, I found an answering service that could connect to my phone and take messages while I was gone. Interestingly, the call that really changed my legal career came to my home number at night.

Working in the State of Paperlessness takes less time.

The singular benefit of a digital practice is the time savings. This time savings comes from the automation of many of the tasks in a papered world. For example:

- The time spent electronically searching an entire file or disk compared to manually searching page by page through a table full of documents and or through boxes of files is equivalent to the difference between riding a bullet and crawling.

- The time difference between searching for relevant case law, finding, and reading it in electronic format versus manually pulling books and turning pages is equally spectacular.
- The time to get a file, find the wanted document within it, and transmit it to someone else digitally takes a minute or so compared to the minutes or even hours it did before.
- The time to find a deposition that has been removed from the file and is piled on another lawyer's desk at home is forever. The digital deposition is online and available to everyone all of the time.

The paperless office brings greater accessibility to the law, faster. Early in my career, I had a case that relied on a remedy in real estate partition called "owelty" (an old equitable concept in partitioning of land that calls for equalization of parcels by use of personal property). Today the lawyer can use any online legal research service, enter the word, and within seconds—minutes at the most—have a list of all of the cases and materials discussing it. Such online services were prohibitively expensive for me then. Instead I spent hours in a law library. The bulk of the time was consumed not in identifying and reading cases, but in the physical finding, retrieving, carrying, and opening of case books, digests, and *Shepherds* to then find and retrieve the cases to read. At one point a large library table was filled with every decennial digest and dozens of case reporters opened to the case. Literally hours were spent doing everything other than reading or note-taking.

Time lost commuting to and from the office—transportation time.
Depending on the mode of commuting, the lawyer can accomplish some work while commuting. For example, while taking the ferry across the bay, he can check and respond to morning e-mails from the East and those from the night before. On the train from Connecticut to Manhattan, he can draft and edit documents and research the law. Except for a tablet or laptop, nothing more needs to be brought along.

While driving, hands-free phone conversations are also an option. Obviously, anything requiring reading or typing is forbidden—not just as a matter of law or ordinance, but out of necessity for your own life and safety. Also, avoid long and serious phone conversations, which divert attention needed for driving.

On longer commutes (such as long plane flights), the opportunities to find work time are even greater.

> In my early practice, I routinely brought work home to tackle either in the evening after others were in bed or early the next morning. I purchased a trial case just for that purpose. I could stuff it with the case files and, more important, the law books needed. My first set of Ohio's statutes came in four-inch binders. Today I still work at night and in the morning, but without the lugging or even carrying anything.

Time lost because other circumstances (work, family, travel) separate the lawyer from the office—dislocation time.

Something calls the lawyer away from the office and the files and books. Even though during this errand time was available to work, separation from the paper made it difficult at best. In a digital world, those papers travel with him. On those occasions when the lawyer has to be away from the office, when time permits, he can still work. For example, the lawyer's wife is the maid of honor in her friend's wedding across the country. She needs to arrive several days before the wedding day. Though away from the office (and clearly not needed for wedding preparation), the lawyer can work either on his laptop, on a computer at the hotel business center, or at a FedEx Office.

The time lost may not be in the actual travel, but in preparing for it. Road trips no longer require collecting copying, binding, and packing paper. Instead the lawyer can work or spend time with family.

> Almost from the beginning of my adult working career, I have traveled. Not only did I suffer by being away from home, family, and the office, but prior to the trip, rather than spending those hours with the family, I spent most evenings gathering papers, books, binders, and other materials to take with me to work on or finish projects. One of the first revelations of the wonder of the digital practice came when I noticed that preparation for trips was reduced by hours.

Time lost because the day is fragmented into different tasks and
   responsibilities that result in inefficient movement from place
   to place—fragmentation time.

It is not just that a lawyer has to be out of the office; it generally
follows that if there is a day in which he needs to be out of the office,
he needs to be in two or three places. For example, he has a hearing
downtown at 10 A.M. and his daughter is in a school play at 3:30. If
the routine was to the office to the hearing to the office to the play, a
lot of time is spent commuting. Instead, with the laptop or tablet, he
can go to a coffee shop near the courthouse and spend the early morning working there, and after the hearing go home to work or at a place
near the school.

Fragmenting the location during the day also leaves gaps in time.
Two hearings, for example, before the same judge, or in the same
courthouse on the same day but separated by several hours, provide
enough time to get work done but not enough to travel to and from
the office and get anything done. No longer does he need to go to the
office to work.

Obviously, some of that time is required to prepare for the hearings. Doing it near the courthouse and walking to the hearing with
the preparation fresh beats feverishly completing it, fighting traffic,
and parking in time for the hearing.

Time lost in scheduling and attending meetings with others to
   collaborate or communicate within a matter—collaboration
   time.

**The availability of time for two or more lawyers to meet
and collaborate or confer over matters in the case is the
inverse of the number of lawyers and locations squared.**

As the number of participants increases, the windows of meeting
times become fewer and smaller. The place where all of the documents
or materials are located counts as one of the participants. Without
paper, there is no specific place for the physical meeting and, in many
cases, no need for a common space between attorneys or even a common time.

With everything available digitally, the documents or other materials can be viewed anywhere. So if a face-to-face meeting is required, finding a common time between the human participants is

much easier because the meeting place can be determined after that is set. But with the data available from any computer, and the ability to communicate through videoconferencing, telephone, or webinars, many of these meetings can be done from wherever the participants are.

Collaboration in the State of Paperless requires fewer face-to-face meetings. By a variety of means, participants access the same documents and collaborate on their own individual schedule rather adjusting to everyone else's. Documents can be reviewed and annotated on each person's schedule.

As the number of participants that have to meet decreases and the place requirement disappears, the number and length of opportunities to meet increase geometrically. As a consequence, collaboration contributes to the product, not to the stress from scheduling.

THE PAPERLESS PRACTICE MAKES THE ATTORNEY MORE COMPETENT.

The speed of practicing law in the State of Paperlessness also empowers the solo practitioner and small firm to compete with the big firms. Technology brings more parity. Though he may not be able to marshal an army of clerks and associate lawyers, at his fingertips he has the power of many attorneys who are completely in sync with him and his needs. With electronic legal research, computer-assisted discovery, and powerful tools to build documents, those legions of attorneys and assistants become less necessary.

> As a reformed workaholic, the experience of practicing in a State of Paperlessness has been new and refreshing—less work, more thinking, better product, and more life away from the practice. With near-instant access to all information, I now accomplish far more than when I was carrying paper. As an example, the number of matters I handled by myself in a recent year was a handful short of all of the matters that my two partners and I combined had done a few years earlier. Because of the quick retrieval, concentration remains, and the work product is better.

THE ANVIL ON THE FOLDER IS LIGHTER WHEN IT IS PAPERLESS.

Over time there remains that file or task that does not get done. The lawyer knows it needs to be done. The longer he thinks about doing it, the heavier the file gets, and the harder it is to open. At some point the imaginary anvil sitting on top of the folder becomes so heavy it keeps the lawyer from doing anything with it. For some lawyers, it is a small nuisance. For others, this anvil-laden file and others become threats to clients and careers. Failure to take care of a file when needed is a major source of ethical complaints and malpractice.

Even though the lawyer does not address the file, its demands on his time grow, and as it grows it takes the lawyer out of the zone in other cases. In the paperless practice, the anvils can still exist, but they are not as heavy.

Here are some suggestions for lifting the anvil on a case:

- Reduce the expectations from "take care of the case" to much smaller tasks. Look at individual pieces rather than the whole. In the digital world, the ability to quickly do a lot of "little things" but have them connected to the matter is much easier than in the papered world.
- Plan to do one thing on the case first thing in the morning, before starting anything else. This could be just to start a needed letter by entering the name and address, the purpose of the letter, and a signature block. Or send an e-mail to someone asking them a question. Just do something.
- Find and do other simple tasks.
- Leave the folder and promise to do something on *it* the next day.

Over time, the matter will begin to take shape and completion will come quickly. Often just actually *starting* results in completion.

Notes

1.   Abraham Lincoln, Great-Quotes.com (Gledhill Enters., 2011), http:// www.great-quotes.com/quote/15743, last visited May 26, 2011.

2.   John Geirland, *Go With The Flow*, WIRED Magazine, Sept. 1996, *available at* http://www. wired.com/wired/archive/4.09/czik_pr.html (last visited Oct. 1, 2011).

3.   M. Csikszentmihalyi & K. Rathunde, "The measurement of flow in everyday life: Towards a theory of emergent motivation," *in* J.E. Jacobs, *Developmental Perspectives On Motivation*, Nebraska Symposium on Motivation (Lincoln: Univ. of Neb. Press 1993), 60.

4.   Gloria Mark, *Too Many Interruptions at Work? Office distractions are worse than you think—and maybe better*, GALLUP MANAGEMENT JOURNAL (June 8, 2006), *available at* http://gmj.gallup.com/content/23146/too-many-interruptions-work.aspx. (last visited Oct. 10, 2011).

5. *See* JONATHAN B. SPIRA & JOSHUA B. FEINTUCH, BASEX, THE COST OF NOT PAYING ATTENTION: HOW INTERRUPTIONS IMPACT KNOWLEDGE WORKER PRODUCTIVITY (2005), *available at* http://www.basex.com/web/tbghome.nsf/23e5e39594c064ee852564ae004fa010/ea4eae828bd411be8525742f0006cde3/$FILE/CostOfNotPayingAttention.BasexReport.pdf (last visited Oct. 10, 2011); Jonathan B. Spira, *High Cost of Interruption*, KM WORLD Magazine, Sept. 1, 2005, http://www.kmworld.com/Articles/News/News-Analysis/The-high-cost-of-interruptions-14543.aspx (last visited Oct. 10, 2011); R.M. Ratwani & J.G. Trafton, Beyond the Time Cost of Interruptions on Primary Task Performance: Understanding Errors, Poster presented at the 29th Annual Conference of the Cognitive Science Society, Nashville, Tenn., Cognitive Science Archive Proceedings, 2007, p. 1842, http://csjarchive.cogsci.rpi.edu/proceedings/2007/docs/p1842.pdf.

6. Gloria Mark, *Too Many Interruptions at Work? Office distractions are worse than you think—and maybe better*, GALLUP MGMT. J., *available at* http://gmj.gallup.com/content/23146/too-many-interruptions-work.aspx.

CHAPTER 3

THE FIRST STEP TO BEING PAPERLESS IS REPLACING PAPER WITH PORTABLE DOCUMENT FORMAT (PDF)

Before the lawyer purchases another piece of equipment or program, she can move almost all the way to a paperless office by using the software found on virtually every computer (or easily added). Every time she prints a document, she simply prints or converts it to portable document format (PDF). Instead of filing papers in folders, she stores PDF documents on the computer. Instead of being mailed or overnight expressed, agreements or letters are converted to PDF and e-mailed. Instead of pleadings being shipped to the clerk of courts, PDF versions are uploaded to the case management system.

> **The lawyer shall use PDF in every instance instead of paper unless paper is absolutely required. Even then a PDF version shall be retained in lieu of paper copies.**

PDF SOFTWARE REPLACES PAPER.

PDF stands for "portable document format," a format that displays and produces documents in the original font, margins, justification, and other characteristics independent of the generating program, hardware on which it was produced, or the operating system. It makes the document "portable" from one machine, program, or system to another. In this way, a document produced using WordPerfect on a Windows 2000 environment can be read by someone who operates exclusively in Word 2007, or a Mac user can read something prepared on a main-frame computer. At the same time, the text, fonts, layout, and graphics are captured for retrieval. There are no size limitations, which permits unlimited formats for storage. Originally proprietary to Adobe, which created it, it is now a universal product with ISO standards.[1] Other companies, such as OmniPage by Nuance (which markets Dragon Naturally Speaking) and Adobe, have programs that process PDF. Most word processors and spreadsheets now produce PDF directly, and a PDF printer can easily be added to the list of printer options for a computer for use by any program.

> **PDF shall be the official "paper" in the State of Paperlessness.**

PDF goes beyond being a paper replacement in two-dimensional form. PDF also can contain hyperlinks and video, and even stores 3-D information. PDF document management provides:

- Representation of document;
- Structural modification of documents through page deletion, extraction, compilation, addition, *and* portfolio creation;
- Document editing, including deletions, insertions, comments, and rearrangements;
- Document oral reading;
- Document modification, cropping, and size and orientation changes;
- Forms that allow for input and then submission;
- Real-time collaboration with others;
- Securing the contents by digitally locking them;
- Signing digitally; and
- Bates stamping of documents.

CONVERTING PDFS INTO USABLE TEXT

Documents become PDF by being scanned to PDF, created by the computer to PDF, or printed to PDF. Documents that originated as scanned documents lack the utility of those prepared by a computer in that they are not rendered. That is, the PDF is a photograph of the document, and the words are not separate but part of that larger picture. Rendering converts the information in the document into characters that can be searched, copied, deleted, edited, and highlighted.

Text Conversion

Adobe and OmniPage have programs that perform OCR, or optical character rendition. Some document management programs will also render a PDF upon scanning to create a searchable database. To render a document is to convert it into a digital character capable of being searched, copied, and used like characters generated by a word processor or spreadsheet. Scanned documents can be rendered by choosing the OCR function for the opened document. Batch or multiple-file renderings can also be performed. OmniPage also will identify up to 120 languages in doing the OCR.

> For those documents that are locked and will not allow rendering, the lawyer can print them to a PDF or paper, then scan them. These latter documents can be handled by OCR.

Even if the lawyer does not intend to use the information within the document itself in a digital or rendered form, converting the text can provide searchable data to find the document later on. Rendering the document also has the benefit of cleaning up the document.

> Court rules for electronic filing of documents in PDF require that they be in text-searchable format or "rendered." Preferably the PDF is generated by Word or WordPerfect and not prepared by scanning. In cases where the document has been scanned and filed, or snapshots have been inserted, courts have struck the filing and, if timeliness is an issue, denied timely filing. The courts have reminded counsel that the ECF Manual regarding filings in text-searchable .pdf format is not a petty requirement and that "[c]ompliance was not optional."[2]

Tables and Columns

Capturing tabular data has other challenges. In some cases the original source has kept the table format within the PDF, and it can be captured as a table. In others, the information has to be rendered and then copied to a spreadsheet where the text-to-column function can rebuild most tables. In some cases, manual corrections are required. OmniPage does a better job than most in putting PDFs into a native state, including the tables just as they are on the PDF.

USE OF PDF IN CONTRACTS

- PDF tools aid the lawyer in drafting and negotiating contracts by tracking legible comments and edits.
- Printed versions can be conveyed digitally with no loss of formatting even if all participants do not use the same native program generation.
- Changes and notes can be automatically created and readily available with a hyperlink to the place noted or edited.
- Document comparison can be accomplished without reliance on the native document.
- It is easy to compile agreement with signature pages.
- Documents can easily be assembled into briefs, memoranda with exhibits, contracts with attachments and signature pages, and similar combinations.
- Editing documents and reviewing them during negotiations in PDF bring advantages over edits in the native format.
- All of the notations and changes are done in a format that is readable and not subject to misinterpretation due to handwriting.
- Selective use of color and symbols can categorize and qualify the edits. By using, say, a red text or suggestive, there is a distinction between comments and actual insertions, deletions, and modifications.
- The source of edits and comments is identified by the author or reviser.
- It creates a permanent record of the negotiation process.
- Inadvertent and undetected corruption of the underlying document in native format is eliminated.

TOOLS IN THE PDF PROGRAMS BRING ADDED POWER TO THE LAWYER IN THE STATE OF PAPERLESSNESS.

Mastering the tools in PDF brings the lawyer closer to the goal of a truly paperless office. Of greater value, PDF tools enhance her productivity and ability to communicate in the State of Paperlessness. There are several programs available to manage PDF. Nuance and Adobe are the two main competitors. As the originator of the format, Adobe has the most functions. Some of the more useful are described below.

Snapshot

Snapshot in Adobe will take a snapshot of a document or a webpage in the area identified by the lawyer. The snapshot can then be pasted normally in a document or e-mail. This is an excellent way to quote statutes, cases, contract provisions, or even transcripts. The advantages are these:

- To show exact quotes by showing as found in the transcript or book.
- To show handwritten notes or marks that cannot be rendered.
- To exhibit writings in other alphabets or character systems accurately.
- To copy information from deeds and other documents to ensure accuracy.
- To capture graphs, pictures, and information *from* a webpage or other document.

> There is one major caveat to using Snapshot in briefs and other length-restricted documents. According to court rules limiting documents by number of words, words in the snapshot still need to be counted. The automatic word-counting capability of the word processor will not count words that are within that insertion. Either count manually and add or insert rendered text instead. It would also have to be rendered.

Building documents by addition, deletion, and extraction

PDF gives the lawyer the ability to assemble documents from a variety of original platforms, such as word processing, web, spreadsheets, scanned documents, and other documents (even audio and video), into a single document or a portfolio of documents.

Use in a motion or other pleading

The most common way the lawyer would use PDF is in building a motion and memorandum for filing with attachments, such as copies of statutes or cases, exhibits, transcripts, photographs, and tables. The steps to accomplish this are:

1. Create a folder to store the documents.
2. Digitally sign the document where needed. A digital signature need not be a pen-on-paper signature but can be as simple as "/s/ Attorney's name."
3. Convert the word-processing and spreadsheet documents to PDF and save in the folder.
4. Save the exhibits and attachments in PDF form in the folder and name the files initially by the letter or number of exhibit with a description. For example, Ex A Transcript p.114-118.
5. Use the document-combining function to gather all of the PDFs for the motion and order them in the combining window.
6. To make separation tab sheets for the exhibits and attachments, clear the clipboard and, in PDF, insert from clipboard. This creates a blank page. Using the Text Insert option label it Exhibit A, etc. Repeat insertions until complete.
7. Save as a final document.
8. Optionally, secure the document. Note: as per above, this is not permitted in court filings.

The document can be filed electronically or sent via e-mail. No further printing is required unless, of course, local rules require a courtesy copy or it is to be disseminated in paper form. In that case, it is ready for printing with all of the attachments and no collating.

> Note that in ECF, each of the exhibits and attachments are generally filed separately but connected to the memorandum or motion.

Selectively cataloging multiple documents

Under the Advanced Document Processing—Full Text index with Catalog builds an index of words in all of the specified PDF files. For example, by identifying all of the briefs and court orders, a single search can find and display in a single list, with hypertext to actual documents, the number of times a case is cited or a name or object identified.

> This is a great tool to use in preparing for an appeal. The entire record is indexed and hyperlinked for quick access during drafting. This feature lists every time a key person is mentioned, or every citation to a particular case, as well as the context. A hyperlink takes you to that place in the document.

SECURING DOCUMENTS

The biggest danger in this digital world is the potential for intentional or unintentional modification of documents.

> Over the years there have been different technologies for security. When I first started to practice, a lawyer could purchase a single sheet folded to form eight legal-sized pages. It allowed the drafting of an original will for which there could be no question as to page substitution. Subsequent codicils would be noted on the sheet itself, eliminating any question of another will. For purposes of insuring against tampering, this method would be hard to replace.

In PDF, final and signed documents can be secured so that no one can make any modifications to that document without the right password. The document cannot be altered or supplemented. To maintain confidentiality, the lawyer can limit who can see the document, print it, or copy it.

Signing documents securely

Adobe provides the ability to digitally sign documents. The lawyer establishes places in the document for digital signatures. The document is sent to the signatories with instructions on how to access and protect the digital signature. They can then digitally sign the contracts.

USING THE FORM PROVISIONS

Computers, web sites, e-mail, and the paperless environment have made the old NCR and carbon interleaf forms virtually obsolete. But the idea of a form has not gone away. There is still the need, the utility of collecting information in a standardized way so that those who need that information can quickly obtain it even when there are thousands and thousands of such entries.

Most states now no longer accept custom-printed articles of incorporation or other entity filings, but instead require that the users fill in the forms provided by the Secretary of State or Corporations office. These forms generally come in three formats—a web page, an Excel worksheet that protects all but the entry cells, or a PDF. The latter two are preferable because they permit the user to download the form, prepare it, and submit it to others to edit and ultimately sign.

The Adobe forms facility permits the lawyer to convert an existing document into a form. Additional capability allows the person to "submit" the form, and it is e-mailed to a predetermined address.

> Such a form is ideal internally as a client matter input form. In some cases the client can enter the information and submit it to the attorney.

In addition to providing a totally paperless form facility, submitted forms placed in a portfolio are automatically tallied. In this way, for example, a ballot can be sent via the form and returned, and submitted ballots are recorded and tallied.

READING THE DOCUMENTS OUT LOUD

Among the accessibility options provided, Omni Page and Adobe will both read a rendered PDF document out loud. For those who have limited vision, this is a great advantage and helps lawyers comply with the Americans with Disabilities Act. But for those who are blind, it also aids in drafting by reading back documents, briefs, and other things. By the use of another sense, the lawyer can catch problems in the drafting that are not otherwise apparent visually. This can be simply a matter of cadence but also can illustrate duplications, confusion, and complexity.

> It is important to carefully proofread deeds and other real estate descriptions. Our practice was to have someone read the original as another person read the newly drafted document. This facility can be used by one person in a pinch.

MEASURING AND DRAWING ON DOCUMENTS

In the course of a practice, lawyers will from time to time need to measure the size of areas, the distance between two points, or the relative differences in sizes. Adobe allows the lawyer to mark areas, measure them, and even compute the size of space within that area.

> In an accident case, on an aerial view of the scene (now readily available online), you can mark key locations and then measure them with a great deal of accuracy.
>
> When analyzing brochures or package labels for compliance with labeling laws, it is a great tool to check for compliance, note changes and comments, and even measure to see if the sizes and areas are consistent with the regulations.
>
> An aerial or diagram of a floor plan can then be used to mark up the space that will be subject to a lease. Then, rather than having to write an elaborate description of common areas, private areas, and other considerations, you can simply color code the areas and reference them in the agreement. The floor plan can be put into the PDF and the areas color marked to define them in terms of the lease. The size of that area can then be measured for purposes of rent or assessing costs.
>
> Through this tool, zoning maps can be created, or exhibits dealing with this zoning can be created from existing maps.

TYPEWRITER

Some forms are not designed for the computer or readily filled in. With the typewriter tool, a scanned PDF form can be filled in just as if it was put into a typewriter, but better. Font sizes can be adjusted to fit the box, and the mouse can position the cursor in exactly the right spot.

> For years our office retained a typewriter and used it to fill out forms. Then I learned I could have scanned the forms and filled in the boxes on the computer instead—much easier.

BATES STAMPING

Adobe provides automatic Bates stamping of documents. The numbering, including any identifying verbiage, can be tailored to meet

the requirements of the numbering on your documents. It also allows
the marking of the front and back of a single page by A and B.

> The value of Bates-stamped documents came early to me. In
> one of the first cases that I used it in, the opposing attorney
> had the audacity to rearrange documents, letters, and attach-
> ments to create the appearance of documents that did not ex-
> ist. When I challenged the attorney during a deposition, the
> retort was that I could not prove that. I pointed out the small
> Bates stamp numbers at the bottom and explained their signifi-
> cance.

REDACTION

Identify theft ranks as one of the most expensive and, for some, most
destructive crimes in modern times. The ease of gathering information about an individual makes it easy. Lawyers have access to an enormous amount of sensitive information, from birth dates to Social
Security numbers, bank account numbers, and other identification.
They have that in trust and should take care not to make it available
to the detriment of their clients.

> In a case before me when serving as an acting judge, a man
> had been arrested and imprisoned over the weekend for an
> arrest warrant. It turns out he was not the man who was subject
> to the warrant. Someone else had stolen his identity, commit-
> ted crimes, and, when arrested, provided the stolen identity as
> his own. During the course of arraignment, he explained that
> this was not his first arrest for someone else's actions and he
> was trying to clean it up, but it was not easy. In today's elec-
> tronic age, nothing is erased. The lesson is not just to protect
> *your* identity; as a lawyer, you have a responsibility to protect
> your client's identity.

In response to the growing threat, numerous laws and court rules
have been modified that require the removal of such sensitive information from all filings. The lawyer should, as a matter of course, not
maintain this information unless absolutely necessary for the task.

Not everything contained in a document should be available to
the public or even to others. Documents can be easily redacted to
show only what must be shown. Court rules and statutes now pro-

hibit the publication in a document of sensitive information such as Social Security numbers. The E-Government Act of 2002 requires that such information not be made public.[3] For example, the Federal Rules provide that unless ordered otherwise, electronic filings cannot include the full "individual's social-security number, taxpayer-identification number, or birth date, the name of an individual known to be a minor, or a financial-account number."[4] Merely blacking out portions with a marker and scanning again is not enough. Processing with PDF is better. In the case of PDF redaction, the information is completely replaced by a digital blackened image. The sequence of bits that provided the number are now scrambled and replaced so as not to be found in any circumstance. After the document is saved, the redaction cannot be reversed.

Sometimes the data ends up in metadata on the documents, which is just as available if it appears on the intended document.

If you still must retain the sensitive information, then save an unredacted copy. Once redacted, it cannot be undone. The unredacted copy should be saved where it is not readily available even by mistake, and encrypted.

Notes

1.   Document management—Portable document format, ISO 32000-1:2008.
2.   McDonald v. E-Service, 2010 U.S. Dist. LEXIS 78583 (D. Ariz. Aug. 3, 2010).
3.   E-Government Act of 2002, 44 U.S.C.S. §§ 3501 *et seq.*
4.   FED. R. CIV. P. 5.2(a), FED. R. CRIM. P. 49.1, Bankr. R. 1007, Bankr. R. 9037.

CHAPTER 4

PROGRAMS YOU ALREADY USE HAVE THE POWER TO MAKE YOUR PRACTICE PAPERLESS

Existing programs and equipment commonly used by lawyers can put lawyers into the State of Paperlessness. Digital word processing predominates in document generation. Commonly used word processors include Microsoft Word, WordPerfect, and Apple Pages. There are also other commercially available programs, open source programs, and programs in the Cloud. Because, in many cases, the native file generated by the word processor is the means of communication, not the printed paper or even a PDF, the lawyer needs to choose a word processor that will facilitate document generation and communication, not just something he or she likes.

- *Functionality based on the features the lawyer will routinely use.* This includes the basics of formatting, grammar, and spell checking. The lawyer should find editing, change tracking, automatic footnote numbering, and tables of contents and authorities. A feature-packed program is only valuable if the lawyer uses the features.

> For the lawyer, all of the top suites function equally well. Once you have mastered the chosen program, the differences between them are immaterial.

Universality of file formats. The purpose of drafting documents is to communicate. Unless the lawyer exclusively transmits files in PDF or on paper, the native format should be one commonly used by the recipients of his communications. After all, to communicate in the State of Paperlessness, the formats need to be recognized by the audience. Through its near-universal use, Word documents have became the *lingua Franca* of the law office. WordPerfect persists as a word processor in some law offices and courts. With the development of Open Office XML (.docx .xlsx are in that standard), documents produced on the latest WordPerfect documents are generally readable by the latest Word software and vice versa with formatting retained.

- *Availability of functions.* Some functions are on some programs and not on others. This occurs mostly in the area of spreadsheets.

> Though now converted to Word, I still occasionally use WordPerfect, mostly to handle complex documents that originated before I began using Word. Also, there are times when Word cannot open a .docx document even if Word generated it, but I can open it in WordPerfect. Having both can be helpful. Over time by use and pursuing new skills, I have nearly the same skill level in Word as I did in WordPerfect.

- *Ease of integration with other parts of the system.* The e-mail, calendar, contacts, and documents are all integrated with other programs and the practice management system. Because of the greater popularity of Word, many software programs that integrate with word processing are designed to integrate more easily with Word.
- *Access to the program outside of the lawyer's office.* Using an obscure or less than fully available word processing program can hamper the ability to recover after a disruption of service.

> Today, most business centers use Microsoft Suite programs. Trying to work in a format not familiar to it can be challenging. The Open Office XML overcomes this in most cases.

WORD-PROCESSING SKILLS

Word processing goes beyond typing text. It provides powerful tools to edit, spell check, outline, review, and perform other functions beyond writing in simple word processing. Adeptness at using these functions comes with time and use. The key function, typing text, comes right away. The remaining skills come with use and an insatiable curiosity to find better ways to do things. As a general rule, there are at least two (if not more) ways to complete a particular task. By seeking these other ways, the lawyer will find increasingly better ways to finish the job. A number of websites and blogs provide additional insight into these routines. The lawyer can build greater confidence and skill only through experimentation with the commands on the taskbar or ribbon.

Keyboard practice and use enhance productivity in the paperless office.

The skill that will result in the greatest productivity is mastering word processing. For those who argue that typing is time-consuming and the effort is better spent at research, drafting, and the like, my response is that those are the exact things the lawyer does when using word processing to draft documents. Writing is a thinking process. As the lawyer drafts, he thinks. Thinking results in changes, then more drafting. Concentrated, focused, and, most important, uninterrupted, the lawyer can produce better drafts more productively than by the old method, where the lawyer either hand-writes or dictates, someone else types, then editing, more handwriting, paper dolls, someone else typing, and over and over again. As changes are made, the changes appear in real time while the mind focuses on that point or argument. Age does not mean a lawyer cannot train to use the keyboard; he just has to want to do so. The skills are simple and easily learned.

> I struggle to write well. Over the years I have learned that the difference between an excellent final draft and a first draft is lots and lots of editing. So much so that seldom, for me, do the final drafts resemble the earliest. The process of going from one to the next comes through the changing of words and sentences, which is most easily done on the keyboard.

Dictation

In tandem with keyboarding, another way of providing content is through voice recognition dictation. Dragon Naturally Speaking is the best known of such programs. After decades of research and use, the programs provide the lawyer with the ability to not only avoid typing text, but also to control the computer itself.

In speed alone, dictating is faster than typing by approximately three times. For the first draft especially, such an approach can greatly reduce the production time. Also, when the source document cannot be scanned (such as a protected webpage), dictating it is faster than typing it.

> By preparing an outline to keep me on track, just like a speech, I can dictate the bulk of a memorandum or brief. If I do not have the information for a particular spot (such as an exact cite), I note that and move on, filling the pages. Later I come back and fill in that information as I am making final edits. The time savings are significant.

Using dictation brings another element to the practice. The brain thinks differently when the person speaks than when he types. The former is generally simpler and more direct. The language is more conversational and easier to understand.

The dictation software is intelligent software. It learns by use. As the lawyer dictates and corrects words while dictating, the software remembers what is said. In this way names, acronyms and terms of art are acquired and seldom need to be spelled out in subsequent dictations.

For dictation at the desk, the lawyer requires a headset with a microphone. The higher the quality, the better the experience will be. Wireless versions permit the lawyer to move around the room while dictating. While on the road, digital recorders allow the capturing of dictated letters, briefs, or notes to be processed later as if dictated into the system.

Dictation, when practiced, also trains the formulation of ideas and how to voice them in better ways.

Using dictation does not relieve you of the responsibility to read, edit, and revise what you write. Dictation can and does make mistakes. There are a lot more homophones in speech than show up in the dictionary. For example, once when I dictated the phrase, "The actions of your client constitutes fraud since he was well aware that what he was saying was false" came out "The actions of your client costs two or four cents. He was well . . ."

Handwriting

A third way of writing is, of course, handwriting. This too has creative benefits. The process of putting pen to paper uses a different thought process than fingers to keys or voice to dictation. It needs to be done sparingly. All of the creative centers can come together to provide a finished document.

Mastering the commands in word processing

The lawyer in the State of Paperlessness is in the best position if he develops skills in word processing—the more skills the better. The ones that follow are found on the major word-processing programs, but details will tend to reference Word unless a more direct reference is given.

Tracking and comparing changes to documents

During negotiations, group drafting, and editing, merely changing a document and sending its result is not enough. Courtesy, and even ethically demanded candor, requires that the editor indicate the changes rather than return a changed document. This can be done by saving the original, then comparing the revised document with the original to create a "redline."

Word, WordPerfect, and some of the other word processors also provide for real-time change tracking that creates change indications as edits are made. These utilities not only show the recipient any changes made, but also provide the ability to choose acceptable changes individually or *en masse*. The reviewing panel shows where the changes are and will move the cursor to that place in the document. Tracking changes replaces the messy, sometimes illegible, blue pencil or pen on the draft.

During some drafting and editing, it is possible to lose track of the most recent or best version. By using the document compare function, you can isolate the changes and make a judgment on which, or whether even both, of the documents is appropriate to build further on.

Comments and balloons

Not all changes require actual changes to the document. The editing option provides the capability to comment on the document. These comments can be located anywhere and, unless otherwise put into the document, do not become part of the edited document. Balloons, which identify specific text, also allow highlighting of text and raising issues without any editing of the underlying document.

Spell check, grammar check, thesaurus

Documents prepared by modern word processors generally have fewer misspelled words, better grammar, and more accurate punctuation in legal documents. The real-time tools that check spelling and syntax while typing ensure cleaner documents right from the start. Some even correct misspelled words as the typing is done. Most office suites and other programs include these functions in emailing, presentation, spreadsheet, case management, and other programs.

The writing and language skills of the lawyer remain important. Not every error is caught. Take, for example, the following sentence, which Word passes: "It tells what kinds of legal writing you badly due." At the same time, it identifies errors that do not exist.

Styles in Word

The cornerstone of the architecture for Word is its paragraph and styling. This is, no doubt, one of the most complex and counterintuitive aspects of using Word, particularly to those of us who started with WordPerfect. Since styles underlie so much of the functionality and power of Word, the lawyer should understand and master this important function. Style in Word allows the user to easily create documents that look good.

Style in Word allows quick setting of font, size, spacing, justification, numbering, and other attributes of a paragraph or word without having to select the whole paragraph or word. It also allows the quick change of all paragraphs with that style throughout the document.

This is both good and bad—good when the lawyer wants to change all of the headings to a sans serif type, bad when, as a consequence, every paragraph in the document is changed as well. Once understood, it is as useful as powerful.

There are three kinds of styles: paragraph (¶), character (a), and linked (¶a). Put the cursor any place in a paragraph and select a paragraph style, and the entire paragraph conforms to that style. If the style is character, then the selection will change the selected characters or word. Portions of words or several words can be chosen. Character styles address formatting that applies to characters and words but not to paragraphs.

Paragraph styling includes the functions of character with those addressing paragraphs, such as justification, tabbing, line spacing, borders, framing, and numbering. Virtually every court in the country today has rules that spell out limitations on those very items. Violations can have consequences. In a Florida case, a theme park filed for a writ of prohibition in the district court of appeals. The opposition moved to strike the petition on the grounds that it had failed to comply with the rules of the court, noting it was not double-spaced, but used 1.5-line spacing. This allowed for 25 percent more text than was permitted by the rule. Spacing in the footnotes and quotes within the brief were at 0.7 lines instead of a full space, allowing 30 percent more material than was permitted by the rule. The court dismissed the petition because the violations were excessive, and the attorney had a prior warning regarding failure to comply with the formatting requirements.[1] In other cases, the court has imposed fines.[2]

Similarly, some statutes and rules impose specific font requirements in documents. For example, the statute may require that certain portions be in a larger and darker font than the rest of the text.[3]

The linked style means that the style functions as both paragraph and character. This is critical for those paragraphs that always start with an underlined header or numbered item but the text is in the regular font.

> During the writing of this book, I ended up with a dozen or more styles, including headings, body text, footnotes, and framed sections like this. Word would provide me with a "hint," I would select that style and move on. WordPerfect in its Word mode provides similar functionality.

> First-time users of Word, including especially those who know WordPerfect, should take the time to understand how style works. It will reduce anxiety and the use of single-syllable Anglo-Saxon words. Here are some key pointers from experience:
> - When setting a new style, base it on "No Style." This will reduce a lot of inadvertent mass changes.
> - Turn off the automatic update on the style when creating it.
> - When selectively changing the font of a style, such as bold or italics, and the system changes all of the paragraphs in that style, hit the "undo" icon once and it will be only where you selected.

Fundamentals of font selection, size, color, etc.

How a document looks is important. Fonts, typefaces, sizes, spacing, and margins are more than just for looks. Most courts, especially appellate courts, specify which typefaces can be used. For example, the Supreme Court requires:

> The text of every booklet-format document, including any appendix thereto, shall be typeset in a Century family (*e.g.,* Century Expanded, New Century Schoolbook, or Century Schoolbook) 12-point type with 2-point or more leading between lines. Quotations in excess of 50 words shall be indented. The typeface of footnotes shall be 10-point type with 2-point or more leading between lines. The text of the document must appear on both sides of the page.[4]

Headings and automatic paragraph numbering

The most powerful tool with styles is the ability to number paragraphs and subparts with automatically generated numbers and letters. "List" styles format lists. These can be multilevel lists, such as articles and sections in by-laws, or simple numbered lists. Legal documents are commonly numbered. Some have multiple levels, such as Article, Section, Paragraph, or Clause. Briefs are set out in an outline form. During the editing process, these get rearranged or others are inserted. Finally, tables of contents are required. By using the heading styles with automatic numbering, this powerful tool provides, among other things, the following abilities:

- Numbering is maintained consistently and correctly.
- Table of Contents can be generated automatically.
- Sections within the outline can be moved, promoted, and demoted quickly without relying on the risky cut and paste.
- The document can be quickly navigated for drafting, review, and reading.
- Numbering style can be changed once with universal application—for example, to change "Section" to "§."
- If the outline is done in sentence form, the user can collapse the document to just the outline and easily see the flow, or lack thereof, of the argument.

> In brief drafting I see this as essential. I firmly believe that the brief outline should be done in sentence format, and the outline alone, which ends up being the Table of Contents, should lay out the argument by itself.

- The Navigation Pane will allow the lawyer to move quickly from one place in the document to the other without having to scroll or page through the document.

> It is frustrating when I draft a document that uses a list style and the other contributors manually insert paragraph numbers. It slows down the process and incurs a risk that the paragraphs will be numbered wrong.

Page numbering

The numbering of pages is simple, but it needs to be done correctly. For straight-numbered documents (start at one and go to the end), putting the page number in is easy. For those with multiple sections (like a brief), it is important to know how to change sections, restart numbering, and change numbering formats.

> For Word, changing numbering from, say, small Roman for tables to Arabic for the body requires the insertion of a section break (Page Layout Ribbon). For WordPerfect, the program allows you to insert page number style changes wherever you want.

Page numbering also permits insertion of the chapter number as well as the last page of the document. For wills, contracts, and other documents, identifying the page number and total pages adds another level of control.

Cross-referencing

In the drafting of contracts and leases and other similar documents, it is common to reference other sections or subsections. The challenge is that as the drafting goes on, paragraphs are rearranged, added, and deleted. Unless care is taken, the references are wrong. This can result in some unintended consequences.

> Word provides a limited utility in cross-referencing, and WordPerfect is more powerful. In both cases it is easy to forget to update the cross-referencing and leave the wrong reference. As part of drafting, when referencing a paragraph or section, use a different font, such as italics, or underline. These act like highlights. As a final edit, check each of these for correctness.

Merging and mailing

Simply stated, the mail-merge function fills in a typed template with the data from a table. It permits the printing of labels, letters, pleadings, envelopes, and a whole host of documents in which a standard verbiage is populated by data from a table. Today's mail-merge programs also allow for conditional insertions as well as pauses to allow the user to type in missing information. The mail-merge with other utilities also permits the lawyer to develop standard letters, agreements, wills, trusts, forms, and pleadings that can be easily filled in from a table of information.

> While this function is headed "mailing" in Word, I have used it more in other functions. For example, I use an Excel spreadsheet for the names, certificate numbers, values, etc., for stock certificates and use the merging function to generate certificates. For ballots and signature requests on minutes, I use the merge to generate the documents from the Excel or other table.

Another use of spreadsheets and mail merge is to generate standard documents, such as powers of attorney or nondisclosure agreements. At the same time, cataloging these and tracking deadlines and expirations can be handled with such a spreadsheet. Simply set up a worksheet where each of the labeled columns represents a field in the standard document. Open up the standard document and link it to the spreadsheet. In Mailings, insert the column label as a field. Now the program will generate a document with all of that information. When the document is complete and saved, link it to the spreadsheet.

> Use the mail-merge to generate the first draft. In many cases it can be a final draft, but the lawyer should read the document completely to ensure that it does in fact create the relationship intended and has not been corrupted.

Footnotes and endnotes

Automatically numbering and placing footnotes and endnotes greatly facilitate a task that in the pre-word-processing days was a nuisance. Numbering the footnotes and endnotes accurately is virtually automatic, as the lawyer merely notes where to insert the note. When a footnote is required, simply appropriately mark it and fill in the information. Editing options allow letters and numbers or both, unlimited editing options, and the ability to restart numbers on each page or chapter. As paragraphs and sentences are moved, the footnotes move also, and the numbering is correctly changed for all footnotes or endnotes.

> I actively eschew footnotes except for providing citation information. If something is valuable enough to be put into a brief, memo, or even a book, then it needs to be in the body of the text. Text buried in footnotes is text forgotten. At the same time, the use of footnotes for citations makes the text easier to read and follow. Citations in the middle of a sentence or thought disrupt the reader's flow.

Citation, tables of authorities, and bibliography

One of the tedious things about drafting memoranda and briefs is the citation and conforming to the proper form. WordPerfect has a built-in program that provides one of the better generators. Some stand-alone programs, including Best Authority, another Corel product, generate tables of authorities (TOAs). A number of research programs, such as Lexis/Nexis and Westlaw, will provide the properly formatted citation to be used. Many of these programs are designed to automatically search the document to identify items that should be part of a TOA and then build the table. Some, particularly those with legal databases, will check the citations and report if there has been any change in the efficacy of the cited statute or case law.

Indexing the document

Some documents contain key words that users look for to answer questions. The goal of information writing (that is what a contract or by-laws are, for example) is to get the user to the information he wants and answer his question as quickly as possible. Tables of contents are the initial help, but the use of an index is equally helpful.

The process of indexing begins generally during the writing of the book. Indexing in the process of writing forces the writer to identify and mark key words or key concepts in the document as it is drafted. This helps keep the use of key words focused. An index in a completed document such as bylaws make it easier for the reader to quickly get to the place in the document he wants to be. The marking of words for indexing also provides for main and sub-entries. For example, the word *attendance* may be marked under the heading "Quorum" and the sub-heading "requirements."

The types of words to index are nouns representing persons, places, or things and verbs representing processes. Adverbs, adjectives, prepositions, and other types of words have no place in the index. For example, the word "many" will not assist in finding a concept.

> The word in the index does not have to be in the agreement. For example, there could be an index entry for "renter" or "lessee" when the term used in the lease is "tenant."

Concordance

An easier and even more powerful way to index transcripts, briefs, e-mails, and anything with words is software that develops concordances. A concordance differs from an index in that it looks at the actual word, not its synonyms or categories. It looks at all words, including adjectives and adverbs. It does not substitute for an index, but it does provide a way to analyze the document and make sure the language is appropriate. The program is not just for word-processing documents but for rendered PDFs as well.

Concordance software, whether looking at the work produced by the lawyer or someone else, builds word lists, word counts, comparison of word uses, keywords analyzed in their context and use, phrases, and idioms. In the case of litigation, especially when analyzing an expert's reports and transcripts, a sense of word choice can help prepare questions or identify weak spots in testimony.

Another value of a concordance is that it will print out the word in the context of where it is to permit reading the whole sentence and other writing in the vicinity. It provides a different kind of spell check because it lists all of the vocabulary.

> The concordance can flag unusual words or uses of words that would otherwise pass the spell check and grammar check of the word processor. For example, in a lease I was drafting, at the last edit, I ran this and we found "hazardous sustenance" instead of "hazardous substance." How it got inserted I do not know, but I suspect that as it was being drafted, the word was misspelled, and the trusty spell check "corrected" the misspelling. In the meantime, spell and grammar checks never caught it. Neither did several passes by good lawyers!

ONLINE OR IN THE CLOUD FORMS PROGRAMS

A wide range of forms designed for single-entry input and distribution throughout the form are available online. Most of these are for a fee. Occasionally, a purchased form may be great place to start, but the lawyer still must know what is permitted in the form and what is not. For example, in some states cognovits notes or confession of judgment clauses are allowed,[5] some require the clause to be in a certain font,[6] and some make the note void or voidable.[7] While a consumer who finds such a form on the web uses it at her own risk, it is inexcusable for the lawyer to grab a form and not research its applicability. Some bar associations have forms available and identified for specific state use.

Notes

1. WeekiWachee Springs, LLC v. Southwest Fla. Water Mgmt., 900 So. 2-D, 594 (Fla. App. 5th Dist., 2004).

2. Kano v. Nat'l Consumer Coop. Bank, 22 F.3d 899 (9th Cir. Haw. 1994).

3.   *See, e.g.,* Chalfonte Condo. Apt. Ass'n v. QBE Ins. Corp., 526 F. Supp. 2d 1251 (S.D. Fla. 2007) (holding that insurance contract that failed to conform fonts to statute (Fla. Stat. § 627.701(4)(a)) was unenforceable).

4.   Sup. Ct. R. 33(1)(b).

5.   Ohio Rev. Code Ann. § 2323.12.

6.   Ohio Rev. Code Ann. § 2323.13(D) ("appears more clearly and conspicuously than anything else on the document").

7.   N.M. Stat. Ann. § 39-1-16 (Cognovit notes prohibited and provisions void).

CHAPTER 5

HIDING THE INVISIBLE DIGITS FROM PRYING EYES AND PURLOINING FINGERS: CONFIDENTIALITY AND SECURITY IN THE STATE OF PAPERLESSNESS

CONTROL THE COMING AND GOING OF CONFIDENTIAL INFORMATION.

Data goes in and comes out of a computer equally fast. The ability to copy massive amounts of data quickly from one media to another is one of the great advantages of a digital office, while at the same time it provides its greatest risk. With a few strokes, anyone can move huge amounts of information from the computer or network drives to a thumb drive or to the cloud. Massive information in case files, information that would fill hundreds of filing cabinets, can be stored on a media small enough to carry or even hide in the palm of a hand or pocket.

What makes such loss of data so serious is that it can be done without the lawyer even aware that the data has been copied, removed, or corrupted. Today that adversary would not need to physically break into the office but could electronically enter through the Internet, gain access through the computers, search to find a file he wants, and quickly download it.

There are a number of products available that enable the lawyer to track the use and access to documents. In short, the data loss from the computer can be controlled by the computer. A data loss prevention package monitors the access to confidential files. It is able to determine whether or not confidential files are being viewed by anyone at the same time. If the person viewing confidential files is not authorized to do so, it notifies appropriate individuals. In the meantime, the program denies access to that document. It also will scan any document that is being copied onto a thumb drive or to some other downloadable medium. If the document is identified as confidential, it will deny access to make that copy and again notify appropriate individuals.

Considering the dispersion of equipment and files through PDAs, laptops, and the like, it is necessary that such data loss protection go beyond a central processing system. Rather, it should be incorporated into all of the equipment that everyone is using. Such software will block the use of e-mail and e-mail attachments based on content restrictions, limit confidential information displayed, and stop or greatly limit the use of any kind of removable medium to obtain data. In other words, it acts as an around-the-clock, everywhere security agent that ensures that the confidential information is not being accessed by people who are not entitled to see it and that the information is not being copied for use elsewhere.

Today's more sophisticated software of this type also keeps such files from being encrypted or zipped or converted into some other format. This works in much the same way as a central filing office operates. That would control the access to files and also provide those opportunities to tailor the accessibility to files depending on their level of sensitivity and the persons who need to know.

> One company, InterGuard Management of communication (e-mail, correspondence, phone, and notes), has a product called DataLock that provides all of these services.

The lawyer should employ safeguards on the release of confidential digital data, as would be the case if the information was spoken or submitted in visual form.

The digital practice brings information to the lawyer at near lightning speed. What she needs and when she needs it—the documents or other information appear. A few strokes in a search mode and seemingly lost documents are found and displayed. The lawyer can reach all of the information quickly. So can others. And it can disappear, even permanently, just as quickly as it presents itself. The technology in the State of Paperlessness empowers the lawyer to obtain, analyze, copy, and process documents with amazing speed. It equally empowers others to knock the lawyer out of practice.

From the start, those who venture into the State of Paperlessness should not let the wonders of that state blind them to the risks.

The forces that increase productivity in the State of Paperlessness equally increase the capacity of those who would do harm. Small intrusions, otherwise innocuous, can destroy a practice. Someone a thousand miles away gains access to the practice database and, within seconds, downloads and disseminates hundreds of files around the world, never to be retrieved. A virus from an infected e-mail enters the computer and reformats all the hard drives. In a millisecond, a single lightning strike sends millions of volts through the wires of an office and wipes out every digital file while leaving the walls, furniture, and paper-stuffed file cabinets untouched. A walnut-sized meteorite hits a satellite 25,000 miles above the earth, ending the connections of tens of thousands of users relying on the "cloud" for their data. A lawyer e-mails a complete trial notebook for the trial tomorrow with all of the strategies and analysis to co-counsel—and opposing counsel, and the judge, and the press. A chemical spill on the road near the office forces a mandatory evacuation, denying access to the office for days.

Risks—to the practice and even career-ending—continually haunt lawyers in the State of Paperlessness. Technology helps, but also increases the risk. The lawyer must deliberately and constantly consider the risks to the practice, protect herself from them, and ever seek to avoid them.

> The lawyer's primary responsibility in managing her practice is to secure the firm, its people, its clients, and its data.

Security goes beyond keeping bad people away from the lawyer's confidential information; it also means having the data readily available for the good people. That means protecting it from corruption and destruction by other forces, such as electromagnetism, storms, earthquakes, fires and explosions, downed power and Internet lines, inactive towers and satellites. It means having backup copies when the original files are destroyed or corrupted.

> The lawyer shall take all steps reasonably available to protect the data in the practice from known and knowable risks.

The security basics

The lawyer should have in place at least the following:

- An unending awareness that threats capable of undermining the practice exist everywhere and can arise at any time.
- Equipment location and connections protected from surges in electricity from any source.

Over the years, my offices have experienced two lightning strikes in two different buildings and in two different ways. Early in my use of electronics, in my naiveté, I believed there was no need for surge protectors on everything. During a particularly violent storm, lightning hit a nearby power pole, sending millions of volts through electric lines into office equipment, wiping out network cards, fax machine, copier, phones, and printer. It was not just the cost in dollars (insurance covered much of that) but also in the downtime until new equipment was acquired and installed.

Years later, when we built a new office, we thought we had learned our lesson. We put surge protectors between electronic devices and the outside source of electricity. The office sits on a slight hill. The red metal roof on the barnlike structure (intentionally, due to the nature of my practice) has lightning rods on top. These adornments are not for effect, but for real function. During a severe storm one summer, they saved the building and its contents by directing the electricity into the ground. Most of the electronics survived, but not all. We had recently converted to digital phone with Voice Over Internet Protocol (VoIP). For some reason the fax machine, rarely used, was not part of the system and connected directly to the outside phone line. Internally it was part of the intranet. We theorize that the electrical charge hit the underground telephone lines, came into the building on a single line, wiped out the fax machine, and continued into the intranet, zapping the router, the phone processor, and half of the phone sets. Now everything has surge protection on it.

- Routine and frequent copying of entire databases and storing those copies securely in multiple sites.
- Use of a continuously updating antivirus program that monitors the entire system to protect against unlawful entry into your programs and files. These malicious viruses, worms, and other electronic vermin damage systems by:
  - Changes to the passwords and controls of *the computer* operater.
  - Access to information on the computer that leads to greater access to other data, such as birthdates, Social Security numbers, and other sensitive information.
  - Access to passwords used to access other programs and websites.
  - Access to sensitive information about you or your client.
  - Changes to your operating system to become a robot of a master computer to send e-mails under your e-mail or ISP.

> Often these robots will also hijack the contacts used in the e-mail system. To thwart that, we have at the beginning of our contact list a contact called "!VIRUS" with that as the e-mail address, followed by about a dozen other bogus e-mail addresses.

> On too many occasions I have received e-mail with the address of someone I knew but which was clearly destructive spam. While it did no damage to me, it did tell me that I could not trust the security of that person's systems.

  - Destruction of data and programs.
  - Modification to files to make them unreliable.
  - Denial of access to the lawyer's own data.
- A second antivirus program, manually activated, to sweep the system with a different set of threats.

> Do not have both programs run in the background at the same time. They will fight each other and severely degrade performance of the system.

- Access to the system only through password or bio security at all levels and all times.

> Passwords are only as good as their secrecy. Using obvious words or numbers or displaying them in obvious places makes them less effective.

- Firewalls on networks to limit unauthorized access into the system through the internet.
- Encryption of files. Data storage, particularly storage that is off-premises and accessible offsite, should be encrypted. RSA algorithm (from the first letter of the surnames of the inventors, Ronald Linn Rivest, Adi Shamir, and Leonard Max Adelman) converts information into unintelligible gibberish with an encryption key, normally a character screen, and then converts it back to usable form with the input of the correct key. When others need to use the encrypted data, they are given a key.

> Virtually all word-processing and spreadsheet programs, as well as other programs, have the capacity to have files stored in an encrypted manner. The challenge to this methodology is that once encrypted, it cannot be unencrypted without the code. Because there is no way to retrieve this code, you need to save it someplace where you can get it (preferably somewhere protected).

> Freeware and commercial programs are available to encrypt a USB drive, hard drive, or other data storage.

- The ability to store highly confidential information "offline" or with limited access.
- The ability to remotely wipe data from a device that is compromised. For example, an employee leaves the firm but retains the phone containing client data, or the lawyer leaves the phone in a taxi.
- Limit access through traditional physical security, such as doors, gates, locks, etc. Because so much can be taken with so little weight, this protection remains one of the most important.

In my early years of practice, I briefly practiced family law. Once I represented the wife against a controlling, abusive, and psychopathic husband in a divorce. He was trying everything to find out what she was saying. Among other tricks, he paid a woman to join a support group to spy on his wife and report what she shared with the group. One night he broke into my office to get her file. I had it with me, so he came up empty. We found out about it later when he told his ex-wife what he was doing. If that file had turned up missing, we would have immediately known that it had been compromised. But if he had gotten into our system and copied files, we might never have known. We fixed the locks on the doors and used the locked filing cabinets.

- Frequent audits and checks to see that all of the precautions taken *perform* as designed and expected.
- Regular reviews of new technology *to keep* current.

The lawyer does not need to fully develop these skill sets. She should instead bring the mind-set that preserving the confidentiality, integrity, and availability of the data is job number one when practicing law in the State of Paperlessness and seek professionals who will assist her in meeting that goal.

Part of any legal team today should be the tech-savvy person who can keep things running smoothly and securely. This can be an employee or a contractor. In the same way, the lawyer should not be repairing her copier, and she should not be the one who gets into the details of operating a computer system. A function of that person should be to keep security systems up to date and protective.

PASSWORDS ARE THE BEST DEFENSE.

Practicing good password creation is the lawyer's best defense. "Brute force" computer programs can break passwords by simply generating all of the possibilities. The strength of a password, sometimes called entropy, is a function of the number of characters and the number of characters usable. The higher any of those numbers, the higher the entropy. Similarly, a shorter password with larger character count can be stronger than a long one that only uses the 26 letters of the Latin alphabet. Symbol counts are numbers (10), non-case-sensitive alphabet (26), case-sensitive alphabet (52), and all other printable ASCII characters (33).

Some very secure systems will generate passwords for the user. These will tend to be long, with all kinds of symbols and numbers, and hard to remember.

The passwords should be at least 12 characters long and, where permitted, include upper- and lower-case letters, as well as numbers and symbols. They should not be words or logically derived passwords from those who have gathered basic information about you. Longer is better. Based on assumption of intruder computer power, an 8-character password using case-sensitive alphabet can be broken by computer brute force in hours, while a 12-character password takes seven plus years! Using numbers increases that almost tenfold, and a 12-digit password that uses numbers, case-sensitive alphabet, and symbols can take six to seven thousand years. [1]

The challenge is having both a password that is hard to crack and one that is easy to remember. Since the number of characters used from a mix of numbers, letters, and symbols defines difficulty, create "pass phrases" instead of passwords. A pass phrase such as "Myredcar_costs$!" would be extremely difficult to crack by brute force. If that is too many characters, take the first letter of each word from a short memorable phrase "Oh say can you see!" and four numbers, "1812," and interleave and add an author (Francis Scott Key) to form a password, "Ols8cly2s!=FSK." That takes about 57 million years of brute force.

Some things should not be done in making passwords: use of number or alphabetic series, repeating only one character, using your name, family names, company name, street, or other identifiable information, Social Security number, or birth date.

Notes

1.   Jason Fossen, "How Long to Crack a Password Spreadsheet," SANS Windows Security Blog, *available at* http://www.sans.org/windows-security/2009/06/12/how-long-to-crack-a-password-spreadsheet/ (last visited Oct. 1, 2011).

CHAPTER 6

ORGANIZING, ANALYZING, AND DISTILLING DOCUMENTS AND INFORMATION IN THE STATE OF PAPERLESSNESS

A million documents have no meaning in themselves. Within those documents, however, answers exist. The lawyer's job is to bring not only meaning from those documents, but also understanding to those unwilling or unable to go through the raw information. The lawyer's job is to mine that mountain of documents and to retrieve its ore, smelt it, and form it into a piece of art. But that is what lawyers do. Better lawyers do it better, and the giants among us do it the best.

> In an unorganized mass of documents, if a document disappears, no one will know it.

In the State of Paperlessness, tools give the mute mountain of documents the ability to speak and the lawyer the ability to hear. Organization provides this voice.

- Organization takes attendance of documents present and tells the lawyer what is there and, more important, what is missing.

- Organization presents the right document to speak to the law-yer when and where he requires it.
- Organization allows the same set of documents to speak to multiple persons and multiple persons to speak back through coordination and collaboration.
- Organization provides the lawyer the ability to analyze what the documents say and let them say even more.
- Organization of the documents coupled with the lawyer's analysis brings a chorus of information that leads to understanding.

This is the essence of being a lawyer—making simple and under-standable what was otherwise complex and unordered.

> The lawyer shall possess the tools and the skills to use them to bring understanding to enormous amounts of data.

In the papered world, lawyers ordered papers, filled file folders, built notebooks, made checklists, tagged pages, highlighted phrases, cataloged notes, drew diagrams, and made outlines. In the State of Paperlessness, lawyers do all of that, but on steroids.

Almost any program the lawyer uses can be used as an organiza-tional tool. Word processing provides outlining and highlighting func-tions, for example. But there are tools specifically designed to organize, annotate, and tell.

> As a boy, I loved to build things. My brothers and cousins and I would clean the lumber from pallets that brought paper to our fathers' printing shop. With that lumber we built tree houses, towers, playhouses, go carts, and numerous other things. I had a 12-ounce hammer. It was hard for a boy to pound a 16-penny nail into an oak board. I got it done, but with more than a fair share of "bend-overs." Later I had the chance to use a 16-ounce with a longer handle. What a difference that made! When I built a garage as an adult, I used a 20-ounce framing hammer. If I did that again today, I would use power hammers.
>
> While I could very roughly beat a board into two pieces with a hammer, it was not cutting. I needed a saw. Go into any woodworker's shop and you'll find a variety of tools, hand and powered, each with a purpose. The skilled craftsman knows the difference and employs that difference to get the best out of the projects he makes.

There is a variety of digital notebook formats. Each has its own strengths and weaknesses. A lawyer may use more than one depending on the project. Among the tools available to convert the digital mountain into understandable information are the following:

Spreadsheet program. This program's strength can be found its inherent structure as a tabbed notebook capable of accepting unlimited data in many formats, its ease in making and shortening lists that can hyperlink to other documents, and its ability to manipulate and compute data to provide information on its own.

Microsoft's OneNote.™ Microsoft OneNote offers the lawyer a digital notebook with the look, feel, and functionality of the traditional three-ring binder but digitally supercharged. Absent caps on number of pages, restrictions on formats or media, or limits on size of the file, the lawyer can place everything in tabs and subtabs. In addition to documents, OneNote also can capture information from Calendar and Contact items and links to websites. Just like in a real binder, the lawyer can mark, draw, graph, or highlight anything on any page or scribble comments in the corner. Its automatic rendering of all documents will convert a scanned PDF image into searchable material. It even does it on photographs, picking up street names, highway numbers, billboard messages, license plates, and other material.

Adobe Portfolio. Adobe Portfolio provides the lawyer with a digital form of organizing documents in notebooks and file folders similar to those used in the papered world. Coupled with the inherent power of the PDF program, which allows combining of documents and deletion and insertion of pages, Portfolio allows the lawyer to organize documents to be found easily. It permits limitless additions of documents in native formats, not all of which are two-dimensional (think a three-dimensional model of a lift truck). Different users can add, modify, replace, and remove items from the portfolios just as a team would do in a physical sense.

Lexis/Nexis CaseMap.™ Where programs like OneNote and Portfolio take whole documents and organize them, CaseMap tears down documents to their elements, marks those elements, and links them to other elements as well as persons, organizations, and time. It also layers in the lawyer's analysis and understanding of the case to provide an organization of not just information but thoughts on that information.

MatchWare MindView.™ MindView organizes thoughts and processes and, within the structure created by that organization, incorporates documents. Its map provides a single display command center that gives the lawyer direct access to all of the elements of even the most complex projects, such as a merger or patent litigation. It facilitates the reorganization of the information. Its ready integration to and from Spreadsheets, PowerPoint, and Word give it more flexibility.

In writing this book, I did not want to get down to "step-by-step" or even particular product reviews. There are several programs, however, that in my experience are so uniquely designed and powerful that nothing else really competes with them. CaseMap™ is one of those. OneNote™ and Matchware's MindView™ are two others. These three programs take digital into different places than programs that merely replicate pen-on-paper functions digitally. Adobe PDF Portfolio™ in many ways is like the traditional paper systems, but its ability to merge multiple formats and automatically develop sophisticated linked concordances and indices puts it into the class of programs uniquely adapted to the digital world.

I will be the first to acknowledge that other programs are available that can meet or even better these programs in some areas. I expect that by the time this book is published these programs and others will have advanced into even greater power; such is the greatness of the digital age. In short, I note that these programs have worked well for me, not that other programs will not work as well or better for others.

THE LAWYER AND NOTEBOOKS

Notebooks, those three-ring binders designed to pinch the ends of fingers and hold paper, help lawyers organize all kinds of things. Some notebooks are not hard-back with rings, but pressboard folders with clasps to hold documents that are two-hole punched at the top. Lawyers use these tools to organize matters for quick reference (like a real estate closing file that has separate sections for correspondence, executed documents, title opinions, and the like), such as case law for briefs and motions and exhibits and notes for depositions; to hold corporate minutes and documents; to prepare for speeches; and many other uses.

In the State of Paperlessness, the notebook remains an important tool for the lawyer. The differences go beyond not having three shiny rings and hard covers. A paperless notebook holds more and disparate things, not all of which can be reduced to paper. Try putting a globe or a defective jet engine into a notebook.

Different approaches can be used to make a paperless notebook. One option is to take a particular document format—say, .DOCX—and make an electronic binder with everything in that format. But everything is not a .DOCX document. Typically a lawyer will have documents in .DOC, XLS, .PPPT, XLSX, .PDF, .JPG, .TIFF, and dozens of other formats.

Then there are the contacts and calendar entries. It is not just the electronic format, but the size and shape of the documents as well. Not all are 8½ by 11. Not all are two-dimensional pages; some may be three-dimensional objects or video and audio recordings. Fixing on one medium forces the lawyer to compromise on what and how information is kept. A PowerPoint presentation could be displayed without any soundtrack in PDF or word, but if the purpose is to use the material again, having it in the native format is important.

Paperless notebooks give more function than papered ones. They develop indexes and tabs dynamically. Multiple users can access the same notebook at the same time, even when separated by thousands of miles. They come with no bulk or weight. One person can carry hundreds or even thousands of them in his pocket or in the cloud. And they do not snag clothing or punch skin when inserting pages into them.

Building a notebook with spreadsheets

The digital spreadsheet provided the world with the first paperless three-ring binder. The name "notebook" fits its purpose. The spreadsheets automatically provide tabs, which the user can label and color. Its size is limited by the capacity of the machine that uses it—effectively unlimited. Each sheet can be separately formatted to handle a different orientation, size, or function. A letter-sized spreadsheet can follow a legal-sized form, which follows a square chart. It accepts insertions from other formats.

The spreadsheet provides functionality for handling and managing data. It can link to other documents irrespective of format. For example, if the case involves matching invoices and checks, the spreadsheet can contain columns showing the dates and amounts of the invoices and checks and, at the same time, link to PDF copies of those actual documents. The functions of the spreadsheet can count, add, subtract, average, and perform any number of other operations on the data.

> The spreadsheet combines the ability to organize documents with the ability to compute and manipulate some of the data.

Building a notebook with PDF portfolio

In the papered world, lawyers commonly use pressboard folders. The multiple-tabbed folders have embedded fasteners at the top. Such folders provide ideal organization for real estate, probate, bankruptcy, and similar matters. Portfolio ideally replaces that papered function paperlessly.

Portfolio does not exclude other formats or impose rigid sizes. The lawyer or his staff can put native documents in Portfolios regardless of size. A set of 36 x 54-inch maps, video or narrated PowerPoint, or a 3D depiction of a building fit in the Portfolio as readily as a letter-sized document.

Portfolio goes beyond just organizing the documents. PDF Full Text Indexing generates a complete word index of all of the documents within the portfolio. For example, in doing legal research, reduce the selected cases to PDF and add memoranda and briefs to the portfolio. The index will allow the lawyer to link every instance where a particular case is identified, or key term is used, and move quickly between these cites. As explained, later it has other benefits as well.

Use of the Portfolio provides a hyperlinked table of contents. Appropriately labeled documents will result in a usable table of contents.

The Portfolio can replace the corporate minute book with digital pages. Typically, all of the contents are documents of the same size and use the same electronic format. This would be a Portfolio for the whole book, with separate folios for each of the tabs in the book and subfolders for other divisions, such as years for the minutes. Audio or video recordings of the proceedings could be included in the Portfolio if they were available. While it contains all of that information, it has no physical weight, can be of unlimited length, and is available anywhere it is needed.

> Adobe Portfolio's strength is in organizing a multitude of documents of many formats into a readily accessible form for reference or presentation.

Building a notebook with OneNote

Microsoft's OneNote represents the best transition into the digital age for lawyers who use notebooks. It has the look and feel and utility of the three-ring binder. It fully integrates with other Microsoft products as well as PDF and other programs.

Because of its tab function, OneNote not only helps bring together documents but also helps identify what is missing. If the notebook is used for a real estate closing and tabs are created for each of the required documents for closing, a quick look will tell if all are there.

OneNote assists lawyers by organizing documents in some of the following ways:

- Replaces those multitab pressboard folders or accordion folders for cases such as probate and bankruptcy.
- Creates a trial notebook with tabs for required information and, as the case develops, inserts the documents.
- Provides an appellate notebook with everything needed to draft a brief and prepare for oral argument.
- Creates a binder for all of the odds and ends that come across the desk every day. Every random note or phone number can be saved into daily or weekly folders. OneNote goes one step further than the slips of paper with sorting, arranging, and searching.
- Records audio and video. It not only provides the voice playback, but also will mark notes made in the dictation and automatically makes a searchable text for finding comments later.
- Renders PDFs, including pictures, automatically to create searchable database. Insert a photograph with street names and automatically those street names, the billboards in the background, and other words are rendered and available for search.
- Organizes transactional matters. This allows the lawyer to have in one place the contact information, the calendar, the to-do list, drafts of documents, notes, letters of intent, e-mails, final drafts, and eventually signed documents for reference in the future.

OneNote organizes and displays documents much like a traditional three-ring binder. It provides the means of bringing and organizing disparate formats and types of information together to complete a matter or case while leaving the documents in their native format.

ORGANIZING THE ELEMENTS AND THOUGHTS THROUGH CASEMAP

Documents do not win cases. A sentence or so within a document makes or breaks a case. Finding and tagging those sentences is what brings out the value of a document. Rather than organizing documents, which it does, CaseMap organizes thoughts and elements.

In the same way that Word does not write briefs, CaseMap does not analyze cases. Documents do not just appear fully profiled and analyzed. The work, primarily at the front end, shines in the back end when needed the most.

> Understanding that the benefits of using CaseMap are deferred creates a barrier for many who try to use it. There is more front-end work, and the initial benefits do not seem worth it. It is the development of the case and analysis over time that builds a formidable knowledge base that brings together the facts, the analysis, the law, and the unknown to show a case for what it is and can be.

The lawyer has to view CaseMap less as a program and more as a power tool that, combined with discipline, breaks a case down to its bare essentials while putting in the structure to rebuild it later for trial. It forces the lawyer to not just identify a letter or a photograph, but to analyze them in terms of when and who and where and why and so what. Then it helps him preserve those thoughts for use later on. As the case develops, the lawyer visits the facts and the documents and the people over and over again as he edits, augments, moves, or removes the information. Brick by brick he adds material, and thought by thought he brings architecture; when combined, they bring understanding to the case.

These are living bricks. In time they speak to the lawyer, they grow, they connect to other bricks. Nothing stays the same. As the case develops, the new information is added. Over time the case begins to take shape. Strengths and weaknesses expose themselves. Gaps in the structure become clearer and their importance more pronounced. The issues develop themselves. It identifies the needed witnesses and those to fear. Among the tens of thousands of documents, the handful that really count stand out and the key one screams out.

As a sentence or paragraph strings unrelated letters together to express a thought, the lawyer puts the details and the analysis into

CaseMap, which in turn expresses the case's meaning. It goes beyond telling him specific facts or times or places and puts them together to tell that what a person did when, where, and how implicates the case.

Although it is possible to automatically create concordances of every word use, that does not help find and mark the critical words. Imagine that the case involves Hector suing Joan for breach of contract. A key element in the case is showing that Hector gave Joan notice of a breach. Throughout all of the documents, pleadings, and transcripts, Hector is variously known as Hector, buyer, idiot (by Alexander in frustration), or Leonardos (the name of his company). The contract is called in various places the contract, agreement, sale, understanding, Exhibit A, Defendant's Exhibit 31, Deposition Exhibit 5, or Sales Agreement of 7/11/2011. Joan is known in various places as Joan, Joanne (by a less than careful stenographer), seller, manager, Ms. Walden, Joanie (by friends), and Sis (by her brother). The written document at issue is known variously as the notice, the letter of August 14, 2011, or the demand letter. In a deposition of Alexander (or is it Alex, brother, salesman), the questions focus on whether Alexander received the notice from Hector and gave it to Joan. After identifying the written document as Deposition Exhibit 5 and Alexander's relationship both familial and business with his sister, the questions come down to this:

Q: Did you receive it?
A: Yeah, the idiot there gave it to me.
Q; Did you read it?
A: Yes.
Q: What did it say?
A: It complained about Sis not delivering the goods on time.
Q: What goods?
A: The ones that he claimed he ordered.
Q: Did you show your sister?
A: I laid it on her desk.
Q: The desk in her office?
A: Yes.
Q: Why did you put it there?
A: That is where I put everything for her to read.
Q: When did you put it on her desk?
A: The day after he gave it to me.

Aside from some less than careful questioning, the above example illustrates how often key points in a transcript are less than clear. Obviously, it would have been preferable to get an answer like "Hector gave me the notice of default for defective goods provided in the Sales Agreement of 7/11/2011 and I put it on Joan's desk on August 16, 2011."

No search of the key words will find such a phrase. Pronouns and nicknames and other avatars will hide the answer. Exact dates are far from clear. But in CaseMap, part of the process is to actually link the various names to the single name so that as time goes on, whenever something is required about the agreement, all of those instances come up, even if labeled "it." The dates can be determined.

The lawyer can view the case at 10,000 feet or at a fraction of an inch, from the top or the bottom, from the viewpoint of his client or his opponent. Pen on paper notes are two dimensional. With some cross references they can be three dimensional. CaseMap builds a 10 or even 20 dimensional structure that cannot be expressed or done in paper. As a consequence, the lawyer has that many ways of looking at his case, and his opponents, to see strengths and flaws invisible otherwise.

Diligent use of case management forces the attorney to fully comprehend the facts and issues in the matter and not only making them more accessible in digital or visual form, but it mentally prepares the attorney for hearings, depositions, and trials.

Not only does it build a database that can say all of that, but the very act of building that database with bricks of facts and analysis grows within the mind of the attorney for rapid reference in the heat of a deposition or trial when no opportunity exists to even look at the CaseMap.

In the first case in which I used the software, several farmers brought in a copy box full of documents, letters, and other information they had gathered to support their claim of bad feed. I scanned and numbered all of documents. One by one I analyzed each document and filled the database. By the time I was done, I had a complete and detailed list of the history and through the letters identified the factual issues. As the lawsuit developed, I learned less about facts but could concentrate on filling gaps, reinforcing points, and understanding how all of the facts fit together.

By disciplining himself to analyze every item placed in the file, the lawyer accomplishes three important things—he is fully exposed to all that is in the case, he is forced to organize and reorganize all of that information so that it makes sense, and he has as a by-product a handy, easy-to-use reference to the entire case all the time.

> CaseMap does not organize documents; rather, it distills the documents and other information and organizes the distillate to establish the case. CaseMap allows multiple lawyers to review and analyze the same information differently so that rather than trying to figure out what the other lawyer thinks about a document, each lawyer can key in what he thinks.

ORGANIZING THOUGHTS WITH MIND MAPPING

The lawyer cannot describe everything in terms of documents or even elemental facts. In the end, the lawyer has to organize a matter in terms of the processes as well as the thoughts. Where notebooks and other organizational tools are linear and hierarchical, Mind Mapping provides a means to organize ideas, facts, arguments, and law graphically and without the constraints of hierarchies. The connections between thoughts can be treelike or even connections between branches. Because of the nonlinear approach, the use of Mind Mapping encourages an "outside the box" analysis of the issues.

> If you are one of those people who like to draw out what you are working on or to stand at a whiteboard and visually display an argument, Mind Mapping is for you.

Mind Mapping is a process that begins with the end (manage and complete an appeal, things to get done today, a winning argument on a given issue), identifies the different things that would contribute to that result, and then orders them. Depending on the nature of the parts, it also identifies times, completions, priority, resources, and even subparts. Here is a sample of things to do today.

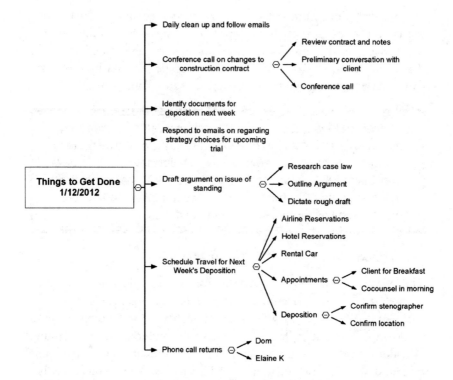

Not apparent are the links to documents and the deadlines and other information in there.

Mind Mapping is ideal for the following tasks:

- Brainstorming
- Building, maintaining, and using time lines.
- Identifying and organizing ideas
- Visual display of written documents
- Building storylines and presentations
- Acting as a command display to navigate through complex projects
- Gathering concepts and organizing arguments for an outline to draft a document

This particular map provides a command display during the process. As things were completed, they were coded, new things were added, and, where they existed, lengths of documents and other material were provided.

> Mind Mapping provides a way to easily organize thoughts and tasks.

LITIGATION AND THE TRIAL NOTEBOOK

At trial, the lawyer has no time to process the mountains of documents, transcripts, exhibits, and pleadings of a case. He needs the right page at the right time during the fast pace of trial. A war room filled with boxes of files, folders of pleadings, and binders of legal research plus files of notes need to be reduced to something he can handle. Preparation for trial means turning that amorphous mass of information into organized, sorted, categorized, and easily found and used. They call it the Trial Notebook.

The Trial Notebook remains one of the most powerful tools for the trial lawyer. Organized fundamentally in the flow of a trial from commencement of litigation to post-trial motions, it gives the lawyer places to put the pieces of a case together as they will unfold in litigation, providing context. Over the years, many different lawyers and legal suppliers have provided such outlines commercially. Other lawyers have created their own. The process is simple: Acquire a standard three-ring notebook, insert tabs labeled for each of the stages and sub-stages of the trial, and fill the space between the tabs with notes, transcripts, exhibits, and other material as it is gained. The result is a dynamic script from complaint to verdict. With those in mind, the lawyer starts at the beginning of the notebook and makes sure that everything needed to get to the desired end shows up in the appropriate place in the trial. In the process, he discovers that some of those pieces, such as exhibits, have their own prerequisites. As they are identified, he places the needed witnesses and questions in place.

Besides the great advantage of making sure that the requirements of winning are in the notebook, the notebook permits the lawyer to rehearse the trial from beginning to end and adjust the order of witnesses and exhibits, add or subtract arguments, develop lines of questions and, most important, hone it all down to the necessary.

For those lawyers who built and used such notebooks, the idea of giving up the physical book upon which to write, rip out pages, tag notes, and the like is hard to consider. In the State of Paperlessness, the reliance on a tablet or laptop instead of a three-ring binder in the courtroom is possible, but the final form of a notebook does not explain the power behind building it without paper.

Some lawyers I know have used notebooks as a matter of course for almost every case. They open a case, they start a notebook. Many of these notebooks come with prepared check-lists, questionnaires, and predefined tabs to help the lawyer identify, gather, and organize the material with the goal of pre-paring the basis for each step of the litigation process. Lawyers also have their own style of organization.

My first "trial notebook" was nothing more than a blank legal pad. I outlined the case from "All rise!" to adjournment with the voir dire, opening statements, witnesses, exhibits, motions, closing arguments, and jury instructions. Then I labeled clean sheets of paper with each of the outline elements and pro-ceeded to fill in the space. Exhibits and other information would be attached. I originally paper-clipped it, then went to the three-ring binder. But I always kept the outline. I pasted it to an over-sized piece of tag stock or cardboard so that it never got lost. It was my road map through the trial. At each stage's completion, I checked off that it was done.

Then I changed to the use of file folders instead of tabs. I had a file folder for each witness, settlement, closing argu-ment, voir dire, and so forth. The folders had the metal clasps so that I did not lose any information. The problem came late in a multiday hearing when all of the file folders began to look alike and I could not find the one for the next witness. In use during the hearing, it had been misplaced. Then I went to the notebook.

The challenge for practitioners who use the old-fashioned low-tech notebooks in switching to paperless is leaving that com-fort zone so critical during the stress of trial. But abandoning the physical notebook for trial is not necessarily the first or even a required step. The State of Paperlessness provides the means to build better notebooks, which, at time of trial, can be reduced to paper—or not.

In the State of Paperlessness, the lawyer can build her own super trial notebook. The SuperTrial Notebook combines all of the programs and facilities available within the confines of a notebook structure.

- OneNote is the primary notebook, with tabs and pages laid out for all aspects of the trial.
- Excel Spreadsheet creates the time line, responsibility, and status report.
- Pleadings are placed in an Adobe Portfolio with a table of contents and an index of all key words.
- Depositions and exhibits are also combined with Adobe Portfolio with a link in the OneNote to that portfolio.
- All of the depositions, documents, interviews, and research are distilled into CaseMap, which is connected via a hyperlink in OneNote.
- Individual documents and notices are inserted into the OneNote book.
- Using the function in OneNote or inserting Word documents, notes are made and pages annotated.

Example of using OneNote in the State of Paperlessness: Appeals

As stages of litigation go, appeals hold one advantage over other stages— the material to be considered is tightly defined (the record), much less than the mass of discovery and trial preparation. Combining the power in OneNote with the PDF catalog and CaseSoft, the appeal brief drafting will be just that: drafting without lots of wasted time, focus, and thought looking for information.

- Create OneNote notebook named by the client or case being appealed.

> When more than one person is working on an appeal, all can access the notebook, particularly if it is saved in the cloud or on an office network. Create a tab labeled Key Information with pages such as the following:

- Insert case information, such as the style, number, court, and attorneys.
- Deadlines, key dates, and checklists.

> This calendaring does not replace putting the dates on the main calendar. They appear here for convenience while working on the appeal.

- Contacts for attorneys, clients, clerk, courts, and others. One Note provides icons that will move these from the Contacts in Outlook.
- Create a section for the Court Decision from below being appealed.
- Create a section for notices of appeal.
- Create a section with separate subsections containing the docket, all relevant decisions, journal entries, and orders from the case being appealed.
- Information on the judges as their identity is learned.
- Create a tab for the record, including transcripts and pleadings. These can be actually inserted as documents or create links.

As the case moves along from preparation to discovery to motion practice to trial to appeal, the issues and relevant facts narrow. In cases where I filled boxes of documents in preparation and days of trial and depositions, the court of appeals accurately summed up all that had gone on in two or three paragraphs or a few pages in its decision. In one case, I filed a petition for a writ of certiorari with the U.S. Supreme Court. As I was holding the finished booklet, I noticed that a few dozen pages held everything about the case. The total folder at that stage, including all working documents, relevant items from the lower courts, research notes, and so on had filled a large expandable file folder. The court of appeals case, which included the transcript from the trial and all of the exhibits and notes and research in preparation for the brief, copies of the briefs, and the decision, filled a couple of copy boxes. The trial material was larger still, and the information prior to trial was enormous.

From then on, I tried to get to those kernels sooner in the process by removing the unneeded information.

- Combine all of the documents from the trial, including pleadings, transcript, and exhibits, into a PDF portfolio. *On a page put a link to the portfolio. Using PDF Full Text Indexing, gen*erate a complete word index of the entire record. Insert that into the notebook.

> While the complete word index can help find some words, it will not detect when the same thing is called something else (for example, John Smith, defendant, recipient, Johnnie Smith, and misspellings such as Jon).

- Insert link to CaseMap from the trial.
- Analyze the transcript, record, and exhibits. In this case, CaseMap of the trial can be modified, but it should be new work looking only at what is in the record.
- Create a Section for Brief Drafting with subsections for Issues, Facts, Outline of Brief, Notes, and Drafts.
- Create a Brief Section with subsections for the appellants Brief, Appellee's Brief, Reply Brief, and Opinion.
- Create a Law Section with subsections for Court Rules, Statutes, and Case Law.
- Now that the notebook is created, work on the brief can move rather quickly. All that is needed is there.

Over years of appellate work, I have come to believe that no matter how much work was done at the trial level, annotating the trial record and doing new legal research are essential. The record and issues facing the appellate court differ from what faced the lawyer preparing for and participating in the trial. The trial lawyer could plan based on what evidence he thought would get into the record; the appellate lawyer must rely entirely on what the record actually contains.

This is a living notebook. It is designed for augmentation, deletion, and rearrangement. The facts can be gathered by listing them or taking snapshots in Adobe of the transcript or exhibit. Issues can be listed as the lawyer thinks of them. Over time the list can be revised and reordered.

During research, key cases and statutes (annotated on the PDF with highlights, notes, etc.) are placed in the notebook. Besides what is annotated in the PDF, OneNote allows notes on the side or the inserted documents themselves.

By printing the case or statute to a PDF and annotating it using the various editing tools available, the PDF also builds a table of all of the notes and comments. During drafting or preparation when you need a particular note, rather than rifling through the pages, use the annotation index; it will get you there faster. For me, using visual memory to find things fails on electronic viewing is but corrected by this index.

This indexing also allows for multiple participants to make their own mark and notes. The result is a single copy of relevant law that has all of the annotations from everyone readily available.

In Mind Map, list the issues. Then, with each of these issues, identify and label elements of the argument. Put them in free form, unconnected to others. Whether they are key or secondary is unimportant at this stage. After all of those are entered, attach the key ones to the issue and the secondary arguments to the key ones. Look over the display. Are there missing points? Put them in.

Once the Mind Map is complete, export as a Word outline. Convert the thoughts into sentence outline. Reading the outline from beginning to end should fully describe the argument. Add to the outline other requirements of the brief as required by the rules.

Either by dictation or typing, fill in the body text to the outline. Add the required sections, such as jurisdiction statement. The result is a great first draft of the brief.

As drafts are prepared, they can be saved in the file. Using the collaboration tools available in the word processor or PDF, the work of multiple participants can be combined to produce the drafts. Without ever printing a single piece of paper, the brief can go from building the record to a finished brief.

In counting words, make sure that the words that are entered through SnapShot are included in the count. Also, most courts require a rendered PDF, meaning there are no images unrendered.

CHAPTER 7

COMMUNICATING AND TRANSMITTING DOCUMENTS IN THE STATE OF PAPERLESSNESS

Every organized society has had its means of transferring information. Rome established elaborate roads. The Incas had a sophisticated organization of runners. In the United States we had the Pony Express, part of a large enterprise known as the U.S. Post Office. Once a cabinet office, the Postmaster General now presides over a paper delivery service more and more replaced by the information service in the State of Paperlessness, e-mail. Paper no longer carries communication. Digits do.

> E-mail is the official mail service of the State of Paperlessness.

E-MAIL CAN DO ANYTHING PAPER DOES WHEN IT COMES TO
    COMMUNICATION.

What was once sent by mail is now e-mailed. Any item that is not an object can be conveyed by e-mail. E-mail now reigns as the vehicle of communication. Virtually every lawyer today communicates through e-mail. It replaces not only paper but phone calls and face-to-face conversations. It is so ubiquitous that it needs no introduction or explanation. It just is.

Communication with and through e-mail is as comprehensive as use of an envelope and a stamp, but without either of these. As a consequence, when using e-mail, treat every e-mail as if it were formerly sent first class, because no legal difference exists. This means that the lawyer should provide the same information in e-mail that she would in a letter, such as name, address, and other contact information. If it will be lengthy (generally more than a few paragraphs), actually draft it on a letterhead in PDF form and attach it to the e-mail.

E-mails with the attachments can and should be saved together in the PSM. In this way the lawyer knows exactly what was sent. The same goes for incoming e-mail. If the document that is attached has an independent basis to exist, such as an invoice, a memorandum, a lengthy communication, a contract, or the like, the lawyer should save it as a separate document that can be filed independently and separately from the e-mail itself.

In the class of e-mails are other technologies, such as text messages and instant messaging. So long as the latter is truly private and can maintain that status, then it can be a professional way to communicate with clients and others. Text messaging is great for short messages, but the speed of texting brings even greater risks of violating confidences or sharing with the wrong people too much anger or other thoughts.

THE LAWYER CAN RELY ON E-MAILING AS SHE WOULD FIRST-CLASS MAIL.

The law now provides that generally an e-mail is deemed sent when the user hits the Send button and is received when a server places it in the lawyer's inbox.[1] The Uniform Electronic Transactions Act (UETA) has been adopted by all but three states, Washington, New York, and Illinois,[2]. Those states have adopted electronic transactions acts of similar effect.[3] Among the provisions of the UETA is default times of sending and receiving e-mails. Generally an e-mail is deemed sent when submitted by the sender to an outside service to transmit and received when the outside service deposits it in the recipient's e-mail account. Issues of intelligibility or content remain questions of state law.

THE LAWYER NEEDS TO TAKE CONTROL OF HER E-MAIL.

With hundreds of e-mails coming in, most unsolicited and even unwanted, controlling what comes in and goes out of the lawyer's e-mail account requires effort and determination. It does not just happen.

The lawyer should establish e-mail addresses.

Each lawyer—not the firm, but each lawyer and staff person in the firm—needs his or her own e-mail. This openly advertised e-mail should use the professional name and firm name to provide a professional and businesslike image. If the firm has a logo, use it. What the lawyer does on her own time is one thing, but an avatar for a lawyer's professional account has no place in professional communication. To use such a made-up name can provide an unflattering impression of the lawyer.

> For this one, at least, use a professional service to host and handle the e-mails. Preferably it should use your firm's domain name rather than the free ones. In that way, messages for advertising are not inserted. Why would an auto dealer want to have you as an attorney if the e-mail he received from you included an ad for a national auto sales company?
>
> It speaks volumes in terms of professionalism and a serious attempt to be part of 21st-century business practice. These are easily obtained and cost little. The commercial, free domain names are great for personal use, but undermine the professionalism or credibility of the lawyer.

In addition to the general account for the lawyer, she should have other e-mail accounts as well.

- Personal or home e-mail. The business e-mail address is for clients, other attorneys, judges, would-be clients, and even strangers. It should be business-related. While some personal communication can enter into the business mail just like one makes or receives personal calls at work, it should be the exception and not the rule.

Within the business, have several accounts for different purposes.

- Purchasing e-mail. When purchasing online, use this e-mail address. It will reduce the junk mail that comes from vendors who sell the e-mails of their customers.
- Information or news mailings. This account is where you can direct your subscriptions. This way they will not interfere with your business communications. In this case, an avatar is appropriate.

- Other e-mail addresses for specific purposes or cases. There are some matters— administrative, for example—in which more than one person in the firm is involved. This could be for new-client inquiries. By routing those e-mails into each attorney's mailbox, you can be sure they will be addressed.
- Secured e-mails. There are some situations, such as banking, e-mails regarding your cloud file storage, etc., which should have e-mail addresses that are not obvious and more akin to pass-words to limit hackers and protect your digital property.

Not in contradiction of earlier advice, when you get a firm name for a website, also buy the domain name for .org, .net, and other extensions. Further, consider getting e-mail addresses in some of the free places with the same name as your business one, such as mylawfirm@gmail.com. Some people learn slowly and will inadvertently try using these extensions on your name.

Passwords are the lock and key even for e-mail.

To protect information being sent by e-mail, put it under lock and key—virtually, that is. Password security can be in the documents themselves. When finishing a PDF, secure it and send a password-encrypted document via e-mail. Then, in a separate e-mail or orally, inform the client of the password. Another option is to upload the information to a password-controlled and -secured website the client can access.

Some of those websites allow you to limit viewing of docu-ments only to specific URL addresses to avoid someone else getting the website and password.

As for the information you have, limit all access to pass-words—your computer, the network, the management programs, and some files themselves.

KEEP THE E-MAIL BOX CLEAN.

Despite all efforts to judiciously use different e-mail addresses, and saying no the ubiquitous question of whether the lawyer wants to receive additional spam, there will be spam—and lots of it. Some companies lie and really do market e-mails. Robots roam the Internet seeking e-mail form websites and membership lists. So if the lawyer has an e-mail address, spam will come.

It is a problem for lots of reasons, not the least of which is that amidst that clutter are very important missives. Here are some ways to keep it cleaned up:

- Learn to use the Rules function in Outlook. This tool allows the lawyer to identify spam and automatically remove it or redirect it before it shows up in the end box.

> I use it not only to get rid of spam, but to direct messages I do want to read but with different priority than others (some more, some less). For example, special clients' e-mail will be flagged.

- Practice the 60-second rule. When an e-mail is opened, if it cannot be answered in 60 seconds, send it to a task list, calendar item, or somewhere it will get the attention it deserves.
- Do not use e-mail Inbox as a to-do file. That is, unless you can keep it down to a dozen or less. E-mail messages should not be left on the server.
- Use e-mail for e-mail. Do not supercharge the e-mail program to provide you with an archive of messages and documents.
- Make it routine to spend time to clean the Inbox every day.
- Program the PDA, tablets, or laptops that access the e-mails to delete from the server just as if it were on the main computer. This particularly applies if the lawyer travels a lot.

> Many servers will delete old e-mails. In other cases, old e-mails with attachments can quickly fill memory limits.

ORGANIZING E-MAILS

With hundreds of e-mails coming in each day and a couple dozen of those worthy of being saved, finding a way to organize saved e-mails is a challenge. As noted above, doing this as part of the Outlook or other e-mail program folders is not a good idea. Rather, the lawyer should use other organizing tools.

- Use the e-mail profiling and saving module in the practice or document management program. As a minimum requirement, any practice management program should integrate with the e-mail to save e-mails and retrieve them as needed. Save them to the same case matter file as if they were a document. Where there are multiple cases, e-mails can be saved multiple times.

- Convert to PDF and save as a document. There is an Adobe add-on available for Outlook and other e-mail programs that will convert a message (or the entire folder) and attachments to PDF. Once converted, these PDFs can be saved in the document management system.
- Acquire an e-mail management program. A number of vendors provide programs that will allow the user to profile, save, and retrieve e-mails. While integration with documents is better, if that is not available, these programs are invaluable in handling the mass of e-mail communications.

Take care with e-mail language.

When drafting an e-mail, expect that it will multiply and reach all corners of the digital world instantly. Once sent, it cannot be withdrawn. It remains forever in the digital world to be resurrected at the most untimely moment. The use of e-mail is so user-friendly and informal-looking that some wrongly assume that the drafting of an e-mail can be equally informal. It is a formal, on the permanent record communication.

The lawyer shall carefully choose words when using e-mail.

E-mail fights can get ugly, public, and permanent. A Boston attorney applied for a job with another Boston attorney. At first she agreed to the job, but changed her mind. In her e-mail she said, "The pay you are offering would neither fulfill me nor support the lifestyle I am living." The hiring attorney responded with "Do you really want to start pissing off more experienced lawyers at this early stage of your career?" To which the applicant responded "blah, blah, blah." And the hiring attorney hit the forward button. Forward followed forward, and seemingly the whole world knew. After all was said and done, the new attorney admits she is "more careful about how I word e-mails and the content of them."[4]

A real danger comes with the small, handheld e-mail generators, such as BlackBerries, PDAs, and iPhones. The keyboard
is so small that getting an e-mail that is clear, spelled right,
says all the needed words and nothing more is nearly impossible. Though excusable, the results can be difficult. In a matter I was handling where we were buying stock, we proposed
an offer, and one of the shareholders responded, "I reject your
offer of $400 but agreed to sell all of my shares for $100 per
share." Under the circumstances, the client could have accepted
that offer. Instead we wrote back, "We accept your offer of one
hundred dollars ($100) per share." He responded quickly that
the earlier one was a mistake, he had typed it on his Blackberry and did not confirm that he was saying "$1,000."

Watch the tone in language you use in e-mail. Seek always to be
professional. Sometimes one may be absolutely livid, and rightfully
so, over something that someone has said or done or sent in an e-mail.
It is absolutely imperative that you do not respond in kind within an
e-mail. In drafting e-mail, you should respect all persons as valuable
human beings. Choice of tone must be at the forefront in all use of the
computer. If you are uncertain whether the tone is right, have a trusted
individual look at before it goes out or exercise the 24-hour wait rule
before reviewing again and mailing.

One way in which I try to maintain a more professional and
direct approach is to begin my messages by naming the recipient. If I know them well, I address them by their first name,
otherwise by their whole name. Then I insert a simple statement, such as "Good day," "Good Morning!" or the like. That
helps set a tone of respect within the e-mail.

THE LAWYER NEEDS TO PRACTICE E-MAIL ETIQUETTE.

The new technology brings its own ethics and rules for lawyers.

- Promptly respond to e-mails. The expectation is that an e-mail
  will receive a response within a day, or even hours. When an
  immediate response is not possible, return an e-mail with a note
  that it was received and a response will be forthcoming within a
  certain period of time. In this way, the lawyer projects a high

level of responsiveness. If the lawyer is out of office on travel or vacation and will not be responding to e-mails, insert an "out of office" e-mail to let the senders know.

- Conversely, when the lawyer sends an e-mail that requires fast response, call the individual to confirm receipt.
- Depending on the relationship with the sender, the lawyer may want to deliberately delay response in order to slow down that sender's demands on the lawyer. In other words, send a response that is timed to establish a pace.
- Limit the Received and Opened message options on e-mails. Consistent use of these features will reduce the responsiveness of recipients.
- If the lawyer does not like responding to e-mails, let senders know. Use the auto reply to every message and explain that e-mail is unreliable and that the lawyer's response will be erratic. Direct them to where they can reach her, such as over the phone or through another person.
- Attach a voice mail. When the communication is best done with a human voice, dictate a voice mail and attach it to the e-mail.
- Establish e-mail expectations up front. As part of an opening discussion of the attorney-client relationship, even better in a follow-up letter or agreement, explain how you use e-mail and what kinds of responses to expect.

> I worked once with a professional who made it clear from the beginning that his e-mail responses would be unpredictable and delayed. I knew it, respected it, and the relationship worked out. Without the warning, it might not have.

> E-mails are not only easier to use, they can be used to avoid a direct confrontation with the other person in the conversation. So common are e-mails, that some people view a phone call as an intrusion (the caller defines when the conversation occurs) and will e-mail a request for a time to make a phone call.

Things that will help avoid e-mail gaffes

Try as the lawyer might, there will be gaffes. Here are some suggestions to reduce them.

- Remove the "reply all" icon from the e-mail toolbar or ribbon.
- Use the "rules" option in e-mail to delay the actual sending of messages for a period long enough to let you undo if necessary.
- Type all your messages in your word processor and save drafts as a Word file, and when really sure, cut and paste to the properly addressed e-mail.
- Enter addresses for sending after typing the message.

RULES A LAWYER MUST FOLLOW WHEN USING E-MAIL

When we learned the law, we were taught the elements of the various torts, the rationale behind constitutional law. We were given the *Blue Book* for rules on legal citations. We need the same kind of fundamental framework for e-mails. Here is a start:

Anything posted in an e-mail never dies.

Regardless of whether it was sent, put in a draft folder, or deleted, every e-mail you produce is potentially Exhibit A for a lawsuit against you, your firm, or your family. E-mails do not die or disappear; they merely hibernate until they are called upon to inflict harm on you or your clients. It could be today, tomorrow, or years later. If you typed them, they were saved somewhere, only to be retrieved by an e-discovery software package. Retrieval and exposure of e-mails, even when illegally hacked, can have major consequences. Consider the effect of hackers who broke into the e-mail server at the University of East Anglia's Climatic Research Unit and posted over 1,000 e-mails and 3,000 documents retrieved online. The information went viral and was used by opponents of climate change to show that much of the reported data supporting climate change was part of conspiracy and a cover-up on the part of some of the most respected scientists behind the global warming movement. As one commenter noted, "The biggest environmental movement of the last decade may see a resurgence in opposition thanks to a few potentially innocent e-mail messages."[5]

Don't say anything in an e-mail you could not say in person.

Wisecracks, sarcasm, and dry humor just don't communicate the same in e-mail. The context that provides needed understanding for the comment is lost in the black and white text of the e-mail or forgotten as days, months, and years pass before it is thrown back at the lawyer. The humor or sarcasm or irony that was so obvious goes missing, and what was thought of as a peach of a joke becomes a stinker of an insult.

Think twice before hitting Send—maybe three times.

Every e-mail should have thought behind it. Despite all the technology that we can use to control access to confidential information, there are still some communications that are just not worth the risk of client exposure by release. As part of routine practice, as the lawyer transfers documents and communications to a client, co-counsel, or other individual via e-mail, she should ask herself, should this document go? Should it go to this address? Should it even be sent by e-mail? After all, for some very highly sensitive information, other alternatives would be best.

An example of why thought comes first, consider this errant e-mail: On July 14, 2011, an employee at the risk-control group office of Chevron sent to the media an e-mail that contained spreadsheets, tables, and charts detailing that energy giant's trading. According to the news media, "Six minutes later, the employee attempted to recall the message. Five minutes after that, he sent a more personal plea to Dow Jones & Co., Bloomberg News, and Argus Media Ltd.: 'Please delete the information from the e-mail which was accidentally sent. Thank you very much.'"[6] They not only did not delete it, they disseminated the information in news reports.

One of the dangers of having highly sensitive information online and in filenames is that in the speed of transmitting data and attaching files to e-mails, it is easy to mistakenly attach the wrong document to an e-mail going to the wrong person.

> Before I send an e-mail with an attachment, I open all of the attachments in the e-mail to make sure the right ones are there. I also created a rule in Outlook to delay the sending of e-mails by two minutes. This would allow you the chance to correct the e-mail if you realized it was going to the wrong party, for example.

> For the really gaffe-prone e-mailer, short of abandoning e-mail entirely, another brute force approach would be to turn off "automatically send" e-mails but store them in the outbox. Then open each one and inspect addresses and attachments before being sent or have someone else check them.

Saving in draft folders is really sending.

It is too easy for the unfinished, and terrible, e-mail in a draft to be sent later without your even knowing about it.

Always check the "To field" before sending.

Do you know everyone in that e-mail list? Is it necessary to send that e-mail to each and every one of them? Fill in the "To" field after writing the heated/personal/jokey e-mail.

> When working with a client, make sure that the e-mail address you have is the proper place to send attorney-client communications. Do others have access to the e-mail account? Will it be received on a business computer and subject to storage and retrieval by third parties?

This applies to addresses in the "CC" and "BCC" fields.

Think twice about hitting "Reply All."

The words "Reply All" really mean to tell the e-mail server to find every e-mail address in the universe and send the message there. As far-fetched as that might sound, it really works that way, and very efficiently. Within seconds, those who should not receive it (that is, for your own well-being) will have the e-mail in their hands.

Read the whole e-mail, including all of the parts of the previous messages in the string, before responding.

Forwarded and reply e-mails contain other e-mails embedded in them. Before forwarding to others, make sure you understand what is in them. Though it may appear to be simply a reply to an earlier message, a number of others may have been included. By sending it, you implicitly make it your message as well.

Know the difference between reply and forward.

When forwarding a message from opposing counsel to your client with your comments, make sure that you hit forward, not reply.

Text messages and instant messages should be used sparingly.

Due to the rapid-fire, short, compulsive use of these types of messages, use them only to confirm a date, say thanks, or the like. Communication requiring thought should be by e-mail or phone.

Do not convey by e-mail anything that is dishonest, pornographic, or insulting to anyone.

When sending anything, the lawyer must assume that others besides the recipient will read it. This includes other attorneys and their staff. Even to friends it is risky. That outrageous X-rated video sent to a college classmate may be read by his children or his wife before he knows it is there. Then there remains the danger of the wrong e-mail address inadvertently being used.

Do not broadcast.

There are names in the mailing list that should not receive the e-mail, guaranteed. The risk is that the broadcast list is later mistakenly used. Imagine the result when a salesman who unwittingly sent to all the contacts in his list (customers, family, government employees) some choice pornography.

Remember that sometimes the e-mail contains too much information.

If there must be an intimate conversation with someone, do it by phone or old-fashioned mail. An e-mail can quickly be distributed to the world. It is like a postcard. Lawyers who have reviewed e-mails in e-discovery all have stories of steamy or unseemly e-mails captured in the process.

Do not spam.

Yes, that was a great article, but that does not mean it should be sent to everyone on the contact list. Keep e-mail to the essentials.

MAILING TO THE MASSES, SOCIAL NETWORKING AND COMMUNICATING IN THE STATE OF PAPERLESSNESS

Where e-mail generally is one to one or one to definite few, it fulfills the functions of first class postage in the papered world. There are times when mass mailings may be appropriate. Depending on the nature of the practice and degree of professionalism, promotion of the lawyer's practice electronically through social networks is certainly an option.

> Social networking is not a substitute for using e-mail in client and other private communication in the same way that an attorney would not communicate through the newspaper, radio, or billboard. Social networking has its place, and knowing its limits is one of its challenges.

The development of social networks has radically changed the landscape of law practice. It is almost imperative for a lawyer developing a practice, particularly one geared to small business and individuals, to fully use Facebook, LinkedIn, Twitter, and other social media for advertising. These media certainly are paperless, but they should only be used for information that the lawyer would shout in a crowded mall or publish across national television.

An added danger of lawyers using Facebook is the risk that by "friending" someone, they create potential conflicts of interests with existing or prospective clients.

> Communicating on social networks is like having a conversation with an open mike while broadcasting on a global TV program.

> **The lawyer shall not convey confidential information via social networks.**

> Because this information is open 24/7 for anyone to view, you need to make sure that it always puts you in a professional light. Repeated photos of a drunk smiling at a party is not in that category.

LINKEDIN, THE PROFESSIONAL NETWORK

LinkedIn is a networking system for professionals. To get the most out of it, the lawyer needs to consider it at the same level as appearing in court or with clients, not at a party or a bar. Include a professional portrait of the lawyer—not her pet, grandchildren, a design or symbol. The system may be paperless, but it should not be faceless. People are hiring people to be lawyers, and the portrait needs to show that the lawyer fits that requirement. Other things to include are:

- Provide a complete profile showing education, court admissions, bar associations, and committees.
- Identify reported cases and other cases of note *you* participated in.
- Post recommendations, but keep in mind any ethical rules regarding those.
- Use groups or create ones that are consistent with the practice.
- Seek to link in to those you are already working with. For example, if you focus on estate planning, connect to accountants, life insurance salesmen, brokers, and others who share the same client pool. In requesting to be linked, explain why the linkage is good for everyone.
- Be selective about the people with whom you link. Go to their sites and see if they have blogs, twitters, Facebook, or other accounts, and look at those. Ask whether, as a lawyer, you are comfortable being associated with their content.

> The beauty of network connections is connections. The evil of network connections is connections. Quality, not quantity, is the key.

- Include your LinkedIn url in e-mails and other communications.
- Keep the profile up to date with recent articles, news accounts, *and* cases.

These social networks provide a means to quickly let the world know what the lawyer does, what she knows, and who her clients are. Anything bad about the lawyer will go viral in minutes. While she can rejoice in good publicity, it can hurt her with bad publicity. One aspect of Facebook is that people think they are among friends and can tell a ribald story or display some off-color images and everyone will laugh and forget.

> *Forget* is not a word that means anything in Facebook. Would-be clients, opposing counsel, and even judges will go to Facebook pages and see stories about you away from your work and public image. If they do not jibe, then you are in trouble.

WEBSITES

The difference between websites and e-mails is that the reader must make an effort to go to the website to get information, and the information tends to be more general. On the other hand, search engines are visiting the site and building search codes that will direct individuals to the site. It is a way of promoting the business. It is also the first place attorneys, clients, and judges will meet the lawyer. The website should provide a good image.

Using the website to convey information

A firm website is a necessary part of today's practice. Here is what should be on the website:

- The firm name.
- How to contact the firm by physical, mail, phone, and e-mail address.
- The names and phots of attorneys along with their areas of focus, their education and experience, and how to reach them.
- All certifications earned by attorneys in the firm.

> Some state bars require that any mention of focus contain a statement that the attorney is not certified in that field.

- Highlight key cases or matters in which you and your firm have participated.
- Make the website informative. If the firm focuses in a particular area of the law, then provide information such as statutes, regulations, articles, pointers, and the like which would be helpful to an individual seeking those services. Content, content, content.
- Make short video presentations of issues that the firm regularly handles and wants to provide services in. *A probate lawyer, for example, could have a video explaining the probate process.*
- Do a blog that is associated with the website.
- Archive the firm's newsletters.

> We all want the greatest website. But on a scale of one to ten, functionality counts for eight, fancy only two.

- Carefully check to ensure that no confidential information is released.

Websites that receive information

Websites are places where documents can be filed with the lawyer. In addition to use of the web to do court and government filings, lawyers can set up websites to receive information from clients. For example, the web can be used to obtain client information in a bankruptcy.

Use online vaults.

Websites can provide another means of communication. By establishing data vaults through the firm website, the lawyer can store information that is available only to a client with the user name and pass code, and sometimes only at the designated computer. This allows the lawyer to safely transfer sensitive information to the client and *only* the client. Restrictions on the documents through PDF security that are saved also can limit what documents can be copied or printed—further assurance that confidential documents are not improperly disseminated.

Another version of this vault is to use it as a library of sorts where information that may need to be referenced from time to time is always available to those who have a need and right to know, such as a client or co-counsel in a case. For example, during a major financing project, hundreds of documents may have to pass between parties to be reviewed and considered. There are also foundation documents that are always on demand, such as the letter of intent or corporate organization documents. All of these can be placed in the online vault.

BLOGS

Another way the lawyer can communicate one to many (one lawyer to multiple clients or others) is a blog (a combination of "web log," which explains that it is a web-based program). The blog, a website that is routinely updated with commentary, calendar items, documents, graphs, video, or any other digital item, provides the lawyer the opportunity to communicate with a wide range of audiences. The lawyer communicates either to the general public to gain recognition or, in a more limited version, to a client or group of clients who have access through ID and password.

> A limited-access blog that keeps clients up to date on the course of complex litigation can save everyone a lot of time. All the pleadings can be kept up to date. The calendar of upcoming deadlines, motions, and hearings can be displayed, as well as contact information for all the lawyers on the team. In addition, you can prepare a diary or journal of events and thoughts on the case. Clients can leave comments and stay up to date without a lot of telephone and back-and-forth efforts to communicate. Calling the client to say "We won the case!" is still permitted.

Blog websites also allow readers to comment on what is written. Some more sophisticated websites permit visitors to send messages to one another.

The lawyer can use the blog he creates in some of these ways:

- A blog on a subject matter special to the lawyer, such as *a* particular area of law available to everyone.
- A blog on a subject matter directed to specific visitors who have been given access, such as sensitive legislative analysis.
- A blog to a client to show progress in a matter or case.
- A blog *that* brings in the group of attorneys and other professionals involved in a major case, transaction, or related legal issue.
- A blog available to all sides in a case to share not only docket entries and filings but discovery, and *to* coordinate time lines.

> For more information on social networks for lawyers, *see* Carolyn Elefant & Nicole Black, *Social Media for Lawyers: The Next Frontier*, ABA 2010.

Notes

1. Uniform Electronic Transactions Act §15.
2. National Conference of State Legislatures, Uniform Electronic Transactions Act, http://www.ncsl.org/IssuesResearch/TelecommunicationsInformationTechnology/UniformElectronicTransactionsActs/tabid/13484/Default.aspx (last visited July 31, 2011).
3. 5 ILL. COMP. STAT. 175/1-101 (West 2011); N.Y. State Tech. § 301 *et seq.* (Consol. 2011); WASH. REV. CODE § 19.34.010 *et seq.* (ARCW 2011).

4.   "World's Worst E-Mail Gaffes, Read 'em and Reap Some Lessons," ABC News, *available at* http://abcnews.go.com/Technology/Business/john-lisa-cornell-pair-committed-worst-mail-gaffe/story?id=9080827&page=2 (last visited Oct. 10, 2011).

5.   Chris Hoke, *Ten Worst E-mail Gaffes 2009*, E-MAIL SERVICE GUIDE, Dec. 22, 2009, *available at* http://www.e-maile-mailserviceguide.com/2009/12/ten-worst-e-maile-mail-gaffes-of-2009/ (last visited Oct. 10, 2011).

6.   Brian Baskin & Ben Lefebvre, *Chevron's E-mail 'Oops' Reveals Energy Giant's Sway Over Markets*, WALL ST. J., July 16, 2011.

CHAPTER 8

READING, WRITING, EXECUTING, AND PRESENTING DOCUMENTS IN THE STATE OF PAPERLESSNESS

The single biggest impediment to going paperless is the sense that paper is required to write, read, sign, or present documents. Surely, it is supposed, one of those steps needs to be on paper. Understanding that this assumption is wrong means the lawyer is in position to go all the way to a paperless world.

> Documents can remain digital for reading, writing, executing, *and* presentation.

WRITING PAPERLESSLY

Document generators

Word and other word processors through mail/merge and macro programs can build the basic documents. Some vendors build on this function and offer the macros complete with some standard language. Document generators take a generalized template and fill in the matter-specific information, including correcting for gender and number, to produce a nearly finished document. Rather than move to each place in the document to enter the information, it takes the information from an input table, spreadsheet, or database and fills it in. Other programs, such as HotDocs, ProLaw, and Pro Doc, enhance this capability. The choice is to buy off-the-shelf programs or use word processing and spreadsheets to build a library of templates, or both. In the end, the lawyer should be the one to choose the language and clauses in the documents, so strictly off-the-shelf should be out of the question.

> Word processors also have shortcuts that will insert whole paragraphs or sections. For example, in Word Quick Parts, I put the signature block at the end of pleadings, standard clauses found in most contracts, etc.

Drafting documents, though mechanically aided, still requires a lawyer who understands the issues to guide even the mechanical aspects. When a paragraph is in a contract in a certain way, it is there for a purpose.

> In negotiations, I have asked the drafter a question of what a paragraph means not because I do not know already, but I am looking for the kind of answer given. When the paragraph is explained, I know I am dealing with someone who either takes care in what she does or, if she says it is "just boilerplate" or something similar, then I see a completely different negotiator.

Careful writing recognizes that situations may arise to which the contract language must speak in a way that is not in the standard templates. Careful legal writing requires that the lawyer understand those situations and draft the contract accordingly.

Cutting and copying clauses from other contracts alone does not answer those questions, because these clauses are answers to questions never raised or entirely different questions.

Time and time again people say that a clause is "boilerplate" as if it was or is unimportant for consideration. Some even believe that the presence of the "legalese" brings legitimacy to the document. The term *boilerplate* comes from the days of steam-driven engines. When heated, water expands, and the force of steam is powerful. The goal of a steam-driven engine is to force the power of that steam into a single place where it can be harnessed for beneficial use.

Thick steel or iron was also used for printing. Advertisements and syndicated articles were set in these iron plates. Newspapers could print the whole plate as is or not at all. They could not alter it. This rigidity was used by businesses and others when making public announcements. Because it could not be easily changed, it was printed as the business presented it. The practice became known as "boilerplate." The term has passed into legal jargon to suggest those provisions that are standard and unchanging. But in the digital world the lawyer can, and in some cases should, draft the language for the issue at hand. Certainly there are key paragraphs that should be considered, if not used, in every legal document—but not mindlessly.

The term *boilerplate* suggests a better metaphor. Steam generates tremendous pressure—enough to move a large train or a boat. If steam is not properly restrained it will miss its purpose; or, if the boilerplate is weak or missing at key points, there will be an explosion, sometimes with disastrous results. The contract boilerplate similarly should protect the client from the effects of the pressure of ongoing relationships and extraneous events "blowing up" the contract. Properly designed, it holds the agreement together to fulfill the client's expectation. If boilerplate is weak or missing, disastrous results can occur for the client.

> Let me illustrate how failing to understand the use of boilerplate can haunt you. I had a client who wanted to sell a family business to a company that was buying up such smaller companies. The buyer provided the initial draft of the agreement. Because of the way it was printed (it was on a dot-matrix printer), I surmised that the buyer was working without counsel and had an older agreement within which he merely changed names and amounts. He wanted to save money and do it himself. After all, it was only "boilerplate." What I also learned was that the agreement he was using was one in which he had been the seller of another business. His lawyer in that agreement did him a great service, because whereas the boilerplate included all kinds of warranties of the buyer, there were no similar warranties for the seller. Specifically, there was an expressed waiver of any typical seller's warranty. Customarily, if I represented the buyer, I wanted some warranties, including one from the company and its officers that they had no knowledge of any upcoming event that would materially change the company's finances. It was nowhere in the agreement.

With a few changes we accepted the deal, signed, and closed. Several months later, a major customer of the purchased company went bankrupt. Several other customers made changes in suppliers as well. While none of this was known by my client at the time, we never had to defend. When word came from the other side that they were suing us for breach of warranty, I asked the lawyer to send language where we had made such warranties and directed him to the express waiver. Fortunately for him, or his malpractice carrier, the contract was not his.

Boilerplate counts; understanding what it means is the job of the attorney, and making it work for the best outcome for the client is the goal. Being paperless or not does not change any of that.

Even the speed in legal research does not change the obligation of the attorney to read the whole cited case and determine his relative role, if any, in the case. Search items, even complex ones, can find phrases, sentences, and sometimes whole paragraphs that seem to support what the lawyer wants to say. A quick copy, paste, and citation note and it looks like research was done. Wrong. We have only found one case that had words we were looking for. The whole case needs to be read. What if this wonderful phrase is in a dissent or used to describe an argument later rejected? It would be embarrassing to cite it only to find that out in a filing by the other attorney or the court.

When I cite a case, I try to state the position so as to identify the level of the court, whether it is an affirmation or reversal, the type of ruling below (motion to dismiss, summary judgment, new trial, etc.), and how the argument was framed in those cases. For example, "In reviewing a lower court's grant of summary judgment to the defendant employer, the Sixth Circuit held that . . . ."

That is not new from being paperless. There have always been lazy lawyers, unfortunately. The State of Paperlessness and its power allows these lawyers to look smart even in their laziness, ultimately to the loss of their client. At the same time, good lawyers who are not so lazy become even better lawyers.

> Here, as in all cases, it is important that you proofread all documents carefully, even those that you have used before. A standard of every document should be saved in Read Only format, and after generating a document, the generated document should be compared to the standard. Otherwise, you might have "document creep," by which documents are slowly corrupted.

> Early in my career I did some family law cases. In one of those cases at a pretrial, the judge wanted to know why I was asking for "inequitable division of property" rather than "an equitable division of property." Funny, yes, but it forced me to double-check pleadings and be especially careful about copying and pasting mistake-riddled copy.
>
> In making documents yourself, be very careful that local rules are followed. Some local court rules require that their standard forms be used verbatim without changes to anything, including font, pages, etc. I once practiced before a magistrate who would compare filings character for character, match them for page agreement, and, if they were failing in any respect, return them for edits unfiled.

When getting practice-specific document generation, consider the following factors:

- It is current at the time of purchase.
- It respects and responds to jurisdictional issues in drafting
- It keeps up to date with changes in law.
- It agrees in gender and number with the parties as well as between the subjects and the verbs.

- It protects against change once the documents are executed.
- It provides immediate answers to relevant discussions of the applicable law for choices that are requested.

Be very careful if you take a document that you did for one client and replace the names with a global search and replace. One of my first word-processing documents was for a trust whose surname was Fetter. The next one was Sturgeon. Spell check noted that the latter documents were giving the trustee "unsturgeoned" discretion.

Even in civil litigation, particular types of cases subject to repetitive forms have specialized software that aids the lawyer in gathering, posting, reviewing, and using the information. In the case of software used to generate court pleadings and documents, consider the following factors:

- Does the software automatically upload documents into the ECF system of court?
- Does the software automatically update the forms to conform to new court rules as they are announced? This should include the local rules where possible.
- Does the software prepare documents in PDF or only store in virtual form? While the virtual form (which means the information actually resides in a database and, when called, is displayed in the format of the forms) can save memory, it means that the forms are not necessarily as filed, and access to the forms at later dates may require continued maintenance fees.
- Does the software provide local rule documents and forms? Each court has its own way of doing things. For example, although bankruptcy is a federal practice in national courts subject to federal rules, each court has its own idiosyncrasies, including special forms for different pleadings.
- Do you have access to the input and output even after the software license expires or is not renewed? This may not be a concern during the immediacy of the case, but if filing is required months or years later, resurrecting a license to retrieve a form can be very expensive, and the company may not even be in business to provide the service.

- Does the software integrate with the document management system and word processor? Simplicity in the systems should be a goal, and making the generator a part of the larger system serves that goal.
- Does the software allow clients to enter the data? Rather than sort through a shoebox or grocery bag full of unopened mail and statements, the client should enter this information.

Writing without paper

A blank screen is no less daunting than a blank sheet of paper. Getting started is tough. What follows is a way to use the tools available digitally to write quickly and efficiently.

Writing challenges the lawyer because the mind has a myriad of thoughts trying to get on the page. Going from unorganized in the mind to logical organization on the page means the ideas back up in the slow writing channel. Mind mapping breaks this logjam. For example, open a new Mind Map window. Type the topic, title, or goal, such as "Summary Judgment on Liability." Then with the cursor somewhere on the page other than the subject, double-click. This creates a new subject. Repeat that at least eight times. In each of these nodes type a thought about the subject. This could be single-word notes, an entire sentence, a phrase, anything that identifies the thought. Don't worry about order or dependency; every idea stands on its own. It might look like this:

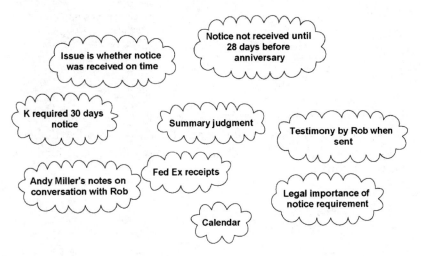

Connect the first-level thoughts to the main subject, "Summary Judgment." Connect those dependent on these branches. For remaining ones, identify branches to which they could connect. It would look something like this:

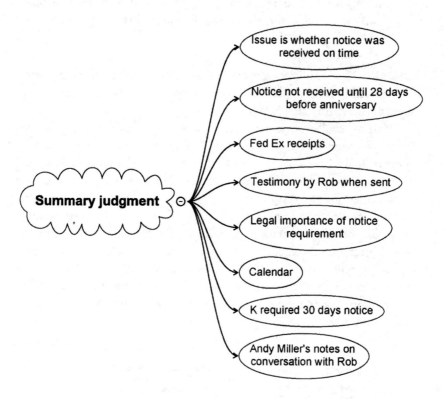

Organize the nodes into priority in a clockwise manner. Where appropriate, move some to sub-branches. Consider if other thoughts need to be added and insert those. The result will be something that looks like this:

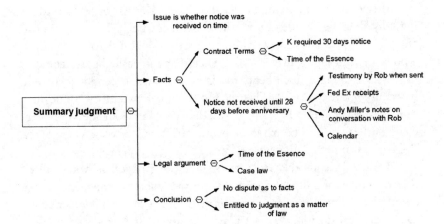

After adding any additional branches, sub-branches or even sub-sub-branches, the map can be converted to an outline in Word. Convert each of the elements into complete sentences. At this point the draft needs simply to be fleshed out, stylized, and headed consistent with pleadings.

This is a simple example, but when faced with writing about an issue or a case, initially there are a lot of things that the lawyer might want to say. Actually drafting something with that in mind becomes so time-consuming that the ideas are lost. Here in free form, while ideas are fresh, they are all identified, gathered, and then organized. Because each idea stands initially on its own, there are no limitations imposed by earlier notes. Also, all ideas can be noted right away. As you look at the diagram, missing parts can be identified and all of them further supported. Then with an outline, after careful thinking, finishing the draft is much easier.

READING DOCUMENTS IN THE STATE OF PAPERLESSNESS

Lawyers read to fulfill different purposes. They read to understand, to analyze, to criticize, and to distill. Reading to understand can be done with equal facility on paper or digitally. Once read and understood, the document no longer has value.

But lawyers read to analyze the argument and the relationship of this fact with this issue and this law. They read to be critical as they edit contracts, letters, briefs, and much more. They read to be informed as they distill the information within the document for later reconstruction as part of their creating a document.

After decades of reading books and papers, the transition to reading digitally does not come easily. The differences begin in your posture and where your hands are. Looking at a screen does differ from holding a book in your lap. But it is a difference that can easily be overcome.

After reading a document, the lawyer creates a second document based upon the one read. This second document retains the information the lawyer wants to keep. It is either an analysis of the argument, changes that need to be made or comments about possible changes, or the bare information the lawyer finds in the document.

Because it is another document, making it paperless brings all of the advantages of a digital document to those edits, comments, or other annotations. This allows for faster retrieval of the lawyer's augmentation to the original document. That is not possible if it is read and marked physically, as in the past.

Everything the lawyer does when he reads paper he can do digitally. He can highlight, underline, point out, leave comments, and indicate changes. Word and WordPerfect as well as other word processors have all those options. Making such comments on the PDF is better because the options are greater for markup, the original is left untouched, and all of the comments, marks, changes, etc., are cataloged for easy reference. Several parties can work on the same document, leaving their comments and notes, creating a single marked-up document.

To distill a document, the lawyer can open a word-processing document and move the elements from the original document that he wants to keep. For distillation, nothing competes with CaseMap. Using CaseMap to distill information found within a document identifies the key information and links it to all other similar information in almost unlimited ways. At the same time, it automatically creates a reference for either later retrieval of the original or a citation to it.

This book is offered to the lawyer as a traditional book or electronically, and without hypocrisy. Each medium has its pluses or minuses, but the productivity—that is, reading the page—remains about the same. That is not the case in processing digitally in the practice of law. The differences in productivity are geometric.

So, the answer to the question whether the book should be read electronically or in paper is "Yes!"

SIGNING DOCUMENTS DOES NOT REQUIRE INK ON PAPER.

One of the challenges against using a paperless system concerns signing documents. With some special exceptions, the general rule allows digital, as opposed to physical, signatures.

Electronic signatures are ubiquitous. The types of electronic signatures include:

- Typing the name of the sender at the end of the e-mail or on the signature line of a pleading or other document—*e.g.*, "/John Z. Smith/" or "/s/ John Z. Smith/."
- Use of digitized images of written signatures where a signature is required. The use of facsimile signatures to sign volumes of checks and letters has been practiced for decades.
- The process of checking a box that indicates acceptance and clicking a button to continue or a button such as "I Accept" or the like at the end of a statement.
- Using the services of an encrypted signature through public key cryptography.
- Providing for a person to actually sign the document, but digitally. This is found in most retail establishments that accept credit cards and by package delivery services.

> For those who want at least the appearance of a signature, a program called SignMyPad will put a PDF on your iPad and allow it to be signed. The result is a fully executed document. The other option, less efficient, is to print the document, or at least the signature page, and then scan it.

Digital signing is legally binding.

Such signatures are legally binding. The law generally recognizes an electronic signature equally with a written one. The electronic signature is an electronic sound, symbol, or process attached to or logically associated with a record and executed or adopted by a person with the intent to sign the record. The way in which a signature is done electronically can range from clicking "I Agree" on a web page to the name typed at the end of an e-mail to an encrypted signature.[1] A signature in electronic form can be given full force and effect.[2] Under the comments for electronic signatures, the act of handing out a business card with an e-mail address or the use of the e-mail address on the letterhead can be construed as permission to use electronic transactions.[3]

A New York employment case shows that electronic signatures are as good as hand-written. That case held that the typed name of the sender at the end of the message was sufficient to bind a person in a contract.[4] In this case, the CEO was relieved of his position. The compensation for that position included a salary and the opportunity for an "earn-out" bonus if certain economic targets were surpassed. After the CEO was terminated from his position, the chairman of the board proposed by e-mail an option which he argued to the former CEO was "in your best interest because it offers the best opportunity for you to achieve your stated goal of a full earn-out." At the end of the e-mail was his typed name. The next day, the former employee wrote back accepting the offer. He too put his name at the end of the message.

The question was whether or not there was a "written" agreement to amend the original employment agreement, as required by its terms. The defense was that there was no writing due to the Statute of Frauds. The appellate court agreed with the trial court and held that "[t]he e-mails from plaintiff constitute 'signed writings' within the meaning of the statute of frauds, since plaintiff's name at the end of his e-mail signified his intent to authenticate the contents" and that the chairman's typed name at the end of his e-mail constituted a "signed writing" and satisfied the requirement of the employment agreement that any modification be signed by all parties.

The case result is fundamentally correct. Had this correspondence been done the "old way" in a letter, the formal signing would be there without question. The response is that e-mail is just another form of oral communication, complete with its informality. The mistake is not that the communication is via e-mail, or its legal significance, but with the attitudes toward e-mail as being an inferior and unreliable form of writing. E-mail may not be formal, or even as pretty as a nicely typed and signed letter, but it is all that is legally required of a letter. One forgets that at one's own peril.

On the other hand, if such an e-mail exchange is not contemplated in drafting an agreement, then a clause in the contract make that clear.

According to federal law, a digital signature can be (1) any sound, symbol, or process that is (2) attached to or logically associated with an electronic record, and (3) made with the intent to sign.[5] The UCC defines a signature as "any symbol executed or adopted with the present intention to adopt or accept a writing."[6]

The passage of the Uniform Electronic Transactions Act (UETA)[7] provides the basis for determining whether or not digital or electronic documents constitute valid agreements. The purpose of the UETA is to broadly permit the use of electronic transactions in place of traditional physical documents and signatures in all areas where such were required by law.[8] Only business, governmental affairs, or commercial transactions are within the UETA.[9] Wills, codicils, and trusts are expressly excluded, as are other documents by individual states.[10] According to comments, powers of attorney can be digital documents.[11]

The electronic records are described as "a record created, generated, sent, communicated, received, or stored by electronic means."[12] "Electronic means" broadly includes "technology having electrical, digital, magnetic, wireless, optical, electromagnetic, or similar capabilities."[13] Such a definition includes virtually all ways of handling documents paperlessly now known and practiced.

Section 5 of the UETA provides that electronic signatures are permitted only between parties that have agreed to electronically handle documents.[14] In this context, the construction of the term agreement must be broad in order to ensure that the act applies whenever the circumstances show the parties' intent to transact electronically, regardless of whether that intent rises to the level of a formal agreement. In those circumstances, an electronic signature can replace a signed one.[15]

Legal efficacy of digital signatures requires the intent to assent by placement or putting the sign or taking the step indicating acceptance. The purpose of UETA as regards signatures is to permit digital signatures where physical media are currently permitted.[16] The UETA also provides for verifying the veracity of the documents through the use "of algorithms or other codes, identifying words or numbers, encryption, or callback or other acknowledgment procedures."[17]

The UETA does not change the definition of agreement, but instead simply makes it clear that the use of digital transactions as contrasted with paper or other physical instruments is equally permissible.[18] Though generally now applicable in legal practice, the UETA permits transactions to take place electronically with no direct human creation, review, or acceptance. The rule is that unless someone objects, the transaction is consented to.[19] There must be some indication that the signature is linked to the electronic record.

Finally, the language is broad to include commercial transactions even if otherwise "consumers." The rules apply to transactions between two or more persons. Thus wills, trusts, or health-care power of attorneys, living wills, etc., are not included.[20] Real estate transactions such as deeds and mortgages should not be excluded, though local law may do so, but "an exclusion of all real estate transactions would be particularly unwarranted in the event that a State chose to convert to an electronic recording system."[21]

Various federal regulators have adopted digital signatures. [22] With federal courts adopting e-filing of pleadings and other court documents, they, too, have adopted electronic signatures.

To take advantage of electronic signatures, language within the documents should allow for electronic signatures. In the case of business entities, the governing document (such as corporate by-laws) could also provide for acceptance of electronic signatures. The UETA allows context and other unwritten bases to support the existence of an agreement to use electronic signatures.[23]

Notarizing signatures without paper

One vestige of paper that will die hard involves the notary. The actual signature and seal of a notary can be electronic in some jurisdictions.[24] The notary signature can be digital, but the signer must be in the presence of a notary to either sign or acknowledge the signature. In cases of a sworn document, must be sworn. Once those elements are met, the actual notary signature can be digital.[25]

A lawyer, for example, cannot receive a page signed by his client via e-mail and then notarize that.

Secure the signed document.

Once there is a document that has the signatures attached, then the final step is to secure it electronically so that it is certainly the signed contract. This can be done through PDF programs that will certify the copy to secure it from tampering.

- *Printing:* This is one a few options that generally should be allowed. If it is a top-secret document, then denial of printing might be a reasonable choice.
- *Changing the Document:* This should not be allowed; it is a final and sealed document.
- *Document Assembly:* No modifications should be permitted, and this not allowed.

- *Content Copying:* This option generally should be allowed. Depending on its sensitivity, copying may be restricted.
- *Content Copying for Accessibility:* This permits copying so that the document can be made accessible, such as being read to *the* visually impaired.
- *Page Extraction:* This is like copying and printing but in a smaller portion of the document. *Allowance* depends on choices made for copying and printing.
- *Commenting:* This is a form of modification of the document and should not be allowed.
- *Filling of Form Fields:* This is a form of modification of the document and should not be allowed.
- *Signing:* This option should be allowed *only* if the document is complete except for signature and *should be denied* after signature.
- *Creation of Template Pages:* This is a form of modification of the document and should not be allowed.

TAKING THE STATE OF PAPERLESSNESS TO THE COURT

Handling a hearing without paper

In today's courtroom, it is possible to completely try a case without paper. The tools the lawyer uses—notebook, note-taking, legal research—can be done without paper. So can the presentation. With displays located for jurors, judges, lawyers, and the public, there is no longer any need to ask the court for permission to approach the witness to give a document; the lawyer simply calls for it to display. Documents generated in the courtroom can be done on a smart board and saved for later use by the jury or the court.

In taking advantage of this technology, the lawyer should consider the following:

- Early in the case, visit the courtroom. Ask the bailiff or other officer if you can practice using it.

> The lawyer should be as familiar with the technology as she is with a pen and legal pad.

- Assign a person on your team, other than a lawyer trying the case, to handle the technology. It is her responsibility to have the equipment connected and operating. At the last minute the lawyer should be thinking about the opening statement, not opening a file.

- Prepare a script and give it to everyone on the team. Plan how documents will be displayed. For cross-examination this may have some impromptu events, but in most cases the cross-examination can be planned.
- Practice using the script and the technology with this technician. This is a team effort, and the team should work as one.
- Have backup equipment available in case something happens with the main units.
- Make sure computers connected to the system have nothing that the lawyer would want withheld. If it is on the computer, it risks being displayed.
- Do not surf the web or check e-mail while in the courtroom.

Despite the sophistication, every courtroom has its differences. The lawyer should understand the technology in use by the court in which he is practicing.

Filing paperless documents with the government

Virtually all federal courts except the Supreme Court use Electronic Case Filing, or ECF. Other state courts are doing the same. This furthers the advance to a purely paperless state in which there is no need to file paper. This brings all kinds of efficiencies to the firm.

I recall one of the first cases in which I was involved with online filing of federal documents. I had a summary judgment motion due on last workday before the Christmas holidays. That generally would mean a full staff on that day or the day before to print, collate, bind, and ship out the documents. Instead, I finished the document before then, printed it electronically to PDF, attached the exhibits, and filed it online. Copies were e-mailed to clients. All of that was done without staff and in 10 to 15 minutes.

This contrasts with another deadline in the Eighth Circuit Court of Appeals. The matter had been scheduled for accelerated consideration. Our briefs were due to be mailed by December 31. During that entire holiday period, there were times I was physically present but mentally still drafting. On the morning of New Year's Eve, we went to print the brief (nearly 50 copies) and our copier died. No service available. We called around and the copying centers were closed or closing. We found an office supply store open and were able to get the copies printed in time to ship.

> Some courts, or judges within courts, require a hard copy for their consideration to be delivered to the judge's chambers. The deadline for this may or may not coincide with the deadline on which you have to actually file it with the court. Check that out.

Led by the Electronic Case Filing (ECF) system of the federal courts, other state courts, and federal and state agencies, too, are providing for electronic filing. Filings with the United States Patent and Trademark Office are fully automated, providing almost no opportunity to send in paper.

Such electronic filings come in three forms: uploading of PDFs produced by the lawyer, submitting forms created by the agency with information filled in by the lawyer, or providing detail online. The ECF is an example of the first form; business filings in some secretaries of state, such as Illinois, are examples of the second; and the USPTO exemplifies the third.

One of the challenges is to make sure that the documents are proofed and corrected before filing. For the ECF and other document upload, the documents have to be finished before filing so the lawyer has the opportunity to ensure accuracy. For the second approach, generally the form can be downloaded, completed, proofed, and approved before filing. If so, that should be done. For the third, sometimes the form can be printed, or the lawyer can at least go through and print the pages for the information. The lawyer should prepare the answers offline before the online filing can be done.

> In every instance, PDF copies to be stored in the matter files are required of all filings.

Paying attention to publishing forms in this environment is extremely important. Filing the wrong PDF can be harmful to you or your client. In a bankruptcy case, the abundance of clients and the rapidity by which filings could be done through the ECF created a problem for an attorney. He filed a number of bankruptcy petitions via ECF prior to the effective date of the Bankruptcy Abuse Prevention and Consumer Protection Act of 2005 (BAPCPA). BAPCPA specifically provided that petitions filed before October 17, 2005, would be subject to the less strenuous standards of the earlier act. On October 15, the Hammond, Indiana, Bankruptcy Court received an ECF for a case captioned "Donald Lee Austin," but the petition that was contained in the PDF was for a David Randall Bradley. The address on this petition meant that it belonged in another division, where it was transferred and docketed in the name of Bradley. The Bradley petition had already been filed, and the court issued a show-cause order for explanation of why there were two such filings. In response, counsel filed "Debtor Donald Lee Austin's Motion to Substitute Voluntary Chapter 7 Petition and for Order Confirming the October 15, 2005 Filing of Debtor Donald Lee Austin's Voluntary Chapter 7 Petition, and for Order Transferring Case Back to Hammond Division."

The final conclusion was that no petition for Austin had been filed, and the Cinderella date had passed, meaning the filing would bring the petition under the stricter standards of BAPCPA.[26]

> While filing via ECF is certainly fast, don't wait until the last minute to to learn how to use it. The websites provide manuals, FAQ, and other information. In addition, trial sites are available in some jurisdictions. Practice, become familiar, then file.

> To avoid this, we set up a simple file in the root directory called Filings. When a document was ready to file, we moved it to the folder and uploaded it from there. We also tried to have two people do the filing together to make sure that quick fingers did not finger the wrong file. Mistakes can happen, but extra care is required here.

STORING RECORDS ELECTRONICALLY RATHER THAN ON PAPER

For documents produced and used electronically, storing them electronically only makes sense. There is no requirement to reduce electronic documents to paper and file the paper. For purposes of saving documents, the Uniform Electronic Transaction Act allows electronic records of business, commercial, or government transactions to be retained. The requirements are simple: the electronic record must accurately reflect the information set forth in the record in its final form and remain accessible for later reference.[27] The requirement of accuracy is derived from the Uniform and Federal Rules of Evidence. The requirement of continuing accessibility addresses the issue of technology obsolescence and the need to update and move information to developing systems. It is not unlikely that within the span of 5–10 years (a period during which retention of much information is required) a corporation may evolve through one or more generations of technology. More to the point, these versions may be incompatible, necessitating the reconversion of information from one system to the other.[28]

The electronic record of commercial transactions can be a substitute for the original even if the original is required by law.[29] The Uniform Rules of Evidence permit the treatment of electronic records and electronic information as originals.[30] Consistent with this, evidence of a record or signature cannot be excluded solely because it is in electronic form.[31]

> One of the interesting footnotes in storage history is that during much of the first half of the 20th century, including World War II, most of the service records were on punched cards. All of these punch cards were reduced to 16mm microfilm as "microfilm copy of the Army serial number file, 1938–1946."
>
> As ridiculous as this seems, these microfilmed files became invaluable. After a 1973 fire at the National Archives and Records Administration, the military records of approximately 80 percent of the men and women who served from before World War I to the eve of the Vietnam War were destroyed. But the information on the microfilm rolls was electronically scanned, and almost all of those rolls were converted to a digital format which can be accessed today in the Access to Archival Databases, or AAD, found at http://aad.archives.gov/aad/.

ePublishing provides the lawyer access to "printed" material without the paper.

One way to further reduce paper in the office is to adapt to the use of electronic papers. The ABA is moving to almost exclusively electronic publishing of section newsletters. Many newspapers and trade journals are either sent via e-mail or available by going to a website to view material. There is a whole universe of paperless books available for reading either on readers or on computer screens in general.

And there still is paper

At least at this time, the lawyer cannot completely get away from paper. Valuable correspondence and information still comes on paper. While that can be converted to digital for paperless processing, there are those documents that must remain on paper.

There are also times you must communicate in paper. Some courts and agencies are not equipped to be paperless, and some clients can only be contacted that way. Then there are those special documents, such as deeds, wills, trusts, and the like, that must be reduced to an original paper that is physically sealed and secured.

Paper will still exist, but it should exist as little as possible. Those times are:

- The document arrives in paper form through the mail, delivered by a client, at a meeting, etc. Convert it to digital. Depending on its purpose, you may need to retain the original, return it, or recycle the paper.

> When given a document, ask if it is in digital form and whether the person can e-mail you a digital copy.

- The rules of the court or agency require paper filings. Comply, but you do not need a lot of extra copies for yourself and your clients.

> Some courts that do not use ECF may permit parties to agree to service via e-mail in lieu of mail. It may require a stipulated order.

- The law requires that the document be actually an ink-signed paper, such as a will, deed, or certificate.
- The person to whom you are sending the document cannot receive documents digitally.

When I tell people that my office is paperless, some ask with an incredulous look, "You have no paper in your office at all?" My answer is, "Not very much." Most of it remains from pre-paperless existence. For example, there is a drawer full of legal pads, almost all of which were put there four years ago when I ordered the last package. I have not used up a single legal pad since then. I have a drawer in my desk full of scratch pads. They will not be used by me. The source of the paper is from outside. I occasionally print something, but it is seldom for my office or use.

I still like to look at the diplomas I worked so hard for and my parents sacrificed to get. The certificates showing admission to the various courts around the country are also in paper and proudly displayed.

While some documents must be in paper and original, such as wills and trusts, copies for retrieving can be online. The UETA permits the use, retention, and enforceability of electronic documents and does not require paper ones for commercial transactions. This does not apply to nontransactions such as wills and trusts. Individual state law may also limit the uses. There are also documents that were created and executed in a physical, traditional way. Those documents cannot be replaced by digital documents unless re-signed.

Just because retaining the hardcopy original is required does not mean a digital copy of it cannot be used within the system. Careful thought shows that except for the exact moment of proving the authenticity of the document, lawyers almost always work with copies, both hard and digital. Copies are attached to correspondence, pleadings, motions and briefs, and in depositions. Except in special circumstances, the copy, if authenticated by testimony, can stand in place of the original. So for those originals, scan them, add to the matter database, and profile for use as any document. Meanwhile, save the originals in a fireproof cabinet.

Courts commonly require a complimentary written copy of all briefs, even if they are filed online. This somewhat interferes with the efficiencies of online filing. What has happened is that the lawyer's printer has moved from his office to the clerk's office or to the judge's chambers. Often—and in the cases of some judges, always—the electronic filings are then printed onto paper for consideration by the court. That immense motion for summary judgment that is a ream of paper can sorely tax the facilities of the court. It is for that reason that many courts that have electronic case filing also request written copies of the pleadings to be delivered to chambers.

Depending on the timing of the filing and the expected ruling (think TRO versus a complaint for damages), the delivery may have to be contemporaneous with the electronic filing or immediately thereafter. Knowing this before filing can certainly make life easier.

> The challenge comes when you consider this question: If I print out a copy of what I filed electronically, do I also need to print and serve the adversary? This is one of those thorny issues that can be argued either way. The easiest way to know is to discuss it with opposing counsel and the court and come to an early agreement. Picking up the phone and talking is still a more efficient way to practice than a paperless office, especially when it eliminates the need for any filing at all.

Notes

1.   Unif. Electronic Transactions Act, Comment 7
2.   Unif. Electronic Transactions Act, § 7.
3.   Unif. Electronic Transactions Act, § 5, Comment 4, example B and C.
4.   Stevens v. Publicis (App. Div. 2008), 854 N.Y.S.2d 690.
5.   15 U.S.C. § 7006(5).
6.   U.C.C. § 1-201(37).
7.   Uniform Electronic Transactions Act (1999), drafted by the National Conference of Commissioners on Uniform State Statutes, *available at* http://www.law.upenn.edu/bll/archives/ulc/fnact99/1990s/ueta99.htm (Aug. 1, 2011).
8.   Unif. Electronic Transactions Act, § 3(b).
9.   Unif. Electronic Transactions Act, § 2(16), Comments.
10.   Unif. Electronic Transactions Act, § 3.
11.   Unif. Electronic Transactions Act, § 3, Comment 2.
12.   Unif. Electronic Transactions Act, § 2 (7).
13.   Unif. Electronic Transactions Act, § 2 (5).
14.   Unif. Electronic Transactions Act, § 5.
15.   Unif. Electronic Transactions Act, § 7.
16.   Unif. Electronic Transactions Act, § 7 Comment 7.
17.   Unif. Electronic Transactions Act, § 2 (14).
18.   Unif. Electronic Transactions Act, § Comment 4.
19.   Unif. Electronic Transactions Act, § Comment 2.
20.   Unif. Electronic Transactions Act, § 2 Comment 12.
21.   Unif. Electronic Transactions Act, General comments.
22.   *See, e.g.*, FDA, 21 C.F.R. Part 11.
23.   Unif. Electronic Transactions Act, § 5(b) Comment 4.
24.   Unif. Electronic Transactions Act, § 11.
25.   Unif. Electronic Transactions Act, § 11, Comment.
26.   *In re* Bradley, 342 B.R. 783, 789 (Bankr. N. Dist. Ind. 2005).
27.   Unif. Electronic Transactions Act, § 2(a).
28.   Unif. Electronic Transactions Act, § 12(a) Comment.
29.   Unif. Electronic Transactions Act, § 12(d).
30.   Uniform Rules of Evidence 1001(3), 1002, 1003, and 1004.
31.   Unif. Electronic Transactions Act, § 13.

CHAPTER 9

STORING AND FINDING INFORMATION IN AN OCEAN OF DIGITS

If the lawyer needs one document, the fact that millions are available to her makes little difference if the one she wants is not. File cabinets with file folders provide the means to store and retrieve documents made of paper. But it is a cumbersome process fraught with real risk that documents can be misfiled and forever irretrievable.

The federal civil rules, and most states that follow them, describe documents broadly as "including writings, drawings, graphs, charts, photographs, sound recordings, images, and other data or data compilations—stored in any medium from which information can be obtained."[1] In the State of Paperlessness, that medium containing information consists of bits—lots and lots of bits. A bit represents a single state, 0 or 1. Eight bits make a byte, sufficient to represent a letter, number, or symbol. Sequential bytes in varying numbers combine to form words, sentences, paragraphs, briefs, cases, tables—in other words, documents. Billions upon billions of bytes make the digital office, one bit at a time—not just bits, but ordered bits. Miss a bit and a whole document becomes a meaningless series of zeroes and ones. Storage of these bits runs from the flash card in the phone to massive storage banks in cages around the world, with thumb drives and hard drives in between. Connected by millions of miles of wire and fiber, or endless electronic waves in the air, they combine to be a mass of innumerable zeroes and ones.

The lawyer sees none of this. Machines translate what she creates into invisible bits and, in reverse, converts them back into something she can see. It just happens—seamlessly, continuously, and reliably.

Somewhere in the State of Paperlessness, the needed document exists—on the thumb drive in hand, in the box on the floor under the desk, in a room down the hall, or in a building full of computers on a system site thousands of miles away. As long as it is there and she can retrieve it, it makes no difference where it resides. Or does it?

STRUCTURE OF DATA STORAGE

Heloise Bowles, during the middle of the 20th century, was a popular columnist who answered readers' questions on how to efficiently do household chores or conquer household problems. Out of that came one of her most famous rules: "A place for everything and everything in its place." Today's wired and electronic world presents unlimited choices as to document placement. This unlimited ability also means that everything is in places, plural, which means everywhere. Because they are everywhere, they are nowhere to be found when needed. In this overabundance of storage, every file must have one designated place where it always resides, and the file that resides there is the only copy.

- An identified place where the documents are stored. Generally this is thought of in terms of storage, such as a hard drive or the cloud.
- A structure that organizes the documents so they can be found. This is done by a management program or folder/subfolder/file organization on the drive.

DETERMINING THE MODEL BY WHICH THE DOCUMENTS ARE ORGANIZED

The lawyer must have the ability to conveniently find and retrieve from that mass of bits the document she needs when she needs it.

The lawyer shall possess the capacity to easily, consistently, and securely create, store, find, use, and maintain the digital information required for the practice.

Technology provides several models for document organization—structured files, database, or searchable open storage. Commonly, actual organization combines some of each of these.

Structured organization uses the folder/subfolder organization inherent in today's computer storage. A common way is to store by client/matter/submatter, or to speed finding files with abc/client/matter/submatter where the abc represents folders for each letter or small groups of letters of the initial letters of client names. Depending on the practice, the filing can be by matter type/client/matter. For example, in a practice with lots of wills, the matter type would be wills, subfolders would be the clients' names, and, if multiple wills or services, sub-subfolders from that. For firms that identify matters by client number/matter number, the matter number can be the name of the folder. With discipline this can be useful, but as files accumulate the structure can become difficult to work through.

Database organization may or may not incorporate structured storage. Rather, each document is coded for client, matter name, matter number, type of document, people associated with it, date and time, and other information. A database records all of this information and saves the location of the document for later retrieval. The database can be searched by matter type or name or any of the other characteristics coded. From those found, the matter or document desired is located and retrieved. It is not important how that is done but rather that:

- information is securely stored;
- the indexes are reliable;
- the indexes can be automatically rebuilt in the case of a failure;
- the indexes are logical;
- the system internally guards against alterations and corruptions of the data; and
- access to the information can be restricted.

Open storage means the files are simply placed *en masse*, one mixed with another. Needed files are found through search engines. These may search only metadata saved in the documents or the entire document contents. Some search the open storage to build a database. Precoding a document's metadata with information on client, matter, and the like is required because it may not be inherent in the document itself.

> Database organization should be used because it also integrates
> the documents with contacts, calendar, e-mail, and billing.

The search capability for open storage should also be employed with database organization or structured storage. To do otherwise will result in extended delays during searching.

> In smaller firms, use a structured file, such as abc/client/matter,
> in conjunction with a database management program. Also have
> a search program that will allow searching through all of the files.
> This will give an additional option to find a file, particularly when
> the system is down and retrieval is on the cloud base

Naming files

The first step in having a place for a document is naming it. The long name protocol now commonly available on all software supplies enough characters to name a file. Except in those systems that do not permit users to name files, the lawyer should have a system of naming documents. Here are the simple rules:

- Do fully identify the record by providing key names, type of document, and, where there can be versions, dates or version numbers. Wrong: "Contract." Correct: "Acme–Gamma Buy Sell Agrmnt 5-6-2011."
- Do try to go from general to specific in the labeling.
- Do not assume that case sensitivity will always be recognized. "Ltr Ben to Patty.docx" is the same as "ltr ben to patty.docx" in many systems. That does not mean that capital letters should not be used; they make reading labels easier. But for purposes of naming, capital equals lower case and vice versa, because not all systems are case-sensitive.
- Do not use any of the following characters: < (less than); > (greater than); : (colon); " (double quote); / (forward slash); \ (backslash); | (vertical bar or pipe); ? (question mark); or * (asterisk).
- Do not rely on the path to fully describe the file. Although the path name can designate where a file goes, it is best to identify common documents with their full name. For example, while c:/ newco/articles of incorporation.docx identifies the file, it is best

to have c:/newco/newco articles of incorporation.docx because the file might be moved advertently or inadvertently into another path. Another example of a common document is a will; naming the file by the testator will make identifying it easier.

- Do not alter the extensions. Let the software that uses the document define the extension. The reasons for this are several. The file may not reopen in the altered extension, the security system may view the altered extension as indication of malware, the system may open the file in another program entirely and unalterably change the contents, or it may not be available for use on other systems.

DOCUMENT SEARCHING

No matter how well the lawyer profiles documents before storing or associating them with the proper client or matter, they are subject to being lost. Digital media facilitates electronic search of documents. Some of these programs automatically render scanned documents into a searchable format.

> Copernic is one such program.

STORING OTHER DOCUMENTS

Besides the information traditionally associated with a matter file, the lawyer also has other paper that is essential to the practice. This includes specialized books, research papers and statistics, collections of statutes and regulations for specific areas of law, corporation minute books, forms, and so on. Today these are on the desk, bookshelves, and credenzas. This information should also be stored digitally on the system to be retrieved.

> I use a practice management program database to store and integrate what was once found on my bookshelves and desktop. If the item is related to a particular matter, it is filed with other documents on that matter. If it addresses issues in more than one matter (like an article or a book), I use a separate series of numbers and names, effectively creating omni-matter files. Notes on the desk are quickly entered into the appropriate calendar, contact, task, note, or other relevant files. (I often

scan handwritten notes or other similar items and then organize them with the appropriate matter). For corporations, I set
up a master matter for each and store the final documents
there much as one would build a corporate book. Then, when I
have need of the current bylaws, I go to the corporate file.
When the corporation has bylaw changes, those changes have
their own matter where all of the correspondence, notes, drafts,
and other documents associated with the matter are kept. Only
the result goes into the corporate book.

**The lawyer should strive to have all documents stored on
the system so they can be recovered. No document
should be a widow or orphan.**

Something will happen at some point to your data no matter
how careful you are. Often the causes are out of your control.
So it is not a question of whether, but how soon and how serious. Preparation and care should make those incidents few
and fully recoverable.

Keep the files cleaned up.

Over the years, computer activity leaves a trail of old files, dozens of
backups, registries, browser history, and other information that is no
longer useful but could be damaging if revealed. A number of system
maintenance programs are available, freeware and for sale, which can
identify and remove unused files, browser history, cookies, and other
digital droppings that clog computer performance and pose confidentiality risks.

Get rid of information before getting rid of computers.

As a matter of course over time all of the electronic storage will accumulate documents. When replacing equipment because it wears out
or requires updating, it is important to treat the data on the old files
properly. This means:

- saving an image of the entire disk for archival purposes;
- doing a complete data removal of the disk. This is more than just deleting folders and files;

> Programs such as Darik Boot, Nuke, and Evidence Eliminator are examples of such programs.

- if the computer will go out for repair, remove the hard drive.

As for the equipment itself, most of these contain heavy metals and other potential harms to the environment. These should be disposed of properly.

Clean up excess copies.

Over time with daily, weekly, monthly and emergency backups plus the occasional change of system or service, a thumb drive here and one there, a large number of duplicate files will accumulate. An overabundance of copies presents as much a danger as too few. The biggest risk is that full copies are forgotten and held by persons who should not have them.

Keep track of where copies are and routinely clean out some of the excess archives.

Note

1.   FED. R. CIV. P. 34(a).

CHAPTER 10

WHERE SHOULD THE DIGITS RESIDE—ON TERRA FIRMA OR IN THE FIRMAMENT?

In the State of Paperlessness, multiple copies of any one file reside somewhere. But when information exists everywhere, the true or normal copy can exist nowhere. Is the final version of the contract on the thumb drive, in an e-mail attachment, a particular e-mail among dozens, on the lawyer's computer hard drive, his child's laptop, the office server, or the forgotten copy in the cloud?

This is no mean question. Digital information replicates, morphs, and moves over and over again at lightning speed. The day arrives when you need the true, last, correct version of a file. Where is it? Is that one really the last version? Is the time stamp when it was created or copied or last viewed?

> **The lawyer shall be able to identify and retrieve the true document, always.**

Working with a media that by its nature replicates so much, the basic decision of the lawyer is to identify the root storage that will, by practice, always have the true file. Because practice makes it the true one, then by definition any file found there is the true one. One rule in storing data is there must be one root storage. Root storage is storage that holds the best, most recent, and most accurate copies of the documents. This is not theoretical, but the lawyer must treat it as so. It is the one that interacts with the user and the one that the user instinctively and routinely turns to for needed documents. Once it is established, this is the default location for storing documents and retrieving them. While this should be copied in several ways and in several places, there can be only one root storage. Some like to use the term "primary" or "base" storage. The concept is the same.

The root storage differs from all of the other copies stored in three ways:

First, documents or files exist in the root storage only because the lawyer deliberately puts them there during document creation, intentional capture of other documents, file replacement, or other acts of file creation and maintenance.

Second, the information in root storage copies out, not in. The root storage is copied to the other drive, never the opposite. Copies, conversely, always copy from the root.

Third, files in the root storage are, absent clear and convincing evidence to the contrary, the true version. Always. Period.

> **The lawyer shall designate and maintain the primary or root file storage for all documents associated with his or her practice.**

To the lawyer in the State of Paperlessness, this requires the lawyer to engage in deliberate processes—identify the root storage, put documents there, and adhere to established practices that respect its preeminence in document storage. This includes determining the place and means of storage, how it is to be done, and then applying the rules as to how storage is organized, accessed, and secured. This, then, is the foundational requirement to practice in the State of Paperlessness: The lawyer must possess the requisite combination of storage devices, document management software, a process on how to use them, and a discipline to always adhere to this process. The constant goal remains to be able to always identify the true document and retrieve it. In a world where the lawyer uses different computers with multiple storage options, that is a challenge. The challenge grows exponentially with the number of individuals who interact with the lawyer and the documents with which he is working.

The lawyer has the choice of two different storage models for the root storage—storage the lawyer owns and controls or storage he does not. The hard drive on his computer or the network server in his office exemplifies the first, or traditional, approach. The second encompasses the use of storage on the Internet, or the "in the cloud."

> There will be times when, temporarily, the true copy resides elsewhere (such as a document created on the laptop). Do not confuse these temporary situations with the root storage. You have to discipline yourself to move those documents to the root storage as soon as possible.

The use of cloud-based storage is growing even for root storage. The cloud provides an attractive choice because it is always there wherever the lawyer may be, at least when the web is accessible. But it is not an obvious choice, nor is it necessarily the first choice.

> A file storage and retrieval system is no more reliable than the weakest link. Generally, the weakest link is the means of transferring data from storage to the user (wireless or cable, for example).

Comparison of Root Storage Options

Cloud	Traditional
A service accessed through the Internet.	Hardware onsite or connected to hardware owned and controlled by lawyer.
Resides on drives owned by the service at locations actually unknown, even unknowable, to the user but virtually reachable.	Resides on drives owned and controlled by the lawyer.
User can access all of the data anywhere and anytime needed where and when the web is available; no access when web is unavailable.	Access is limited to the degree access to the computer holding the root storage is accessible.
If there is no web access, there is no data.	Lack of web access will generally not interfere with access to data.

Cloud	Traditional
Low upfront costs with limited cost on acquiring additional storage. Issue more significant for medium to larger firms.	Larger upfront costs due to acquisition of hardware and software for storage. Minimal for the smaller firms, significant as firms grow.
Low ongoing costs of service rental.	No ongoing costs required, but there will be repairs and replacements.
Data in the cloud is always backed up automatically with no user involvement.	Data on the hard drive or server is backed up subject to local control and user involvement and staffing.
Data on individual unit may or may not be backed up.	Data on individual stations in the network are backed up routinely.
Remote units are automatically up to date.	Remote units are updated subject to user intervention.
Ideal for firms with multiple sites or attorneys who operate routinely out of the office.	Ideal for firms with a single or limited remote sites and attorneys who tend to work at the same site.
Documents not subject to loss due to the risks of local weather or geophysical, political, or other threats.	Subject to local risks to access to and maintaining documents.
Break in service from Internet going down or otherwise unavailable denies all access to the documents.	Disruption in Internet would not affect access on site.
The documents are accessible to multiple users at multiple sites under secure conditions.	Multiple accesses to multiple sites more difficult and generally at greater risk.
Use and retrieval of documents may require use of supplier's proprietary software.	Lawyer can control software used to use and retrieve documents.
Bankruptcy or termination of business can result in permanent loss of data.	Firm can control where data is in cases of dissolution or termination.
Uncertain whether the data is accessed by the government or other third parties without opportunity of lawyer to protect.	Lawyer has knowledge of attempted access by government or other third parties and can more easily protect confidential information.
Level of security is not easily verified.	Security can be audited and verified.
Maintaining and accessibility of data	Archiving and access to data can be at fixed, upfront costs.

The risk of data that is on a server outside of the lawyer's control is real indeed. On June 21, 2011, the FBI, in an effort to halt activities of Lulz Security, a group of hackers who tormented corporation and government websites with scareware, seized servers at DigitalOne's Reston, Virginia, site. In addition to taking servers believed associated with the hackers, the FBI also removed servers belonging to New York Curbed Network, a real estate blog, and others. While the FBI was interested in one client of DigitalOne, according to press reports quoting DigitalOne's CEO, it took servers used by "tens of clients."[1] The service was able, after delay, to switch to backup servers, but the incident shows the risk of extended disruption of service and outsiders having control of documents related to confidential work.

In October 2011, a communications satellite lost "earth lock" and those dependent upon receiving telecommunications. As a result, phone, Internet, and cable service across Canada and parts of the United States were interrupted.[2] That same month, BlackBerry phone users throughout the world suffered disconnection.[3]

Lesson: It can and will happen. The question is whether you can function if it does.

> Generally, use of the cloud for root storage should be done only by lawyers who are truly mobile and whose computers are rarely in one place regularly for the kind of backing-up of data required. It is also a considered choice for the solo practitioner who operates with minimal or no support staff.
>
> The power of the cloud and storage for all firms comes from using the cloud for backup. It provides automatic and offsite backup of all of the documents. When access to the primary storage is unavailable, you can access the online backup for the file.

DOCUMENTS AND SOFTWARE IN THE CLOUD

The model called "software as a service," or SaaS, takes cloud storage to another level. In this case it not only provides storage in the air, but also actually provides software with it. The lawyer has an ongoing contract to pay for not only access to the data, but also the ability to use the data within the software. In some cases this is the database that makes paperless practice possible. Others are more specialized. Online legal research is an example of leasing not only data but the programs to access it, as contrasted with having digital copies in the office.

The programs, not limited to the constraints of local computers, can have more power than a stand-alone desktop or laptop computer. At the same time, the programs are constantly being improved and updated without the lawyer having to do anything, or even knowing about it. SaaS programs can provide highly sophisticated software, such as e-discovery processing. Proper use of the cloud can bring greater computing and storage power, state-of-the-art programs, and anywhere accessibility at prices even the smallest firms can afford. Using SaaS, the programs and data are easily shared with others for collaboration and communication and are available anywhere the Internet is accessible.

But the lawyer has an obligation to protect the data. When using a cloud service or SaaS that keeps your data, ask these questions in addition to those mentioned above for the cloud storage:

- Who owns the data? Specifically, can the service provider sell the data? Marketability of some matters is minimal, but what if the lawyer specialized in cases involving a particular kind of claim against a targeted set of defendants and in the process developed a database of documents regarding these matters? These could have commercial value to other lawyers (defendant and plaintiff) involved in similar cases. Legally equivalent, a bankruptcy of the company with the data can result in the sale of the data to others who have no legal obligation under the contract with the lawyer.
- Can the lawyer retrieve all of his data in a format that will allow him to use other software? If the data can only be used with the software, then the lawyer is forever trapped into paying fees.
- Check to see whether the provider meets industry standards for technological safeguards, password and other access security, and recoverability. *This should be certified by a third-party audit which you can review and rely upon.*

In response to a civil investigative demand, we hired a nationally known firm to capture all of the data from the computers as well. The software allowed us to go online and examine and code all of the documents. Based on the processing, copies and lists were sent to the subpoenaing agencies. After the investigation closed, we ended the contract and requested copies of the data.

A few years later, several civil lawsuits were brought based upon the general topic of the investigation. Parties in that suit sought what we had sent to the government. Much to our chagrin, the company could no longer handle that kind of data. It eventually found a way to migrate the tapes to its newer system, but all of the coding had been lost, and we needed to start again on the document review.

Notes

1. *F.B.I. Seizes Web Servers, Knocking Sites Offline*, N.Y. TIMES, June 21, 2011, *available at* http://bits.blogs.nytimes.com/2011/06/21/f-b-i-seizes-web-servers-knocking-sites-offline/ (last visited Oct. 10, 2011).

2. Brian Daly, "Northern Canada suffers power loss," CNews, Oct. 6, 2011, http://cnews.canoe.ca/CNEWS/Canada/2011/10/06/18791311.html (last visited Oct. 20, 2011).

3. Antony Savvas, *BlackBerry outage floors email, BBM and web access*, COMPUTERWORLD UK, Oct. 10, 2011, *available at* http://www.computerworlduk.com/news/mobile-wireless/3309715/blackberry-outage-floors-email-bbm-and-web-access/ (last visited Oct. 20, 2011).

CHAPTER 11

MANAGING INFORMATION DISRUPTION IN THE STATE OF PAPERLESSNESS

The lawyer must be ever mindful that whatever she is doing will be disrupted sometimes. The disruptions can be merely irritating, like a slow response time or a momentarily misplaced file. Others can be practice destroying, such as a fire, flood, or earthquake. The disruptions can be in one document, a lost brief at time of filing, or the entire data of the practice.

In the State of Paperlessness, the lawyer faces greater vulnerability to disruption because of the speed at which she operates and the fact that all she does is tied together by wires, tiny and invisible, which bring power to process information and links to communicate. A break in the power or the links and the whole system slows, stalls, and stops.

There are several rules regarding information disruption:

Rule 1: It will happen.

Rule 2: It will surprise lawyers in how, when, and where it occurs.

Rule 3: It will have the potential to harm the case, the client, the lawyer, or the practice.

Rule 4: In almost every case, the disruption could have been prevented or the harm eliminated or greatly mitigated.

Rule 5: The harm from disruption is the geometric inverse of how current the activity is in those documents. For example, a disruption in writing a brief due in an hour is far worse than loss of a copy of one written 10 years ago.

The key to disruption management is diverse redundancy. For example:

- Redundancy in file storage and diversity in where and how the redundant data is stored.
- Redundancy in file backup and diversity in when and where the backups take place.
- Redundancy in systems that can handle the data and diversity in where those systems reside and can be accessed.
- Redundancy in ways the data can be accessed and diversity in the means to access that data (wireless or cable, for example).
- Redundancy in locations where the information can be used and processed and diversity in geography and risk profile for those locations.

> **The lawyer shall anticipate disruptions and design the practice to eliminate or mitigate such disruptions and to facilitate rapid recovery from them.**

IDENTIFY THE RISKS.

To determine whether or not the lawyer's office risks serious disruptions:

- Identify the major weather events that have occurred over the years in the area where your equipment is located. This includes severe thunderstorms, hurricanes, heavy rain, blizzards, ice, tornadoes, extreme heat, and extreme cold. How would the disruption occur? Even with existing precautions, backups, offline storage, and other technology, would the office still function?
- Identify the other risks of Mother Nature, such as earthquakes, tsunamis, volcanoes, sinkholes, or floods.

> Check back in the history of your area. I live thousands of miles from the California earthquake zone. Yet 80 years ago an earthquake damaged a school building a quarter of a mile from me to the extent that it had to be replaced and totally destroyed one less than 20 miles to the southwest. In the late 19th century, an epicenter a few miles to the northwest caused the top of the Washington monument hundreds of miles away to sway.

- Identify man-made disasters. What is your office proximity to hazardous cargo via truck or rail? Are there plants nearby that use hazardous materials? If there was a leak, could the office be evacuated?
- Identify the risk of vandalism, theft, or other criminal behavior. The better course is to assume the risk is greater than you thought.
- Identify the potential for equipment failure and the ease and speed of restoring service.
- Consider what the disruption would be from fire in the office or a nearby building, gas-line explosion, or water-main breaks.
- Identify ways in which someone can get access to information from office computers.

> The low-tech land-line phone can be a lifesaver. When an ice storm wiped out electricity and Internet to my office, a power generator and land line allowed me to complete and file some important documents.

- When considering disruption, note that in today's practice, the lawyer and her information can be anywhere. Lawyers have mobile devices at home and in luggage. Offsite storage could be with a company that just got hit by an earthquake.
- Identify the vulnerability to loss of electricity, Internet service, and wireless.

Securing against these involves these considerations for each:

- What losses will occur? Will it be only loss of data or confidentiality, or will there be a physical loss?
- What can be done to eliminate or reduce the exposure? For example, locks on doors and windows are steps to reducing risk of theft, password security for theft of data.
- What can be done to mitigate loss if such an event were to occur? This includes having secured backups available off-site.
- What is the scope of the area to be affected? Is there an alternative office site, temporary or otherwise, that can be used that would not be subject to the same risks?
- Disruptions seldom come in single events. They may start with one, but there is a cascading into other events. For example, a blizzard may deny access to the building personally, but the wind

may have severed power and cable service to the building, making remote access impossible as well. Lack of electricity may have caused the computers to power down, but if they are on the 25th floor and there is no elevator service, and the security systems require power to open the doors, there is no recovery. A storm may make the office unusable, but also may make highways impassable and thus the alternative site equally unavailable.

During the coldest season on record, the frost had gone down four feet or more, freezing water lines. A gas station located next to my business hired a welder to apply heat to thaw the water lines. After hours, the lines had not thawed out. Then a customer complained that the gas pouring into his tank was hot! The welder shut down his equipment and fled. Turns out the water line crossed over and touched the lines from the pumps to the tanks. In sub-zero weather, an explosion was not considered.

Some risks are surprising. A Washington attorney served as co-counsel with me in a matter. A brief was due that day. When he thought it was done, he took a step outside for a smoke and contemplation before he finalized it. When he returned to the office building, he was denied access. Someone in the building overpopped popcorn in the microwave to the point it briefly caught fire. Other staff quickly extinguished the fire, contained basically to the microwave oven, but not before the burnt corn and paper emitted a large amount of smoke to set off smoke alarms. These in turn activated calls to the fire department, implementation of mandatory life-safety measures, such as personnel evacuation, and denial of access until firemen could ensure all was truly well.

Don't ignore the old-fashioned and physical threats.

The lawyer should not be so wrapped up in technological risks that she ignores the common, but equally disruptive, risks from water, fire, and heat. A spilled soft drink on the laptop keyboard can shut the computer down. Heat in an overheated car interior can damage the laptop or tablet. A hard drive can be rendered useless in a room flooded by a burst pipe. Small and not so small animals can burrow into equipment, build nests, chew through wires, or defecate or urinate on circuit boards.

> For beverage use at the computer site, use only cups with lids
> that would not spill or would greatly reduce any spillage.

> **The lawyer shall protect all assets from physical damage
> created by water, fire, heat, or other hazards.**

While major natural or manmade disasters always remain possibilities, it is the smaller disruptions that can do the most damage.

Disruptions come in many ways. The following table suggests some of those.

Disruption Scenarios and Recovery Options

Disruption Scenario	Recovery Options
During the course of using a file, it is discovered that it is corrupted, the user has accidentally deleted large portions of it, or it has been deleted altogether.	Access the previous backup to bring current to today. Mirrored backup may not yet have been updated with the corruption; retrieve it. Retrieve file from the offsite backup. Look for backup generated by program. Rely on thumb drive, e-mail, or other file copies made during generation to get current. Possibly use a file recovery program to find the deleted, earlier version.
The program or operating system "crashes" or the computer no longer operates, any of which make the file unavailable.	Access the previous backup to bring current to today. Use the mirrored backup to retrieve it. Retrieve file from the offsite backup. Rely on thumb drive, e-mail, or other file copies made during generation to get current.
The file is "lost" due to operator or system failure by being stored where it is not expected.	Do a search of all media filtering by date. Look at database log of documents added to see if it is there.
The loss of the file or serious modification is discovered days later.	Look at prior backup versions starting with the recent and working backwards. See if temporary copies were made or e-mailed for recovery.
Access to office is denied due to weather or other situation but power is still up.	Try remotely accessing the system. Access the offsite backup. Use any temporary memory or laptop that may have the file. Use an e-mailed copy of the file.

Disruption Scenario	Recovery Options
Access to office is denied due to weather, fire, earthquake, or other situation and power is down.	Access the offsite backup. Use any temporary memory or laptop that may have the file. Use an e-mailed copy of the file.
The data was put on the home computer, a thumb drive at an out-of-town business center, or laptop but not made part of the regular backup, and that medium becomes unavailable.	Out of luck unless it was backed up on another system, e-mailed, or stored on another thumb or flash drive.
The office systems are stored on the same 40th floor as the office. A natural disaster causes the electricity to be shut off and the building is secured from any access.	If the system was backed up offsite, then access the offsite data. If the only backups are in that building, the lawyer is out of luck. Future thoughts are to use an Internet backup as well as a backup in another building and location not subject to the same natural event risks.

The recurring theme in all of the recovery options is that the best recovery comes from preparation prior to the disruption.

My experience with disruption and recovery began early. When I was a college student a rubber band burst, letting loose a stack of punch cards in the wind and rain. That was my first loss of data and programs. I learned to punch copies. The first computers I worked on had volatile memory. That meant as long as there was power, the memory held. Turn off the power and everything was lost. The lesson was to repeatedly store the information on non-volatile memory, such as magnetic cards and 9-inch floppy discs holding a whopping 256K of data!

THERE IS NO BACKUP UNLESS IT IS DONE IN THREE DIFFERENT PLACES.

A single backup is not enough. If it fails, as it will when least expected, then there is no backup. For example, an in-office backup will do no good if access to the office is denied due to a fire or storm. The purpose of the backup is to mitigate or even eliminate the effects of a disruption in the system that results in one or more needed documents being unavailable or corrupted. A good backup system combines backup stored at different locations, accessible in different ways, and made with different timing to mitigate or eliminate the risk. At least daily the files should be copied to another system within the office.

- There should be an automatic mirroring of files in real time. Most computers today are configured as RAID, or redundant array of independent disks. In simple terms, when something is written to the hard drive, the system writes it a second time. How or where this other place is located results in different schemes. The preferred way is to have a separate disk that is written identically to the main drive. Sometimes called RAID-3, this means that if the first drive fails, the computer can look at the second one as the main drive with minimal disruption.

- Programs that generate documents should have an ongoing automatic backup program operating in backgrounds. Within word processors, spreadsheets, and other programs, the lawyer can choose an option of routinely and automatically backing up open documents, the time between these backups, and whether or not earlier backups are kept or overwritten. The choices should be yes, often, and yes.

- During critical file creation periods, copies should be made to thumb drives, e-mailed to self, or placed in the cloud so that the file is available and usable anywhere.

- A full system backup should be done at least once a year or possibly quarterly. A full backup takes times, sometimes days, to copy over the mass amount of data captured over years. It also severely degrades performance for users during the backup. There is also the risk that newly added material is not properly included. As a consequence, choosing a holiday weekend, for example, for a complete backup would be appropriate.

- An incremental backup should occur no less than daily. Incremental backup captures changes since the last full backup. Because they are generally relatively small, they can be done daily and saved separately. Generally, all one needs to look at for current needs would be on the incremental backup. Depending on the degradation of the service, incremental backup during the day is also possible.

- Backups should be backed up offsite. Offsite backup includes any and all of the following: Full and incremental backup to another computer in another location through the Internet, full and incremental backup to a cloud server, full and incremental backup to an onsite computer and the drives are removed daily to be stored offsite. The latter is better than nothing but risks the physical loss of the backup or disruption in routine (the courier is on vacation or sick).

The system must provide for redundancy in software and approaches to backup and retrieval.

Redundancy in the storage of information cannot be overstated. Additionally, there should be redundancy in the equipment that can access and use the data in the formats in which it is saved and redundancy in how to access and process the data.

Incompatibilty happens because the version of software used to create a document is more recent than the one on the alternative machine. Or special software, such as management software that finds the documents or case management software used for trials, is not commonly available except on the lawyer's computer. Even though the lawyer can reach the documents, she cannot process them without the software.

> This has happened to me too often. I created a file using Office 10, but the system I was trying to use only had 7. As if denial of access to the Word document was not enough, I also had an Excel file with an embedded macro and the business center would not let me run the macro. Although there were programs I could download to remedy the situation, the business center systems I was using would not accept any programs to protect it from viruses, etc. No one at the center knew how to override this.

> If part of your disaster plan is to use a specific business center, try it out on a dry run to see how up-to-date the software is and discuss shortcomings with the manager.

- In choosing alternate sites, consider how widespread the damaged infrastructure is and your ability to reach it. If your accessibility and lack of power is due to a blizzard, the next available site might be a great distance away and one that you cannot reach.

Recognize that data may not be on the system that is subject to routine backups.

As the last scenario above shows, the greatest risk of loss comes from the rogue files that are created and used outside of the system or are disconnected from the protocols for automatic backups (such as a turned-off laptop). Other precautions are needed.

- Documents on laptops and portable media are very easily lost or stolen. Keep the data on encrypted thumb drives and synchronize with the system.
- Routinely e-mail files remotely created or changed and, in turn, put them into the main system.
- Routinely dock the laptop or thumb drives into the main system to have them backed up as part of the network backup procedure.
- Set your home and other stationary computers that are out of the office to back up to a cloud-based server and to a backup drive onsite.
- Laptops that are transported from the office to home might contain data that has not been backed up since the last time it was in the office. Copy to the cloud if possible, copy onto a thumb drive, or e-mail it.

DURING TIMES OF GENERATING DOCUMENTS WITH A TIME DEADLINE (SUCH AS WRITING A BRIEF), FREQUENT AND DISTINCT STORAGE IS ESSENTIAL.

During the creation and editing of documents as deadlines approach, the lawyer is in the most critical phase. Corruption or loss of a file could result in the loss of several hours of uniquely creative effort.

One time I had a brief due for a petition to the Ohio Supreme Court. Under the rules of that court, the deadline was hard. Failure to meet that deadline was tantamount to not having the petition considered at all. I had made arrangements for a runner to pick up my document at noon and deliver it to the Supreme Court. It was all but complete. I went to run the automatic table generations to have the final tables of contents and tables of authorities created with updated pages. By some fluke, my document went from 15 pages to thousands of pages as each line became a new page. Because I had been backing up routinely, I retrieved the most recent version, which at that time was at most only 15 minutes older than the one that had been altered. After successfully generating the tables and printing the document, I had it ready for the runner on time.

Save files being worked on in multiple places during the process. For example, I will save under the formal manner, which is the file I work on, unless it is corrupted. I save to a folder on my computer or the desktop as a temporary file and routinely e-mail myself copies.

- During the creation of documents, particularly those that are long and are the result of the creative process, making copies of the file with different names repeatedly during the creation process protects you against several failures that can occur at a critical time. This is diversity in name and redundancy in copying.
- Incorrect use of the global search and replace. Care should always be taken when using this powerful tool. The series of letters that seem unique may not be. They could be embedded into words.
- Copying and pasting can be done in the wrong order or, if there are more than two documents, on the wrong document.
- Downloading a document for purposes of modification to create a new document but saving the modified document by the old name.

In addition to the backup options described above, periodically change the name of the file during saving. During the drafting of this book, for example, I changed the name of drafts to the date I was writing. When it was a heavy day of writing or editing, I would specify AM or PM and sometimes even the hour. In this way I avoided the risk of overwriting the error onto the file and thus perpetuating it.

For search and replace, sparingly use the global one-step process of change, but, instead, seek each instance and then allow a replace. It never ceases to amaze me the times a global replacement would change an expected word and I would not know it. If you feel you must use the quick method, have Track Changes on so you can actually see all of the changes made.

> Editing longer documents is best done on a separate document and under a different regime. This could be by actually printing out the draft to PDF, reading it, and making notations of the edits or making the editorial notes on a PDF. The reason is this: By making the edits to a document that is separate from the real document, it is easier to ensure that all intended changes are made and no more. By making the edits on the go, even with Track Changes on, there is speed and efficiency, but if the changes are accepted, you may make changes you were not aware of. By changing a separate document, a comparison can be done to ensure that all changes are noted.

PREPARE FOR DISASTER.

Just as preparing for trial makes a trial better, preparing for disaster makes response better as well.

Practice, practice, practice.

Just because the lawyer has purchased the best backup software, established the best system, uses the best equipment, and has created the best process does not mean that at the moment of need the data will be there.

> **Data recovery systems do not just happen; they are created, maintained, nurtured, and used by the lawyer.**

> My administrator and system guru got a frantic call from a neighbor one night. A virus attacked his computer and locked badly needed data in its jaws. Connected to the computer was a terabyte backup drive. He had attached it months ago. When he went to retrieve the file from it, the drive was empty. He had just assumed it worked.

- Do a flow chart of the backups showing when and where they are being done.
- Rehearse how to retrieve data when the system fails under different scenarios. Practice retrieving documents and other data if the laptop fails on the road, the server goes down, or the Internet fails.

When you learn about a disruptive event due to a weather, storm, or man-made disaster, imagine that your office was in the zone of disruption. How would you function under those considerations?

- Do a tabletop exercise working through various interruption scenarios to ensure that needed information is available and recoverable from a source.
- Do a dry run and actually retrieve data from an alternate site and use it. For example, identify three files—one that was done a year ago, one that was done last week, and one you are working on—and seek to retrieve them.
- With as little warning as possible (try when working on a day the courthouse is closed, for example), tell all of the staff to leave the office and go to a place off-site and then work through a scenario and recovery as if the office were unavailable.

Here is a simple drill without a lot of drama. When your staff is gathered together outside of the office for other reasons, such as an office lunch, ask each of them to write down what they were working on when they left the office and what they needed to work on later that afternoon and the next day. After they have made these lists, tell them to imagine that access to their desks and computers—in fact, the office—is unavailable. Now ask how they could finish the project. Bring a laptop along and see if the information they need to complete the job is available from both the office computer and the off-site computer.

Put the disaster recovery plan in writing and place it in the hands of key individuals.

The recovery plans should be detailed. Note that these are *plans,* as in plural. The plan for recovery from a very short office separation differs from a longer-term or even permanent dislocation.

- Contact information for all personnel during off-hours. Include the names of neighbors, family, or friends that can be reached. Keep in mind that during a major emergency, traditional connection to others may fail.

- Directions on how to locate and access alternative sources of data, such as offline storage or cloud-based backups.
- Names and access information for key software, such as the practice management programs. *This should also include passwords or other access information.*
- Names, addresses, and contact information for support in setting up equipment. Note that this may require having names and addresses from out of the immediate area if the disaster is widespread.
- Names, addresses, and account information for acquiring equipment as needed.
- Instructions on how to access data off-site, including urls and passwords.
- Names, addresses, and phone numbers of alternative office sites.
- Names, addresses, and phone numbers of emergency personnel in area of office.

This information should be put onto hard stock and laminated, and treated with the highest security. A copy should be at home and one carried with you.

CHAPTER 12

ACQUIRING AND USING PRACTICE MANAGEMENT IN THE PAPERLESS PRACTICE

In addition to the software generally used by lawyers in papered and unpapered practices, the lawyer requires one specific type of software to move the office to the State of Paperlessness. Its last name is "management program." Its first name can include document, practice, case, matter, or firm. In the non-legal world, there are similar programs known as enterprise resource planning (ERP) systems. These programs combine matter, contact, case, calendar, communication (phone and e-mail), and document management with timekeeping, billing, and accounting. Regardless of the name, this essential system integrates all of that information so that the lawyer can move seamlessly from one piece of information to another regardless of what program generated it or how it was used. It does this by linking all of the pieces of information in multiple ways.

THE LAWYER NEEDS TO DEFINE THE GOAL OF GOING PAPERLESS.

These systems can be comprehensive when fully implemented. Such comprehensiveness can be overwhelming. It is best to focus on individual functions within the practice and move them to being paperless. Then, function by function, integrate them with the other functions. In terms of the upgrading of each function, every lawyer has different priorities (billing, document management, e-mail management, document generation, etc.). And that is how bringing in the management software should be considered.

> I generally recommend starting with the document and case management first. That will bring the most productivity the fastest. Once the firm is running smoothly with that, other modules can be added. Billing should be last, because it is the most important. By the time everything else is integrated, almost all of the information for billing will already be present, and it will be easier to add that module.

THERE ARE DIFFERENT KINDS OF MANAGEMENT SYSTEMS FOCUSED ON DIFFERENT ASPECTS OF THE PRACTICE.

Management programs generally consist of modules. Comprehensive in total, they can be used a module at a time—a recommended approach. These modules are:

- *Document management.* This provides information as well as access to all of the documents that are stored. Based upon internal content as well as the information profiled by the attorney or staff, the document manager provides access based on different filters, such as client, matter, persons, type, date, and the like.
- *Contact management.* Contact management combines maintaining contact lists with logging contacts made. It maintains a sortable file on all of the contacts with e-mail, phone, address, and other information. It logs of all e-mails, phone calls, and other correspondence.
- *Calendar management.* This allows the lawyer and his staff to schedule events as well as rooms (such as the conference room), deadlines, reminders, and other time-sensitive information. Some programs even automatically compute dates based on statutes of limitations, filing deadlines, or the like.
- *Time management and billing.* Time management goes beyond identifying dates; it also logs lawyer and staff activities by date and length of time to provide information for billing and management. The times are sortable by date and time, attorney, staff, matter, client, work type, matter type, and other elements to assist not only in billing but in managing the practice. Time management prepares bills with detail and comments as fine or as broad as the lawyer determines. Tied into accounting software, it maintains accounting history. Some programs also link the billing to trust accounts.

- *Project management.* Similar to case management, project management provides a much broader view of things to be done with sortable to-do lists, time budgets, schedules, and deadlines.
- *Case management.* Case management maintains all of the information and filings regarding the case. In addition to just making such information accessible, advanced case management helps the lawyer build the factual basis for the case and link that to the issues, law, documents, facts, and filings in the case.
- *Document assembly.* In some practice areas, such as bankruptcy, probate, and wealth management, this module can assemble the information already in the database as well as additional information requested and assemble and produce the filings and reports required. Also, based on matter type, it can produce checklists and other matter-specific helps.
- *Accounting management.* This set of programs manages time and costs by associating them with specific cases. In addition, it can provide the bookkeeping and payroll records required.

DIFFERENT FACTORS DETERMINE THE RIGHT PRACTICE MANAGEMENT SYSTEM.

The lawyer making the decision should begin with understanding what his practice is and what he can afford. With so much out there, having a consultant can speed the process of choosing the right program. Just be careful that the consultant is open enough to look at more than one system, not just the one he or she markets.

- *Size of practice.* Most packages will apply to most law firms, but some provide a better fit for solo or small law firms, others fit medium-sized firms better, and some are better for the very large. Their functionality is very similar. Rather, as the number of lawyers grows, so does the number of documents, the amount of information, and the times information is being accessed. Handling very large numbers of documents with very large number of interactions requires a different structure than the smaller systems. At the same time, running a solo office on software designed for a firm of 100-plus brings an unneeded level of hardware, software, and support overhead.
- *Budget.* Systems cost money. Not only is there generally an upfront cost, but most good packages have ongoing maintenance and

support costs. Some even charge a periodic royalty that may or may not include maintenance and support. A sustainable law firm needs a sustainable database which needs a flow of cash to maintain and support it. In short, there will be costs, and they will be ongoing. When comparing costs, look at the cost for five years rather than just the purchase price.

> When the comprehensive system is finally running, the biggest investment will be the lawyer's time, and that by many multiples of the initial cost. Investing in good software, regardless of price, will pay off later.

- *Technical support.* The larger and more complex the system, the more support needed. A program that supplies this from the outset can help a small law firm that has no IT support.
- *Integration with other programs.* Every practice has a huge investment in documents and reports produced by a particular system. This is especially the case with word processing. Integration of these programs with the management database is essential to ultimate facility and productivity. Keep in mind that in spending resources, capturing hundreds of events each month (such as e-mails) deserves priority over connecting one or two numbers (such as accounts receivable balance from billing to accounting). Even though the lawyer may not use a particular word-processing or spreadsheet format, having the capability to store, index, and open those formats should be considered.
- *Operating system.* Windows is not the only operating system being used, but it is the most common. As a consequence, a lot of software is designed for it and not others, such as Apple's OS or Lion, the open-source Linux, or other operating systems. Even though technically a Windows application for Apple may create compatibility, the complexity of some of the database programs may challenge such an approach. On the other hand, SaaS systems that are cloud-based are generally not so system-software limited.
- *Equipment.* There are programs that will work on single desktops or laptops; others require networks, and yet others central servers. Knowing what you will use for the system can sort out a lot of programs quickly. At the same time, deciding on a particular program can limit hardware choices.

- *Practice specificity.* Programs targeted to specific practice areas bring a lot of power and simplicity not necessarily available on more general programs. A practice that is almost entirely consumer bankruptcy, for example, may find a management program written for bankruptcy practice sufficiently powerful and comprehensive.
- *Multiple systems.* Programs designed primarily for billing can be great for that but leave other parts of the design lacking. There are excellent accounting and payroll programs available off the shelf, but these would lack the sophistication to handle all the documents and information of a typical law office. The converse is also true. Having several packages targeted at specific parts of the practice can make sense.
- *Accessibility.* The more mobile the attorney, the more mobile access is important. Those that are cloud-based make this less of an issue. But if the lawyer wants to access the database with a remote computer, laptop, tablet, or PDA, then the kind of programs that will allow that need to be considered.

Having a single system that handles everything well is the target, but getting there is best reached by smaller steps. Many of the master database systems have modules that will allow you to do almost all functions but do not require all initially. The best approach is to get the matter management running with full use. Then incorporate the billing. The document management system is easier to integrate, provides the necessary support for billing, provides virtually immediate benefit and buy-in, and the struggles of installation will not interfere with cash flow. By the time everyone is familiar with it, adding billing will be much easier.

Before buying and installing a system, ask around and talk with attorneys who have successful systems as well as those who have had problems. Take advantage of this wealth of experience. ABA has excellent resources in books and through the Law Practice Management Section. The annual ABA Tech Show in Chicago provides a place not only to attend seminars but to visit vendors with the different kinds of equipment.

It goes without saying that a lawyer should not bite off more than he can chew in the conversion. Over the years successful companies and law firms have been knocked out by failures in technology conversion. One lawyer even lost his license in large part due to the collapse of converting his collection practice to a computer.[1]

> **Preparation and patience are invaluable traits in the process.**

The practice management programs available for lawyers include: Time Matters, Cleo, Prolaw, Amicus, Needles Case Management Software, Prevail Case Management, Abacus Law, Practice Master, Rocket Matter, PerfectLaw All-in-One, and Credenza. Some of these are simple but powerful. While on a small set of cases they display well, when you begin to have hundreds or thousands of cases in your system, some do not perform as well.

Incorporate other databases into the main system database.

In addition to the regular system, which has the database management program as well as other programs, there may be times when it is advisable to develop a separate indexing and access system as part of that database. This may include mapping together different matters, creating a database of specific kinds of documents for easier access, a database of photographs that are exhibits or a case management database, or the like.

Most common programs have the power to do this. Word, Excel, Access, and Adobe all have built-in capacity to build databases and link to files. For example, if, in a particular matter, 100 photographs were taken at the scene of an accident, the photographs could be indexed by frame number and other information in a spreadsheet, with a link to the actual photograph. The placement and indexing all of them within the practicewide database might be overwhelming, and unnecessary if the spreadsheet is itself indexed.

Another example of the use of the spreadsheets is when, as part of a matter, there is a large number of checks or invoices. The detail of these documents can be put in a spreadsheet for analysis and the actual documents hyperlinked. The spreadsheet could be the only document that is documented in the case management database.

> To handle many nondisclosure agreements (NDAs), I created a spreadsheet where I identified all of them by party, date, date of termination, general purpose, responsible party of my client, and other information. Each entry was linked to the signed copy and the original. On another page I used the spreadsheet as an input into a Word merge to create the first draft of the NDAs.

> The danger of self-created systems is that generally only the creator knows how to fully work them, so keep them simple and provide explanations in one of the worksheets.

Practice-specific programs with file management systems

Some practice-specific programs (such as probate, bankruptcy, litigation management, etc.) have their own file management system. How these integrate into the systemwide background depends on the programs and the degree to which they are used. Some of these programs are licensed for periods of time. Thereafter they cease to be operable, making the information stored inaccessible. For this reason, all documents generated by the program should be saved as PDFs and managed through the document database.

E-mail should not be a file management system.

In any event, the e-mail folders should not be used to organize information. They should be kept clean except for pending or new items. E-mails accumulate rather rapidly. It is not uncommon for a typical businessperson to receive hundreds of e-mails per day, and the vast majority of them may have little or no value. In an office with 10 people, that amounts to 1,000 e-mails a day, 5,000 a week, and 2.5 million a year. Aside from creating overwhelming storage issues, it also poses other serious issues in terms of confidentiality, accessibility, and degrading of the e-mail system because of all of the files in storage.

> Instead, daily sort the e-mails and remove, by hand or through Outlook rules, the junk ones, and save the rest through the information management program.

E-mails can also accumulate in the Deleted or Sent subfolders. As the number of these e-mails with all of their attachments grows, e-mail program performance denigrates. If there is a pronounced length of time from launching to access to the program, the cause most likely is such a buildup of old unwanted files.

Notes

1.   Cleveland Bar Ass'n v. Sweeney, 74 Ohio St. 3d 44, 1995 Ohio 125, 656 N.E.2d 619, 1995 Ohio LEXIS 2304 (1995).

CHAPTER 13

FINDING A PLACE FOR THE LAWYER IN THE STATE OF PAPERLESSNESS

While documents can be converted to digits and placed anywhere, lawyers cannot. They remain very much a physical object in need of a physical space. In real estate it has always been location, location, location. In the State of Paperlessness, the lawyer will value location differently. No longer does the lawyer need to work at a location but instead can consider locations. These locations are physical and virtual. Some locations meet several needs of the lawyer; others provide only one or two. The skilled lawyer essentially has an "office" wherever she is in the State of Paperlessness.

The papered office location was defined and limited by:

- The need to be near the files and books needed to practice.
- The need to employ people, space, and equipment to access and use the information in that paper.
- The attachment by cords, cables, and wires to power and enable phones, faxes, and the Internet.
- The need to have a place where deliveries of mail and parcels can be made.
- The need for physical proximity to the client, court, community, or co- counsel.
- The need for a location close to prospective clients and cases.

In the State of Paperlessness, the lawyer enjoys:

- The freedom to access all of the information available digitally, instantly, anywhere.
- The freedom from needing (and thus acquiring) space for cabinets, shelves, desks, and staff to manage paper.
- The freedom to be anywhere, detached from wires and cables but fully empowered with all the data and computing power needed.
- The ability to be reached anywhere from anywhere.
- The freedom to be where the lawyer wants to be, where needed, when needed, to the degree needed.
- The ability to be wherever the prospective clients are, around the world and around the clock.

The "law office" provides lawyers with services beyond location. Not all of these services need to, or even should, exist in the same place. These locations include:

- A place where the lawyer works.
- A place where others can reach the lawyer.
- A place where the information, and those who manage it, is located.
- A place where the lawyer confers with clients, witnesses, and other lawyers.
- A place where the lawyer promotes her practice and expertise.

No lawyer shall be required to practice law in only one place or prohibited from practicing in many places simultaneously.

THE LAWYER ACTUALLY WORKS WHERE SHE WANTS TO.

The public sees the lawyer in the courtroom. Most lawyers are rarely, if ever, found there. Except for those lawyers who routinely are in the courtroom in criminal and family law, most lawyers practice their trade outside these public places.

Not only are the lawyers not in the courtroom, they have little need to be even close by. Consequently, convenience dominates the decision of where to practice law. This includes convenience of the lawyer to the place, convenience to clients, and convenience to the courts or agency. Every lawyer and her practice have different ways of measuring that, but if there is anything that new technology brings, it is convenience— and convenience should be enjoyed.

From the day I first started to practice law, I have always had an office within walking distance of my home. In addition, I had a place at home to work. This proximity to work provided me with many advantages, including a competitive advantage.

The advantage came because there was no commute time. There was no wasting of the intellectual, physical, and emotional energy from the freshest, brightest part of the day in driving or commuting to work. Within minutes of leaving home, or even just being home, I was working at my desk. And with no commute time, the hours out of the house were almost entirely spent actually practicing law.

The home office provided a safe and cozy place to work on off-hours. There were times I needed to work late. After putting the family to bed, I could return to my work either at the office or at the house. Some mornings upon awakening I was "in the zone." Armed with a cup of tea, I hit the keyboard, applying my freshest thoughts to the issue of the day.

Working at or near home provides more time to spend with family and also to work. As I raised my family, I was able to attend almost every school function of my children. For example, I could work until 3 P.M., make the short distance to school, attend the function, and return to work. Only out-of-town travel occasionally interfered. Working out of such an environment did not necessarily deprive me of a good practice. Out of an office in a small village, I have participated in legal matters and tried cases in courts all over the country against some of the best firms in the biggest cities. It gave me the best of both worlds. Technology gave me that opportunity.

THE LAWYER NEEDS A WORKSITE OFFICE.

The lawyer can physically be in only one place at a time, but that does not mean the "work office" needs to be only in one place. Different situations dictate different places. Even then, there should be that fixed place where the bulk of work is done. There can additionally be a secondary office at home or a mobile office when out of the office.

Regardless of whether an office is away or in the home, there must be dedicated space to do the job—a place where the lawyer has trained her mind to expect to work day in and day out. It should be a space that does not compete with other activities. The home office, for example, should not also serve as the bedroom, family room, or kitchen, particularly when others are also at home. Working at home means doing the work normally done in the office. It does not mean doing the work done at home, such as watching young children or extensive housework, for example. It is, or should be, designed to remove the distractions of sights, sounds, and smells that will divert the lawyer from the legal task at hand.

Along with convenience, the work office must facilitate the following:

- Concentration of resources to increase power and productivity.
- Elimination of or limitation from temptations to fulfill other, nonpracticing needs and desires.
- A location that dependably provides services and availability.

An office also helps "sell" the attorney by providing an underlying sense of stability, professionalism, and success.

There are physical requirements as well. Worksite offices have to have access to the phone system (landline or cell), Internet (wired or wireless), and electrical power. All other attributes can vary, but those are essential. The electricity needs to be clean and uninterruptible. That means that there should also be backup power.

When building my office, I went so far as to add a gas-powered backup generator. Loss of power is rare, but those could be crucial moments. The most damaging storm in my experience came from wind and ice. Almost every single strand of cable and electrical line hanging between poles snapped under heavy ice, falling ice-laden branches, or both. For days there was no power. Besides power, there was no staff. They were taking care of their own personal emergencies. Before the power was restored, I had to meet a filing deadline. The agency where the filing was due had not experienced the storm. As a result, there was no appreciation of the seriousness of the situation, and my request for a few days' extension was denied. Fortunately, I had access to an old-fashioned phone line whose connection to the outside world was underground. Using that line, I faxed the filing on time because I had power in my office to access the files and prepare the filing.

> VOIP and cell phone make the old-fashioned land-line phone seem useless and out of date. But in case of emergencies, an old plastic phone attached to a wire that connects to the phone line may be the only connection available.

Using mobile equipment, the lawyer can make anywhere her worksite office.

Practicing law today requires access to the files and law and the ability to read, create, and edit documents. Laptops or tablets, along with wireless technology, take the lawyer anywhere. This includes in the car, on a plane, on a train or bus, on the beach, in a coffee shop, anywhere.

> Once as I was boarding the plane for a long flight, my client called and explained his need for a draft of a contract prior to a meeting in a couple of hours. He really had to have it then. I did not cancel or delay my flight, or call someone to help, but boarded as planned. After I was airborne, I tuned my tablet into the WiFi on the plane. Remotely I went to my office computer's desktop, called up the source documents, typed the required draft, and e-mailed it to my client, when he needed it and hours before I landed.
>
> I took more risk than I should have. On a subsequent trip, I planned to use the same wireless capability to get some less urgent work done. The wireless was down.

The lawyer should prepare for mobile use in advance by gaining familiarity with the mobile equipment and anticipating the use to ensure that data needed is available. Just because technology provides this flexibility does not mean that the technology will work properly the first time without testing the equipment and understanding exactly how it works.

Also, knowing where the work is done determines where the data is. Data residing in the cloud is available anywhere—anywhere there is Internet access, that is. Places like airplanes do not always have such availability. There are areas where signals do not penetrate buildings, mountains, or other obstructions. Anticipating what files will be needed and placement on a secured thumb drive avoids this problem.

All of these tools require that they be tested and worked on before you really need them. If the goal is to take advantage of time in a certain situation, then use it to actually accomplish something other than getting your system in position to do something and training yourself on how to do it.

The measure of ease and speed of technology to complete a task is the length of time available multiplied by the importance of the task, divided by the degree of familiarity the lawyer has with the technology used to complete the task.

The first challenge for the mobile lawyer is to choose between a laptop or a tablet. If the need is primarily checking and responding to e-mail, reading documents, or using the Internet, a tablet can be the preferred choice. But when it comes to real document production, such as typing a brief or editing a contract, the laptop does a better job.

LogMeIn ranks as my top application. With my tablet I touch one button on my screen, answer several simple screens, and I am on my desktop at my office. There I can access everything that I have at the office. Using the finger like a cursor takes some getting used to, but once I had that down I could gather information I needed. One time I realized the address of the meeting was not on my iPad or BlackBerry. Using the in-the-air wireless service, I used LogMeIn to get to my desktop, where I recovered the letter with all of the details. I cut and pasted those and put them in my calendar for that day. With the syncing of MobileMe, by the time I landed, all of the information was loaded onto my iPad so I could find the office.

That was an emergency use, but it can also be a planned use. At a board meeting aof a client, a decision was made to request members to approve major changes to the by-laws. To prepare the resolution, I used LogMeIn to go to my office computer and gather the information I needed. I then developed the resolution at the hotel business center as if I were at my desktop. The project was delivered when needed.

Equipment can also be found in hotel business centers, public facilities such as FedEx offices, and airport lounges and airline clubs. Relationships with law offices or other professional offices in visited cities can also provide access to such equipment. The minimum requirements are a computer that operates the latest version of Microsoft Office and has an attached printer, access to the Internet, and a UBS port.

The thumb drive of choice is a password-protected, encrypted, and remote-erasable memory. This thumb drive secures data against theft and provides a platform to securely use the Internet. All downloads, history, cookies, and deleted files remain on that thumb drive, not the host computer. When the key is removed, all of the data and data trail stays with the thumb drive. It does not reside on the host computer. If the key is left or lost, it will lock out with nonuse, and anyone trying to use it without the password will erase the data sooner than they can break the code. The data is also routinely backed up on the Internet so nothing is lost.

> The actual strength of the encryption on such a device as this thumb drive is less the bit length of the cipher used in the encrypting algorithm than how easy the password can be cracked. The longer it is—the more use of characters, symbols, numbers, and case—the more secure.

> IronKey provides a secure thumb drive and system that also provides for remote wiping and automatic erasure if the password is missed more than 10 times.

> Remote worksites such as FedEx offices also provide a place to print those jobs that need printing. Rather than haul paper when traveling, upload the print job to these sites and have them prepare the documents, often overnight. After a confirming phone conversation, they will be waiting, often at the lawyer's room if specified.

> I still take a digital file with me. This way, if changes need to be made, I can make them easily.

While having the data in the cloud or in an e-mail can replace the thumb drive, the assumption has to be that wherever the lawyer is, Internet access is available when the data is required.

A lawyer needs a place to make contact with clients, staff, and others.

The attorney working in the State of Paperlessness has many contact offices.

A lawyer shall locate her practice so that if she is ever absent, she will be missed.

The single most important and place-specific contact office is the place for receipt of mail, parcels, and packages. In some cases there are two—a post office box and a physical address for receipt of deliveries from parcel delivery services. Whether it is also where the attorney can be found is less important than having someone there who has the intelligence and skill to sort through what is received, make it available to the attorney as quickly as possible (digitally or physically), and communicate with her as special situations arise.

Virtually all state rules of practice for the bar require that attorneys maintain a physical address on file. Practicing in the State of Paperlessness does not change that.

Failure to have such a properly functioning contact office can also harm client interests. In a case accepted by the Supreme Court, two lawyers who worked as associates for Sullivan & Cromwell took a criminal appeal pro bono. After filing the request, the lawyers left the firm. The Alabama court hearing the challenge sent the ruling denying post conviction for relief. Someone in the mailroom of their now former firm returned the notice to the court clerk unopened with "Return to Sender—Left Firm" written on the envelope. The question for the court was whether there was notice sufficient to trigger the 42-day time to appeal.[1]

While this presents an interesting legal issue, it is exactly the kind of case the lawyer does not want to have. An attorney's resources are better spent on merit issues, not on cleaning up mix-ups in the procedure.

Other one-to-one contacts can occur through phone calls, e-mail, and text messaging. These contact locations or offices, known as phone numbers and e-mail addresses, require a physical location. E-mail addresses are totally decoupled from place. The availability of phone numbers with a given area code provides no assurance where the phone is actually located when the call is being made. An attorney can have multiple contact offices through multiple phone numbers and e-mail addresses.

The location the lawyer uses to contact many people also does not need to accommodate so many. The function of contacting for one-to-many exists on the Internet with websites, blogs, YouTube, Facebook, and other social media.

The lawyer needs a place to meet with others, a meeting office.

Meeting with clients is an important function in the practice of law. In the State of Paperlessness, proximity to paper files and books no longer dictates where those meetings take place. Meeting clients outside the traditional office means finding a place where there is comfort, confidentiality, and convenience to all, and one that contributes to a successful meeting. While e-mail, Skype, webinars, and other communications are great timesavers, there are times when face-to-face meetings are best. For one thing, it means a more dedicated effort in making the meeting, rather than a slot to move in and out of based on the calendar. There are also nonverbal signals in body language, actions, and other means of communicating not transmitted by the Internet.

A Cleveland, Ohio, lawyer had an office in his apartment. His only paralegal was his mother. In November 2010 he argued a case before the Supreme Court[2] which eventually resulted in a court victory for his client.[3] Nonetheless, if the expectation is to develop a wealth practice firm, having a contact office that is in a rundown building in a less affluent area may not be the thing to do. Not everyone can pull off what the Cleveland attorney did. Even in that case, the client expressed a certain level of unease at visiting a lawyer in his home.

A place that provides support to do the job

From a practical standpoint, all of the support (library, files, notes, and forms) are, like the lawyer, where the lawyer is. In the past, physical bookshelves and file cabinets dictated where the lawyer worked.

Technology makes all of that material accessible anywhere. In addition to the data support, there is personal support. The need is reduced but not necessarily eliminated. Because a digital file can be accessed by many people at the same time, those who use them can be in different places. Phones can be answered anywhere, documents prepped and scanned anywhere.

The law office in the State of Paperlessness may or not be a "virtual" office.

Being paperless does not mean the lawyer operates a virtual office. Likewise, a lawyer using a virtual office may not operate in a paperless manner. Each can complement the other, but neither requires the other.

In all major cities and many not so major cities, the lawyer can establish an "office" that has a professional address, a dedicated phone line, a receptionist to answer the phone with the firm name, mail and parcel receipt and handling, access to a conference room, and a private office on demand—all the kinds of places the lawyer needs. Though the lawyer need never actually work there, it provides a virtual contact office which presents a positive image and a location. In this way, for example, a solo practitioner working in Indiana can create a high-profile address in Washington, D.C. to attract cases related to federal agency or federal law.

> The practice at the location may be limited to areas of federal agency work, for example, or only in federal courts if not licensed in that jurisdiction. Showing an address in a state without a license to practice there would require a disclaimer on any literature identifying the address.

Another version of a virtual office consists of an office on the web. Increasingly, attorneys in practice areas such as business formation, consumer bankruptcy, and family law use their website to serve as the office to meet with prospective and actual clients. The web page allows the client to provide all of the information needed in the forms, often from home. Elsewhere, the lawyer reviews the forms, makes alterations as needed, actually talks with her client, and files the documents with the court.

At some point the attorney has to have an office or place where she works—where she will review the documents, approve them, and file them in court. She will still need to print documents or make copies, or scan them digitally.

Finally, she needs to meet the client. Filing a document in court without ever seeing the client face to face comes with high risk and is indefensibly foolish. While data posted in the cloud can tell a lot, actually seeing and talking with a person can tell a lot more. The client controls the conversation when answering fixed written questions and on the web without the attorney challenging the answers. In a face-to-face with the client, the attorney should be in control. After all, the attorney has to swear to the court that she represents that the filing is factually and legally in good faith.

The choice of an officeless or virtual office has to be made based on whether or not it improves the productivity and profit of the practice, not because it seems like a cool thing to do. It is a professional and business decision.

IN SUMMARY, THE LAWYER SHOULD CHOOSE A WORK LOCATION THAT IS APPROPRIATE TO THE TASK, THE NUMBER OF PEOPLE SHE WORKS WITH, AND THE AVAILABILITY OF TIME- OR BUDGET-REDUCING ALTERNATIVES.

The options for an office differ from those that exist outside the State of Paperlessness. The lawyer can now put convenience for work, family, client, or the courts above the requirement to fix her current place, which provides convenience to none of them.

Because there are more alternatives does not mean that the lawyer should abandon where she is today. While it may not have the location value it did before, its utility remains. With the new landscape in the State of Paperlessness, she may no longer need as much space for paper or the cabinets to hold it.

While accessibility provides unlimited choices, it does not follow that everywhere is appropriate. While seminars, or maybe even this book, tend to glorify the ease of practicing law anywhere, "anywhere" is a very broad term, and judgment still must be used in deciding where the lawyer wants to practice.

For more information on the office: J.R. Phelps and R. Jon Robins, "Flying Solo: A Survival Guide for the Solo and Small Firm Lawyer," Fourth Edition, Chapter 13 in *Leasing and Sub-leasing Office Space,*" Fourth Edition (ABA); Stephanie L. Kimbro, *Virtual Law Practice: How to Deliver Legal Services Online* (ABA).

Notes

1.   Maples v. Thomas, *cert. granted,* 131 S. Ct. 1718; 179 L. Ed. 2d 644; 2011 U.S. LEXIS 2314; 79 U.S.L.W. 3538 (2011).

2.   Alison Grant, *33-year-old Cleveland lawyer David Mills to argue case Monday before the U.S. Supreme Court,* THE PLAIN DEALER, Oct. 30, *available at* http://www.cleveland.com/business/index.ssf/2010/10/young_cleveland_lawyer_to_argu.html (last visited Oct. 10, 2011).

3.   Ortiz v. Jordan, 131 S. Ct. 884; 178 L. Ed. 2d 703; 2011 U.S. LEXIS 915; 78 Fed. R. Serv. 3d (Callaghan) 827; 22 Fla. L. Weekly Fed. S. 769 (2011).

CHAPTER 14

EQUIPPING AND FURNISHING THE LAWYER IN THE STATE OF PAPERLESSNESS

The lawyer needs equipment to convert digits into usable documents. While absolutely essential, the requirements are simple. All the power that practicing in the State of Paperlessness brings the lawyer comes with relatively simple physical needs. Ignoring wants, a standard-issue desktop computer with display and accessories, a work surface, and a chair fulfill the needs. In most cases, a single visit to an office supply store or even one website online can provide these necessities. The lawyer probably already has these necessities and merely needs to upgrade.

Equipping the paperless office does not include providing places to store or hold paper, pads, pencils, pens, files, or books. The lawyer will have no need for these things. Instead the paperless lawyer equips himself with the following:

- Telephone (at least one)
- Computer with lots of memory and storage
- Displays; one will do, but more can be better
- Wireless and ergonomic keyboard and mouse
- Backup device (another computer or stand-alone)
- Access to copier/printer/scanner/fax
- Battery backup and surge protection
- Video camera
- Speakers and microphone

The Computer

The computer stands as the central piece of a digital or paperless office. It provides the lawyer with access to the files and programs he will use. With prices today, obtaining the latest and most efficient computers should be a priority. There are no points awarded to those who struggle with less than ample equipment or like to brag how they are still using decades-old technology and "it is as good as that stuff they make today." As to the last remark, they are wrong. Modern software development, including the upgrading of existing software, takes full advantage of the hardware power available and the multitude of routines, algorithms, and applications that have just emerged. The lawyer should take advantage of all of that.

The computer should include the following:

Maximum memory for processing
The computer should have at least 4 to 8 gigabytes or more of RAM. The newest off-the-shelf programs routinely require a gigabyte each. The computer uses RAM (random-access memory) for quick, short-term storage of running programs and files. The amount of RAM limits the number of programs that can be open at the same time, the size of the files being processed, and the speed at which programs are processed. Downloads from the Internet and streaming video or high-resolution photographs require a lot of memory. Programs include not just the apparent ones, such as Word, but all of the background programs, such as antivirus and security programs, networking, etc. Memory is relatively cheap, and more is better.

Digital storage—lots of storage
The lawyer should have access to digital storage in the hundreds of gigabytes or terabytes. Files require many, many digits, and that means tremendous amounts of data storage. While the requirements are huge, the price of storage is cheap. The lawyer should get all he can because he will need it. If the files are to be stored on a network drive or in the cloud, the actual storage on the unit used by the lawyer will be less. Whether at the desktop or readily available, obtain access to as much as possible. An average page takes up about 100kb depending on whether it is a Word document, a scanned document, a photograph, or PowerPoint.

Multiple displays with high-speed graphics cards to support them
When drafting a brief, open case books, transcripts, sheets of notes, and previously edited drafts commonly sit next to the workspace. Multiple screens bring this paper function to the digital world.

Operating in the state of paperlessness with one screen is certainly possible. The lawyer can toggle between multiple pages. But real productivity with concentration and efficiency comes when all of the pages needed are visible simultaneously with the writing space.

In a two-screen setup when writing, the word-processing program appears on one screen and the source material on the other. This source screen can include pages with statutes, cases, regulations, notes, transcripts, etc. Multiple sources are toggled as needed.

> Two screens still limit what can be seen. For example, in a typical brief writing, I will want access to the CaseSoft database, legal research, the trial record, and other materials. In some cases, smaller windows can be used so that multiple windows are opened at the same time.

> As I completed this book, a five-screen setup was installed in my office. It gave me more source screens when writing and the ability to check security cameras as needed, or monitor web or e-mail. The key is a larger screen setup to provide WYSIWYG ("what you see is what you get").

Wireless keyboard
Ergonomic design of the keyboard is also essential. The keyboard, also wireless, should have space at the front to rest the heel of your hands when typing. This will reduce stretching of the fingers and yield greater stamina as well as hand health.

Wireless ergonomic mouse
Using the traditional-shaped mouse tethered to the keyboard will add work to doing simple jobs. Concentrated pressure on the right hand and index finger moving and clicking the mouse in an unnatural hand form can cause problems over time, particularly carpal tunnel syndrome. Acquire a mouse that is ergonomically designed. This will allow the outside edge of the hand on the desk surface while thumb

and index finger are in a more natural position. With the ergonomically designed mouse, the need for a wrist rest lessens.

Access to the Internet, wirelessly and through LAN
This connection to the Internet not only provides the ability to communicate through e-mail or to surf the web. In the State of Paperlessness, it is also access to the vast library of resources in the law and otherwise. For programs that use the cloud, it is essential. Obtaining the highest data transfer rate possible is the goal here.

Multiple ports for USB on the face of the computer
Many gadgets, from the printer to the PAD to the camera to the scanner to everything, connect to the computer through the universal system bus (USB) ports. More USB ports on the front of the computer (no crawling on the floor trying to find the openings by touch) make life easier for the lawyer. The permanent connections, such as printers, scanners, and other devices, can use the rear USB ports.

> One handy way to do this is to have a multiple-USB port that sits on the desk or near the keyboard. Thumb drive, camera, phone, and other devices easily connect. Bluetooth and other wireless technologies reduce the need for USB ports.

Slots for flash card memory
A number of electronic tools, e.g., cameras, video and audio recorders, cell phones, and others, use flash cards for memory. Rather than hooking up the USB cord from the unit to the computer, the flash card can be used to transfer the data.

Use front ports for headset and microphone connections.
Cables are never long enough for the headset and microphone input jacks. Locating them on the front is a help. The use of Bluetooth technology or other wireless options should also be considered.

High-quality microphone either stand-alone or part of headset
The ability to enter voice comes in many forms—dictation, telephone through VOIP (Voice Over Internet Protocol) or teleconferencing, voice command through voice-recognition systems. The choices in-

cluded microphones integrated into the system (generally in laptops and tablets, and certainly saves packing extra gear), stand-up microphones at the desk, or microphones in connection with headsets. The latter, particularly using wireless technology, provide a lot of freedom of movement as the lawyer speaks.

Sound card with speakers (woofer optional)

Sound plays an important role in the State of Paperlessness, not all entertainment or games. Replay of testimony and video, VOIP and teleconferencing, and voicemail are some obvious business uses. Increasingly, website material is in the form of speech, as are narrated presentations. The PDF programs offer reading of documents. Since some speech is not recorded professionally, higher-quality speakers and a woofer will help in the listening.

Battery backup with surge protection for all cabling, including phone, LAN, and electric

Discussion of protection from surges of electricity and continuity of power are discussed elsewhere as part of security. These are musts for a computer setup today. Surge protection should exist between every electronic device and the source of any wire connection. This includes not only electrical outlets but telephone and cable connections as well. Power strips provide some protection, as do battery backups. The latter often have ports for devices not being supported by the power backup but do provide surge protection. One option is a "whole house" surge protector that is located at the cable entrance to the office just past the meter. Similar provisions can be made for phone and cable.

There are three measurements commonly associated with a surge protector: clamping voltage, joules, and time. The first represents the spike at which level the surge protector will work by either absorbing the spike or directing it to the ground. The standard for 120V outlets, typical of virtually all computer equipment used by a lawyer, is a clamping voltage of 300V. Devices with a higher rating can handle higher surges.

Joules is another standard. It represents the amount of energy (in amperes) actually passing through the system for one second. The lower the number, the better. Often the clamping voltage of the unit and diversion to the ground sufficiently limit the amount of energy to be handled by the force level. Better units handle 1000 joules.

Many surge protectors will claim speed of response in nanoseconds. Due to the wave characteristics of a surge, the clamping rate or joules rate should be reached early in the wave to ensure that the mechanism triggers as far in advance of the peak as possible. The faster the response, the better.

Redundant equipment

One computer setup is not enough for the lawyer. The complete system should include redundancy so that if a unit goes down, the lawyer has an alternative readily available to perform the functions she is working on. This means it has the programs and access to the information.

Backup storage other than on the computer

Depending on whether or not the lawyer uses the cloud for backup, and even if he does, having another disk drive, either as a stand-alone storage device or as part of another full computer to provide both functional and data redundancy, is important. Of course, it means frequent, automatic, and routine copying to that backup as well as regular attempts to use the programs and data to ensure compatibility

Access (direct or network) to the database holding the information

The power of the paperless office derives from its connection to the rest of the world. The fastest transfer rate with the greatest bandwidth is the goal for this selection. While this seems obvious, there are areas where there is limited or no connection to the Internet. This should be discovered before settling on the location. As a general rule, cable provides more than telephone connection. Wi-Fi provides portability, but wire connection through cable or fiber provide greater speed and bandwidth.

Connection (direct or network) to scanner, printer, and copier (individually or together)

One of the most interesting role reversals in technology is how the copier/printer changed from being the office's primary output device for an office into the primary input device as a scanner. As a consequence, if the choice for one of the scanners is such a three-in-one, the choice should be the one with the strongest scanning power and functionality. The scanner should automatically feed lots of documents, scan both sides, capture color, and produce clean images.

The key requirements of a scanner are speed and quality. Speed comes from both the speed in processing the image and the ability to quickly handle multiple sheets. An automatic sheet feeder is absolutely essential. Image quality should be at least 1200 by 1200 dpi (dots per inch). This is not needed all the time, but when it is, it is available.

Scanners must be integrated into the network. If the scanner cannot be connected directly, storing the information on a thumb or flash drive that can then be put in the computer is a viable alternative.

> Even those documents that retain value on paper should be scanned to be referenced, noted, and maintained as a digital file. The very few times that the original is critical, primarily in some court or public record filing, should not limit the lawyer from otherwise benefitting from a paperless office.

There are stand-alone desktop versions of the scanner. In some cases, because the technology focuses on scanning, higher-end units provide higher speeds and greater functionality.

One of the great advantages of paperless data is that the lawyer is no longer bound by the size of paper, whether a calling card or a huge blueprint of extremely high quality. A small cousin of this desktop scanner is the card scanner for calling cards. These cards can be scanned and then synchronized to the Outlook file.

> In the paper days, I would commonly photocopy a business card so that it would be easily found in the folder of letter-size paper. I asked a new person on my staff to copy some business cards and a small printed booklet that was a union contract at issue in a case I was involved with. She did exactly what I asked. I received a stack of business cards the same size as the originals and a fully duplicated book, including the color of the cover.

> Depending on the kind of material used in the practice, a high-quality scanner for prints and negatives may also be helpful. Such a scanner will create extremely high-quality color scans of as much as 4800 by 9600 dpi. When dealing with large documents, such as construction drawings, the scanning can be done off-site or even generated as a digital file by the producer.

To the extent the scanner is not integrated with printing capability, the lawyer still needs a printer. Here the focus should be more on quality than other characteristics because it will generally be a finished product.

POWER

Digits exist only if electrically charged. No electricity, no electrical state, no digits, and no information. An alternative or backup provision is necessary in order to continue to function in the case of a power failure. There are three options to be able to maintain power to the extent necessary to retrieve the information.

Battery backup

Generally speaking, backup power provides only enough power for computers to complete pending tasks and shut down in a controlled manner. The controlled shutdown ensures that files are saved and not corrupted or damaged.

> A fully charged laptop computer can provide a backup source of computer power when the office power is down.

Backup generator

To keep the office going, this is an investment that deserves attention. It is rarely used, but when needed it more than makes up for the initial cost. As with all equipment, it requires a continual maintenance regime and periodic testing to make sure that when the unexpected loss of power comes, the generator is there to work.

Alternative location

A third option is another site to work from—a site that has electric power and all the computing power you need.

> This highlights again the necessity of having files stored offsite but remotely accessible through the Internet. It also shows the importance of that offsite location being outside of the same disruption-risk zone as the office.

TELEPHONE

The importance of the telephone grows in the State of Paperlessness. It is, after all, the second paperless communication device used today (voice being the first). Phone technology provides better management of the phone calls and the practice. Today the use of a phone menu is more widely accepted and reduces the costs of staff to handle incoming calls. This also allows even a small or solo practice to create the sense of a larger enterprise and organize the calls. A separate extension can handle general information, such as web address, physical address, and hours; another extension can handle payables (this reduces the interruptions from vendors during critical think time); a general extension can be for you; and a special extension should be for "must talk to now" clients.

In practices that deal with clients who call initially on an emergency basis (divorce, bankruptcy, criminal law, for example), having a real person answer the call rather than a programmed menu can provide some needed reassurance. If the firm cannot justify the cost of a full-time receptionist, answering services are also an option.

> If using an outside service, routinely call yourself to see how well it is working.

Other options coupled with the phone service provide multiple phone numbers (including toll-free numbers, or area codes and exchanges identified with other regions), toll-free numbers, voicemail, call forwarding, conferencing, and other tools.

The telephone brings additional paperless tools to the office.

Today the telephone provides a number of functions, which eliminates the need for paper. From no longer needing the lowly phone-message slip to the pad tracking time on matters to the Rolodex with contact, the telephone no longer needs paper. The power comes from how it is integrated into the office. Some of the additional characteristics of a telephone include the ability to handle the following tasks:

- Initiate calls from within contact lists to provide real-time note taking.
- E-mail voicemail messages.
- Manage phone messages as other documents are managed.

- Use the detail stored on the phone to provide date, time, and length of phone calls for billing.
- Record the phone call.
- Convert the phone call to text and save the text.

The incredibly cheap cost of telephony today makes the practice by some law firms of charging clients for the cost of a phone call unacceptable. The practice began when long distance (which was about every phone outside of the exchange) had significant cost. When I first started practice, calls to the county courthouse were long distance and not cheap, sometimes running several dollars for a relatively short call. With a typical billing rate from $15 per hour for criminal legal defense to $75 for higher-valued matters, phone bills for longer calls could exceed the legal fees earned while on the phone. Today those numbers have dramatically reversed. With lawyers' billing rates multiples over multiples of the earlier rates and long distance nearly free, a one-hour phone call could cost a tiny fraction of the hourly rate or nothing.

Why some law firms continue to insult clients by charging appropriate hourly rates in specialties at $500 to $1,200 per hour and add a $3.25 phone charge is beyond me. The cost of the call should be part of the overhead, just like the electricity to light and power the office.

Portable digital assistants, cell phones, and the lawyer on the move

The simple phone, land line or cell, has been replaced predominantly by smart phones or portable digital assistants, PDAs, which provide the lawyer so much function that, coupled with digits replacing paper, he can work almost anywhere most of the time. Neither the phone line nor paper tie him to an office.

On-the-go, at-hand benefits of a PDA include:

- Communications through phone, text, and e-mail.
- Directory of contacts that can be instantly accessed to call or provide identification of incoming calls.
- A dynamic calendar capable of audible reminders.
- Access to information through the web.
- Tools to provide navigation and location.
- Synchronization of calendar, to-do lists, and calendar with other systems.

Other benefits, depending on the need, can become primary tools for the attorney, such as:

- Digital camera to record images
- Video camera capability to film an event
- Voice recorders to record interviews or take dictation.
- Countless other applications now available.

While the PDA is an extension of the computer, programs that are theoretically available on a PDA include the ability to view and modify documents.

> For many of the tablets and PDAs, there are programs that will open and, in some cases, allow editing of common word-processing and spreadsheet documents. Small screen and keyboard limit the utility of these functions to only-when-absolutely-nothing-else-will-do situations.

> This at-your-fingertips power has limits. Recent research as well as personal experience has shown that using a cell phone, even if it is "hands-free," impairs driving and should be avoided. While the State of Paperlessness gives the lawyer the tools to multitask, it does not forgive splitting attention between driving a one-ton vehicle moving at 70mph and negotiating an agreement on the cell phone. Virtually all states now prohibit, or should, texting or e-mailing, while driving and the use of the phone without a hands-free option. Even with the latter, use of the phone while driving should be limited.

Voicemail

Voice is the ultimate paperless form of communication. Today a person can call a single number and have an array of options to continue the call. The lawyer can, for example, set up separate mailboxes for different clients or cases and leave messages or receive calls just to that mailbox.

Whether to have a live, answered phone or use an answering machine is an individual choice. When I operated a general law office I believed that a live person needed to answer the phone. For new clients, possibly in an emergency, working through a phone menu was not the right choice. Today my practice is limited to a very small number of clients who have direct access. For the few calls that come in each week otherwise, I use a phone answering machine and a menu. My message suggests e-mail communication for the fastest response.

When setting up office voicemail, clearly identify who you are and invite information. You do not have to tell listeners they have your voicemail or you are away; it is obvious. In the case of cell phones and private numbers, whether you want to give your name or other identification is up to you.

When leaving voice-mail, slowly give your number, twice. It is so easy to run through it quickly.

I once received a voice message on my cell phone from a doctor's office intending to inform someone that the time of a heart operation had been changed. The call-back number was blocked, and the person making the call so rapidly spoke that the voicemail was unintelligible. There was no identification, and the assumption was that the person receiving knew the context and could fill in the blanks.

Voicemail can be quickly sent to e-mail and text or saved as a document in the practice management program. Also, because the calls with their return numbers and IDs are listed, the lawyer can assert her own priorities to return calls and listen to messages rather than be locked in to the first-in, first-out method dictated by traditional voicemail. Between the forwarding of voicemail and actual forwarding of calls, the lawyer can be anywhere. With remote access to the database, the lawyer can answer and respond as if she were at her desk in her office even when that is far from the truth.

Voicemail software will allow notifications of voicemail being sent by e-mail or text message to one or more places. When the lawyer is out of the office, using the PDA or tablet, he can see who made the call and listen to the message. This ensures that the lawyer is immediately notified, and it also puts him in control of what messages to hear and when.

The lawyer is still obligated to maintain confidences when using the phone.

The obligation to maintain confidential information does not end with using the smart phone or any phone. One characteristic of the cell phone, particularly in public places, is that certain people tend to "cell yell"—they talk louder and louder, which certainly helps those of us listening in the lobby hear what is being said.

I travel a lot, maybe too much. That travel brings me to waiting areas, restaurants, and the planes themselves. I have heard the short end of many conversations. Some are nonsensical, many are trying to impress the listener that the caller is on an important trip to a great destination, but others reveal a lot of information. Luckily for those speakers, I do not know who they are speaking to or about, but that has not always been the case. I have heard conversations about my clients, political officeholders with whom I had a special relationship. I could go on.

IN THE STATE OF PAPERLESSNESS, FURNITURE IS AS SIMPLE OR ORNATE AS THE LAWYER WANTS OR CAN AFFORD.

Furniture primarily provides a place for things to sit—a table for the computer, a chair for the lawyer. The rest is extra.

The workspace or desk.

The most permanent item the lawyer will purchase for the office is the desk. Over its normal life, on a per-month-of-use basis, it will likely be the least expensive as well. It is the workspace—one that need not have space for paper, but somewhere to hold the displays and keyboard. Its requirements are simple:

- A height, or adjustable to varying heights, to comfortably work;
- A solid surface for the keyboard;
- Sufficient space to hold the screens, keyboard, and mouse;

- Sufficient side and overhead clearance to allow for multiple screens;
- Space for accessories;
- Space and means to gather and manage cables;
- Place for battery backup;
- Ample outlets with easy access to the computer and equipment below and at desk-level;
- Lockable drawer or cabinet to place a briefcase, backpack, or purse; and
- Places to put equipment, cables, or other items not always used.

In the State of Paperlessness, there is little to no need to equip the desk for storage or shelves for books, papers, notebooks, scratch pads, and accessories. Without paper, the amount of space required is surprisingly small. Even places for files, such as drawers and cabinets, are unnecessary. The biggest determiner of space beyond the computer is for any scanner/copier or printer, or other accessories. The key is to make them handy.

Standard desks stand at 29 inches more or less. This is supposed to be the efficient height for the average person. "Average" does not describe every lawyer. Height should be set what works best for the individual. Some desks can be adjusted for height, but those adjustments are generally fairly permanent when made. Other desks need modification by either adding blocks to the legs or trimming them off. For those who need a shorter height and modifying the desk is out of the question, building a platform for the chair can be a solution

Having the workspace at standing height, like the old standing tables, can provide an alternative, and comfortable, way to work, particularly for those who have issues with back pain and discomfort. Rather than fixed-height desks, some manufacturers provide desks that can be moved up or down at the touch of a button. This provides the flexibility during the workday to alternate between the sitting and standing. For those who do trial or appellate work, working at a standing height trains the mind to think while standing.

The table space need not be great, as there is no need to hold paper or books. Unless the lawyer has items of interest or photographs for the space, it is better not to take up floor space for unneeded tabletop space. Also, without paper, the need for filing cabinets and other such storage disappears, and with that the surface of those items. Empty surfaces will attract clutter.

> **The lawyer shall reduce surface workspace to eliminate the attraction of unneeded paper and clutter.**

In my office today I have a desk from a bygone era. The surface area is almost 40 square feet in a U-shape. When it was a "papered" worksite, all of that was covered and under stacks of folders, notebooks, and papers. I now use less than one half of that. Even the need for a conference table on which others may place documents is greatly limited. Two drawers full of legal pads and scratch pads are virtually untouched from their last filling almost four years ago. I also located a printer at my desk to print on rather than waste time going to the master printer. It lies silently now.

My first computer table was a 2-ft. x 8-ft. piece of plywood with two-drawer file cabinets at each end. Although the space looks better today, nothing has matched that surface for functionality. There was ample space for my computer and the papers and books I used then. I could move around without risk of hitting knees or shins.

Without paper piles, the piece of furniture will be readily seen all the time. There is nothing wrong with acquiring a desk based on beauty or color, because it will now be seen!

The chair holds the most important part of any office—the lawyer.

The chair holds and supports the lawyer's body for hours on end. This job goes beyond keeping his you-know-what from hitting the floor. Properly positioned, it provides support for the back, takes pressure off of the legs, and provides comfort to increase concentration on the task. As the day goes forward and the concentration and stress grows, the discomfort created by improper seating can add to the tension, interfere with performance by requiring more get-up-and-stretch moments, and actually cause muscle and bone problems.

Difficulties there can affect health otherwise. Do not go cheap! A good chair will last for years and on a per-day basis will be the best investment. A sturdy, ergonomic, adjustable chair will last. The upfront cost can be higher, but over time it will be the cheapest chair you buy, not including the savings from a healthier life. Not all ergonomic chairs are the same. While you can see the initial comfort, color, and controls of the chair in the store, what you cannot see is the durability of the seats. Over time the knobs and levers wear out. Repeated sitting and rising, day after day, fatigues the structure. Generally the quality and durability correlate with the price.

- *Height.* The seat should allow feet to be comfortably placed flat on the floor while you are sitting. Lawyers who are particularly short or tall will need to test the chair to make sure that it provides the necessary range.
- *Material.* This is a seat to sit in comfortably, not a throne to show off. Vinyl and leather can be the wrong choices here. Because of the long periods of sitting, the seat material should breathe. Mesh or fabric is preferable. Properly curved mesh seats can be as comfortable as those with cushions. Those that are cushioned should be made of cloth fabric to allow breathing. Stain resistance is an added plus.
- *Seat size.* This is a question of comfort. From side to side there should be some space; the seat arms should not squeeze. The correct depth of the chair allows your back to reach the back of the chair while leaving several inches between the back of your knees and the seat front edge. Some of this is adjustable; the seat can be moved back or the chair back moved forward to shorten the distance.

> If you find a chair you like but it is the wrong size and not adjustable to the right size, ask the salesperson or e-mail the company to see if adjustments can be made at the factory to make it usable. Some can, and some may even do so at little to no extra cost.

- *Lumbar cushion.* The lower spine naturally curves in. The extended and tense sitting position straightens this curve, putting additional stress on the rest of the back. The chair should have a lumbar support that can be both raised to the right position and adjusted in terms of depth for your body.
- *Swivel.* The chair seat should easily swivel so you can reach for something on either side without having to use your legs to move or twist your body.

> At the same time, do not choose one that spins like a prop in a dance routine. I once had one that spun so easily I was putting a lot of tension on my legs and feet to hold still, defeating the purpose of the chair.

- *Armrests.* The armrests should be adjustable up and down as well as out of the way. The proper height and position of the armrests is when your elbows and lower arms rest easily while leaving your forearm free to type or move the mouse.

Other chair types include the exercise ball, saddle, and kneeling chairs. These are designed to address the specific needs of specific users. For example, a history of back or spine problems suggests looking into these types of chairs.

OTHER FURNISHINGS

Although the world has gone paperless, it is not "humanless," and creation of an environment for the person to be productive should not be forgotten. The chair and desk take care of the necessities; the lawyer does not have to stop there.

Decorate the office to be pleasant.

In the digital world there is no paper clutter, so the carpet, furnishings, and walls are more visible. Making them attractive, comforting, and refreshing are essential to maintaining productivity. There is no need to choose wall paint and fabrics that blend with the reddish-brown and vanilla of file folders or yellow of the legal pad.

Lighting is important.

Most of the work that you will do will be emitted by the display. Therefore, the need to light the desk to look at books or other material is less important. On the other hand, warm lighting, such as from lamps or indirect overhead lighting, enhances the level of comfort to the room. An overhead spotlight focused on the keyboard without shadows can provide important light where needed.

Sometimes, the light needs to be whiter. Seasonally affective depression disorder, or SADD, occurs during the days of the year when the sun is low in the sky and visible for shorter periods—when it is not hidden by clouds. Routinely cloudy weather in certain areas can contribute. Having some rooms that use the whiter light during those periods can help adjust for this.

Have a comfortable chair, couch, or loveseat away from the desk.

A workspace demands comfort for the working lawyer. Another comfortable couch, loveseat, or rocking chair provides an alternative location to work. Sometimes, as part of relaxation, going "remote" in the rocking chair next to your desk rather than under the full glare of the digital workspace provides the change of pace or posture needed to recharge or reconsider difficult issues. And with the speed of work, maybe even catch a deserved catnap.

FURNISHING THE MEETING PLACE

Designing a place to meet with clients and others deserves special attention. This is commonly the interview room or conference room. Where possible, it should not be the lawyer's workspace. Because the lawyer can be anywhere, being in his actual office is not necessary to meet with clients. In some situations, however, it may be all that is available. Thanks to a paperless office, the risk of disclosure of confidential material is reduced. At the same time, an attorney-client meeting space can be designed and decorated to further that purpose.

The meeting place should have comfortable chairs and a work surface. It should be equipped with good lighting, temperature control with frequent change of air, and nicely but not overly decorated to distract from the purpose of the room.

In the papered days, there was a need for a place for pads and writing; this is not necessary with a paperless office. The room could be outfitted with only comfortable chairs. The issue is how to be able to share information ordinarily done by paper means. The options for presenting paperlessly come in several ways:

- *Laptop with a mirrored display.* The laptop display with the client sitting next to the lawyer, or the tablet turned to the client as a pad or document would be, can work. An alternative is to have a second display presented to the client that mirrors what is on the lawyer's display (laptop or desktop).
- *Projector or large screen.* A large-screen display that can connect to a laptop or other computer will provide visual access to everyone. The large-screen TVs are less expensive than the projectors and less noisy. The projector can provide a larger display, which,

depending on the room, makes it a better choice than the TV. The projector, if used, may be mounted above the table or suspended from the ceiling with wiring or wireless connection, which also makes it less intrusive, less noisy, and less prone to shadows from those crossing in front.

- *Smartboard.* Within the same budget as a wide-screen TV monitor and a projector are the smartboards. These are a combination of a projector, a touch-screen monitor, and an easel pad. Not only do these function as a display, but they also provide the ability to call up programs through the touch screen or to write and capture the writing.
- *Speakerphone.* A speakerphone can include others in the call who are not present In addition, a dedicated and specifically designed speakerphone provides greater clarity than the use of someone's cell phone. One of the advantages of a fixed meeting place is to have the specific equipment needed.
- *Videoconferencing.* With a projector, widescreen monitor, or smartboard, all you need is a camera to participate in videoconferencing.
- *The table.* Besides being a good work surface, the modern table should also include outlets and network, telephone, and other connections available to all users.
- Different conferencing opportunities require different setups. Besides the typical conference room setup, smaller, deposition-sized rooms and tables are better suited for small groups of six or less. In some cases an auditorium-type setup may be justified.

In the office I had built, I designed a "public section" completely separate from the work area of the office, complete with its own restroom facilities. There was a waiting area and three conference rooms. The first included comfortable upholstered chairs and a couch, but no table. This was a room that could serve as overflow for waiting or a relaxed and comfortable place to talk. The second was the deposition-sized room that comfortably handled six people around a curved table. The third was the formal conference room with projector, cable connections, and larger occupancy.

CHAPTER 15

LAWYER HERE, LAWYER THERE: EQUIPPING THE ROAMING LAWYER

The State of Paperlessness permits the lawyer to practice anywhere she wants. Mobility comes from a desire or need to be somewhere else other than in the office. Regardless of the reason, powerful and light tools let the lawyer do just that. The key to such mobility is mobile computing power, which comes with a cell phone and a laptop or tablets.

THE LAPTOP

Properly outfitted, the laptop brings almost the entire office along wherever the lawyer may go. When the opportunity to work arises, the laptop is there—so powerful it can be considered a redundant computer necessary for a continuous practice. Some lawyers go so far as to make the laptop into the desktop computer by "docking it" into the network at the desk site.

> While this is an option, the danger of a laptop-only computer setup is that its mobility can work against the need to maintain timely and sufficient backups as well as provide security.

With so many models and sizes, choosing the right laptop can be a challenge. There are, of course, minimum requirements of power and disk storage, which are similar to those for the desktop. For disk storage, the demands of confidentiality, backup, and security demand that the documents be stored in the cloud, on a server remotely accessible, or a secured thumb drive. The remaining choices are: size, mouse, keyboard style, weight, and battery life.

- *Screen size.* You should seek to have as big a screen as possible, limited only by where it will be used and how often the laptop is moved. Weight and display size correlate. The bigger the unit, the heavier it will be. The biggest constraint is air travel. The space allowed on most aircraft, even in first class, makes a laptop difficult to open up. A smaller-height screen provides more opportunity to use on the plane. Screens that are wide but low in height can provide a larger display and sometimes (not always) fit on the plane.

- *Mouse style.* There are two methods used for the mouse. One is a ball in the center of the keyboard. Moving the ball like a joystick moves the mouse. The other is a mouse touch pad. Fingers moving across the pad simulate movement of the mouse. These are a matter of personal choice. The touch pad requires a bigger keypad. The use of a separate, traditional mouse connected wirelessly or through a USB port is also an alternative.

- *Weight.* The longer the lug, the harder the tug on the shoulder strap. The rule is simple: Every ounce counts. Just lifting it in the store does not tell the whole story. It will be the single heaviest item in the brief or computer case.

> To get an idea of how much weight adds up, look up the weight spec in the manufacturer's literature. Don't forget the power cord. Find books, cans, etc., that approximate the weight of the laptop you are considering. Put them in your briefcase and carry it the distances you normally would carry the laptop.

- *Keyboard.* Here is where the laptop can be limiting. The keys can be too small for large fingers and the layout much more abbreviated than the keyboard on the desktop computer. Long, narrow laptops (with low screen height) sometimes provide a better keyboard. As the keyboard grows to equal that on the desktop computer, the weight also goes up. If mobility is limited between several places within the office (workspace and conference room, for example) or occasionally moved, then these restraints are minimized. Alternatively, depending on workspace, you can add an external keyboard through a USB port in the laptop.

- *Battery life.* The longer the better. If extended periods of battery use are required, a replaceable battery adds a little to the weight, but the option to have additional batteries while traveling, especially on long flights, can be a lifesaver.

In the early days, when battery life was about an hour and charging time was a multiple of that, I acquired an external battery pack to extend the life of the batteries by about six times. It worked but came with great weight, and by the time I got situated on the plane I had a long cable plugged into the battery extender and headphones. I also carried two spare batteries. By the time I hooked up all the wires and added my headphones, I wondered if I even needed a seat belt. Technology has reduced weight in ways other than paper.

PORTABLE DATA STORAGE

Besides unlimited functionality and a full keyboard, the laptop provides easy movement of files from the unit to other devices. For the laptop on the go, storage should be in a secure thumb drive, in the cloud, or in a remotely accessible server. The thumb drives should be labeled and inventoried. Periodically make sure all thumb drives are accounted for and synchronized with the root storage.

As I was writing this section, I took time to gather up all of my thumb drives. Over the few years that they have been available, I have accumulated quite a few. Two things about the inventory shocked me. The first was how many thumb drives I had forgotten about, and the second was the amount of material still on those old thumb drives. This was less an issue of having the files properly stored (I was confident of that) but more that if someone had taken the drives I would not have known, and they would have had access to way too much information.

TABLETS

Touch-screen tablet computers bridge the PDA and the laptop. Tablets provide less weight and ease of use compared to the laptop, while providing greater usability in terms of readable and usable e-mail and attachments, document creation, and modification—much of the functionality of the laptops. Though technically a tablet can do everything a laptop can, it does so in a limited way. The full functions of Word, such as outlines, styles, and footnotes, for example, are not as functional on the tablets, even with application software.

Tablets take advantage of the 80/20 rule: They provide 80 percent of what the lawyer needs but with a whole lot less weight, clutter, and complexity. When the remaining 20 percent is not needed or can be deferred, they cannot be beat.

> When first announced, I thought the iPad a useless toy. Then I saw one and bought one. I never travel without it. The reason is simple: The primary purpose of having a laptop is to communicate on the road. With Apple's nearly zero boot time, I can get my e-mails and read them with the attachments .
>
> As this book was written, other manufacturers' tablets have been introduced. As time goes, the functionality of laptops will be fully found on tablets.

The tablet is not for everyone or every task. The lack of a keyboard is both freeing (less equipment) and interfering with productivity. The keyboard, depending on the model of tablet and the options, is split three ways among characters, numbers, and symbols. This significantly slows any typing. The keyboard hides a large portion of the screen. At least a third of the screen is hidden by the keyboard. Sensitivity to touch interferes with fast typing, as merely moving over the keys can result in that character. Before long there is a lot of junk, and editing is very time-consuming.

The other big issue with some tablets is that they do not provide external memory hookups. This concern is being handled by wireless external memory and use of the cloud. The easiest way to get documents in and out of a tablet and even a laptop is to e-mail the document as an attachment.

> When I acquired the iPad, I wanted instantaneous synchronization between key information on the iPad and my office computer. MobileMe gives me this power. This service, available on the web, is an exchange service which keeps computers synchronized with dates and contacts, sharing of files, storage of files, and other services.

> Another important function of MobileMe is that it has a FindMe app that will find your computer. This will allow you to wipe the data off the computer if it has been stolen or lost.

COMPARING THE LAPTOP AND TABLET

The laptop and tablet each are the right tool for different times. The laptop comes with more computing power through available software and options than the tablet. With that, however, comes weight, much longer boot and shutdown time, and generally shorter battery life. The tablet is far easier to use, has an extremely short boot and shutdown time, and long battery life. It lacks in computing power and ability to move files readily from other sources.

> Do I use a tablet or do I stick with my laptop? Tablet? Laptop? Tablet? Laptop? It is a dilemma.
>
> For air travel and day-to-day portable use, the iPad is ideal for me. At those times I have one main purpose—stay in touch. While the PDA delivers e-mail, with the iPad I can easily read the e-mails and, more critically, the attachments. The iPad is easier to travel with. It is significantly lighter and easier to carry. After passing through security (which does not require display of the iPad) and arriving at the gate area, I can instantly turn on the iPad and quickly access the web wirelessly. Fee-based services like Bongo and T-Mobile generally provide service in airports. I use a Mi-Fi (a credit-card-sized device that accesses the web and makes its own hot spot) in the absence of those services. The Mi-Fi also works with the laptop. Because it is a single piece and not folded, I can carry it onto the plane and finish the work until the door closes. During flight it, unlike the laptop, is sized and designed so that it can be used on the plane.
>
> During the drafting of this book, I needed to use the laptop. The tablet document-editing software did not recognize all of the styles and cross-references that I used. It also had a nasty habit of changing the font. There was no time during writing to restyle a 300-page manuscript every time I moved from device to device. Then there was the unproductive keyboard. The split iPad keyboard was no problem for short e-mails, but drafting whole pages and moving from keyboard to keyboard for numbers and symbols was too disruptive.

> So I took the laptop on trips. If I got the exit seat, I could use the laptop and did. I sometimes upgraded to first class, though that did not always ensure enough space to use the computer. But I had it in my hotel room and got a lot of work done.
>
> I reserved time on the plane for tasks that did not require typing.
>
> So I use both, each depending on the task and the opportunity to work.

The biggest disadvantage with the various tablets is that each uses its own software. The iPad uses Apple's, others use Android, and still others use a form of Windows. Because the operating software differs from the tablet to the office computer, power found on the desktop or a laptop is often missing in the tablet. With laptops, the *lingua franca* is Windows, which means that programs and files easily migrate.

The market is responding with the ultrabook, which provides the power and keyboard of laptops and the weight and convenience of a tablet.

Securing the Mobile Office

The smallness of the PDA, laptop, or tablet belies how huge a security risk it is:

- Loss of the unit itself is not just the loss of a machine, but also the access that the laptop provides to the private and confidential part of the lawyer's practice and private life. For example, it could result in access to the office server or the backup files.
- Generated documents residing on it may not be accessible. Sometimes it is original documents not yet backed up. This can be especially poignant during those critical stages of brief writing or other similar projects.
- There is the risk of loss of confidentiality if third persons can actually access the data. This is akin to giving someone a key to the office and filing cabinets and copy machine.
- Because of where they are commonly used (on airplanes, in cafes, on the ferry), individuals can see, either visually or through electronic snooping, what the lawyer is doing.
- Using public Wi-Fi (not recommended), the computer is more susceptible to being hacked or information that you enter retrieved.

Securing the data

Portable data should only be stored in an encrypted form. Preferably it should be hardwired encryption. Rather than store files on the laptop, store information encrypted on a thumb drive. The beauty of this type of encryption is that if the wrong person gets the computer, the data will not be with it. If they get the thumb drive, they need the key. The thumb drive should be a secure-erase as well. That means that if a person has the thumb drive, it will, after a few failed guesses at the password, cause the unit to delete the files automatically.

Properly secured thumb drives use hardware-based AES-256 encryption. This is the standard for the military and provides high levels of security on portable data. Because it is hardware-based, encryption goes on all the time, and every file saved is automatically encrypted.

> If you lost your thumb drive, do you know what is on it? To manage what I put on a thumb drive, I create a file folder on my office desktop computer labeled by date. I copy files I want to take with me into that folder. Once done, the folder is copied to an encrypted thumb drive for out-of-office use. The encrypted thumb drive gives security that no one can get the information. The folder in the office file tells me, if I need to know, what was on it. It also helps me identify what was added or changed when I synchronize.

Cell phone passwords

Cell phone and ATM passwords pose a problem not shared with other passwords. Generally they are limited to four characters, and the only symbols are 1 through 10. This means there are only ten thousand combinations, but research shows that while this should mean there is a 1 in a 10,000 chance someone could guess the number, users tend to use the same common tricks to set phone numbers. A cell phone security firm found that 15 percent of one carrier's subscribers used one of just 14 numbers—"1234; 2580 or 0852 (the keys at the center of the keypad, in order or reverse order); 5683, which spells "love"; or four identical digits, such as 0000 or 5555."[1] Don't use those!

Security Tips

When using laptops, you should wrap them in multiple layers of security. This means physically securing the device as well as the data. A lot of it requires being sensitive to the circumstances, or being "streetwise."

- Protect the laptop physically from being stolen.
- Keep the device hidden. Cover it in the locked car or lock it in the trunk.
- Use less-obvious carrying cases when traveling.

> A photographer friend of mine eschewed the silver camera cases for his expensive equipment and instead carried it in a worn diaper bag. It provided heat and moisture protection and no one wanted to steal it!

- Do not leave the laptop or tablet alone in public places. A coffee shop may look safe, but leaving it on the table to get a refill or use the restroom comes with a huge risk.
- Set up the laptop to require a password at boot.
- Shorten the length of time of inactivity before a secured login is required.
- Use cable locks for those times you must leave it.
- Mark the device with unique ID tags, such as engraving name, phrase, or other information.
- Use tracking software that will find the laptop on boot-up and access to the wireless network.
- Set up the remote wipe or file deletion function. This will allow the user, upon locating the address of the lost unit, to remove sensitive files.

> MobileMe and LoJack are among the programs that provide these tools. Many suppliers of laptops or tablets have similar programs available.

- Do not use the option to save user names and passwords when using the web for programs. This is particularly the case for programs that provide remote access to other computers or connect to data storage in the cloud. Some secure thumb drives, such as Iron Key, allow access to the web from the drive protecting such information.
- Do not store confidential information on your computer, but rather on an external thumb drive that is password-protected or in the cloud.

- Encrypt saved documents when storing them.
- Routinely delete browsing history, e-mail, and files.

Dealing with theft of information

Even despite all of the precautions, upon the disappearance of the PDA, tablet, or laptop, the lawyer should take some steps immediately:

- *Call the police.* This provides both a record of the event and the possibility it may be recovered.
- *Notify your clients.* Here is where it is important to know whose client's information is on the computer and what it was. By knowing specifically what files are on the unit the easier and more complete the information of who to call.
- *Notify your malpractice insurer.* Loss of confidential data may result in an actionable claim.
- *Call your casualty insurer.* If the equipment was scheduled, there will be some reimbursement for the loss. Also some insurance policies provide for assistance in protecting the data.
- *Notify your credit card companies* and others that you do business with. Get new credit cards.
- *Change passwords on everything!*
- *Comply with state and federal laws regarding notification of clients.* The HIPAA Privacy Rule has specific requirements if the information lost includes health-care information such as the hospital records used in a personal injury lawsuit.[2]
- *Take steps so it will not happen again.*

There is less need for travel; everyone can share the same thing at the same time.

Making documents with narrower audiences through meetings is another form of publishing the documents created. Combining the digital documents with the technology of videoconferencing and webinars makes the paperless practice also placeless. Physically attending meetings costs a huge amount of time and money—throwing documents or laptop into the briefcase, getting to the meeting, waiting for others to attend, holding the actual meeting, and then reversing all of the above. While a meeting in a conference room at the end of the hall has extra demands, a meeting that requires real travel is something else.

Face-to-face meetings have their place, pardon the pun, but not all meetings all of the time. From simple conference calls to visual telephone conferences to webinars, there are many ways to provide the same experience without the physical travel and its overhead.

Travel or not, the paperless office provides the means to make the documents available without physically traveling or actually meeting the others in the group. Except for use of different programs, whether the meeting takes place in the lawyer's office or halfway around the world, the documents can be presented the same way.

In physical face-to-face, paper can be avoided by displaying the documents on a mirrored display in the conference room, projecting them onto a screen, using smartboards with projection, using display screens large enough for everyone to use, or making the digital files available to the other person on his or her computer equipment. These do not need to be PowerPoint presentations but can be any document capable of being displayed—spreadsheets, copies of documents, Word documents, magazine articles, and visual and audio media. Interactive display of MindMapping maps can only be done through the use of the computer.

As part of the software for web meetings, the program displays who is on and who is not in the meeting. It allows the coordinator to control who is muted, and also allows changing control of displays to other users.

The other purpose of a meeting is communication by things other than what is on the desktop or over the phone line. Call it body language or facial expression, there is a lot of information that is conveyed other than in pure speech. An online meeting will not make that available. Even the use of videoconferencing has its limits. For example, the camera may be focused on the speaker but miss the action at the other end of the table, where several people are having their "other meeting." Electronic meetings on the computer can permit others to have electronic submeetings over smart phones. The dynamic of the face-to-face is lost.

The other part of the meetings is the informal part—the private conversations during a coffee break, at lunch, or in the hall, where a lot of information can be gained. This represents to me the single biggest loss of information from virtual meetings.

Placing documents in the cloud reduces the need to have meetings at a specific time.

Tools available today allow the lawyer to participate paperlessly not only in a placeless environment, but also in a timeless environment. The collaborators, for example, in drafting an agreement do not have to be in the same place at the same time. Numerous collaborative programs make such asynchronous collaboration possible. This includes simply using the editing and commenting available in PDF or tracking changes in word processing. Programs such as Adobe Buzzword and Microsoft SharePoint take that a step further by allowing the lawyer to control who participates in what part of the project. Different people can have different assignments regarding different documents.

In terms of presentations themselves, if there is to be no give and take, PowerPoint and PDFs can be narrated. The recipients can listen to the presentation on their schedule.

For lawyers who want to provide an experience closer to an actual meeting, the presentation can be videotaped and made available by sending the tape through e-mail, posting on a blog or website, or uploading to YouTube for viewing.

TRAVELING IN THE STATE OF PAPERLESSNESS

When the lawyer must travel, the paperless state of the practice makes it easier.

> **When traveling, the lawyer shall travel prepared, travel light, and travel securely.**

Keep the tablet, PDA, and laptop synchronized for contacts and calendar.

Use the software now available that will sync the laptop, tablet, and PDA with the office calendars and contacts. If this is done automatically, there is no need to prepare in advance.

Have a fully prepared briefcase.

Merriam-Webster's defines "briefcase" as "a flat flexible case for carrying papers or books."[3] The idea of carrying paper is obsolete. Mine generally has next to none. But it does carry a laptop or tablet and gear in support. It provides a place to bring together those items and other assorted sundries needed for a trip. Some call it a computer case, laptop bag, laptop case, or other names. No matter, lawyers carry briefcases even if they no longer contain books and papers.

Keeping the briefcase fully loaded for a trip, to the courthouse or Brussels, is the first step for the traveling lawyer. When the time comes to travel, there may be little time to pack. And travel can come at any time. The case not only carries the laptop but other items that provide support in general and emergency to the lawyer and the equipment she uses.

Support for the phone includes a battery charger, spare charged batteries, and earpiece. Support for the laptop or tablet includes battery charger, thumb drive, and, if available and needed, a spare battery. Support for the lawyer includes extra medication (even a "day trip" can turn into an overnighter), toiletries in the 3-3-1 bag, grooming and personal care tools, a change of underwear, or even complete change if flying separate from luggage, reading material, nutrition bars to fill in when meals are missed, reserve cash and credit cards.

Over the years I have tried and worn out about every kind of briefcase starting with my first hard Samsonite with the latches, leather over the top briefcases, trial cases, wheeled computer cases, bags, and about everything else. What has finally worked best for me is what is called a "boarding bag." It is nearly cubicle in dimensions. The squat design makes it steady when set down, the top load makes access easy, and the flexible material allows me to squeeze it under the seat or overhead. The real advantage is that such a boarding bag has few pockets. Generally there is a small one in front and small ones on each end. The absence of compartments means I can design it to fit my needs and not have the weight of unnecessary compartments. Instead I have accumulated a number of small bags of various sizes and colors from previous bags I owned or specifically purchased. I organize all of phone accessories into one small bag, computer support in another, minimal office supplies in a third, emergency kit and medication in yet another. These free-float in the bag. Even the plastic Ziploc bag provides the ability to keep different cords, supplies, snacks, and other contents of the bag separate, protect them from dampness and spilling, and make them easier to recover.

The tendency is to overpack. An "if it fits, I will take it" mentality means lugging a lot of useless stuff. Generally the destination has the same stores that you have where you live, and you can buy what you need. I periodically empty my brief case and reload it, asking myself every time whether I have used an item on the road or would really need it.

Preparing for the average trip

For trips that will require the use of the computer, or during which there will be time and a need to work on other projects, a full-function laptop or a tablet that can provide all of the needed power is required.

When traveling, I ordinarily take the tablet. But when I started writing this book, I needed to use every moment during traveling to meet the deadline. As a result, I carried the smaller laptop (so I could use it on the small space on planes). I also packed a keyboard and mouse that connected by USB to the laptop, which did not require batteries or their weight. With those I could work much faster in my hotel room or other place where I had desk space.

The full system

For out-of-town trials or an extended stay, such as a conference, a more involved setup provides greater productivity. This setup includes supplementing the laptop with a large full screen or screens, wireless and ergonomic mouse and keyboard, and a surge-protector power cord. This provides all of the power from the office. The computing power comes with the laptop, which can be removed and taken to other meetings or hearings. Optionally, a portable scanner and small printer can complete the office. Properly packaged, it can be shipped as baggage. A better option is to ship it commercially to the site. It will be available upon arrival and not delayed due to TSA searches.

I generally rely on the hotel or office printer and copier for the output.

If it is extended stay and I need an office to work with others rather than use my hotel room, I will rent a separate conference room or suite for that purpose. This arrangement provides separation between the office and the living quarters. It also provides a place where I can interact with co-counsel, witnesses, or others without doing so in my bedroom. It is much more professional, provides a place for confidentiality as compared to the restaurant, and avoids the awkwardness associated with spending time with other attorneys, parties, or witnesses in your bedroom.

Written checklists of what to bring ensure it is all there when you need it.

Notes

1.   Carl Bialik, *Easy-to-Guess Passwords Open Door to Hackers*, WALL ST. J., July 23, 2011.

2.   Health Insurance Portability and Accountability Act (HIPAA) of 1996, 26 U.S.C.S. §§ 9801 *et seq.*, 45 C.F.R. Part 164.

3.   MERRIAM WEBSTER DICTIONARY, *available at* http://www.merriam-webster.com/dictionary/briefcase (July 24, 2011).

CHAPTER 16

ACQUIRING AND DEVELOPING THE SKILLS FOR PRACTICING LAW IN THE STATE OF PAPERLESSNESS

The State of Paperlessness does not just come to you. You have to get there by steps, leaps, slides, and detours. No "ACME Paperless Office System" resides on the computer, requiring only that you turn it on. Rather, you will reach the State of Paperlessness by combining your skill with traditional word processors and spreadsheets, PDF management, e-mail, calendaring, and contact management under the umbrella of a data management system. And you have to possess the desire to get there.

PROFILING, NOT POST-FILING, INFORMATION

In the State of Paperlessness, lawyers profile information and store it. In the papered world, documents are *post*-filed and stored. Electronic data profiled can be accessed by powerful search-and-retrieval systems from the first moment. Post-filed documents provide little benefit beyond archival access because documents are placed in stacks to be filed later, often after their useful life is over.

In the papered world, I had bins for items that needed to be filed. There was some presorting. Generally these documents lay in the bins until time or need demanded that someone individually place them in the proper file. The bins were seldom empty. In 1992 I closed an office. I placed all of the "to be filed" in a box and labeled it as such. Nearly 19 years later, as I finished removing the paper files from the office, we came across this unopened box. Nothing was missed. To be sure there was no value, I went through the box, and while the documents were valuable during the life of the case, filing them now provided no benefit.

Quality data properly profiled makes the paperless experience beneficial. The profiling of data comes at the beginning of handling a document or other source of information. Profiling consists of tagging the document with information regarding client, matter, date, author, and other information. Depending on the management program, much of it is automated. Profiling is not unlike the saving of a document in a word processor where the file folder, name of the document, and document format are chosen and the document is saved.

Documents are not the only thing that is profiled. Matters, clients, other persons, events, matter types, document types, and other information are also profiled. Profiling links all of the documents and all of the other information that is stored. It automatically links a document to other documents in the matter, documents for the client, documents by a certain author, documents used by the same attorney, documents made on the same date, or documents of the same type.

Profiling the documents and other information at the beginning empowers the practice management to instantly make all of that available when needed.

The lawyer shall promptly and properly profile every document, e-mail, matter, contact, and other information.

STEPS IN HANDLING PAPER IN THE PAPERLESS OFFICE

Paper still abounds in the practice of law. Even sweeping an office of paper does not stop the onslaught. It comes by mail or parcel delivery; by clients with documents concerning their cases; by attorneys returning from depositions, meetings or conferences; by courts that still rely (even still require) paper; from old matters that hold information for current issues; and in the office with notes small and large. And of course, there are documents that still have to be saved in the original paper, such as a will.

Converting the paper into digital brings it into the paperless office. It is a four-letter word—scan. But more than just scanning is needed. The whole picture includes scanning, storing, organizing, and retrieval of the documents. But paper documents enter the paperless office first through the scanner.

There are two types of scanning—"day forward" or "back file" conversion. Day-forward scanning takes documents in the course of business and either receives them in digital form (such as e-mail or attachment) and saves them as such or, as paper is received, the documents are immediately converted to digital form.

Back-file conversion occurs either in the process of upgrading paper documentation that already exists into the digital program or as a day-to-day process in which documents are first sorted between those worthy of being saved digitally and those that are not.

Regardless of whether the source is outside mail, internal generation, client delivery, or an older file, it is all handled the same. While the office as a whole can be declared paper-free (or nearly so), one space near the entrance should be designated for any paper that comes into the office—a place to hold, sort, scan, and dispose of the would-be fiber infiltration.

> Some things defy scanning. Physical objects can be powerful exhibits. In one trial, the burn marks on a grain silo door from hot slugs generated by a blowtorch sealed our claim that the silo fire was not spontaneous combustion but caused by smoldering hot slugs that entered an opening near this door. The expert standing in front of the jury holding the door and pointing to the slug burns did more than any photograph.

Sorting the paper begins with a "junk or save" decision. Junk finds the recycling bin. Saved are sorted between documents to be scanned and the rest. The latter includes magazines, greeting cards, etc.

> On larger documents, particularly those that originated as scans, use the "reduce size" option in the PDF software to reduce the size of the file. This will not only save space, but allow for easier e-mailing and faster processing when needed.

After scanning documents, another paper sort occurs. Documents that are to be preserved (original wills, certificates, and the like) are set aside for special handling. The rest are placed in a box. After the box is full, it is sealed and dated. After six months, if the box is not opened, it is sent to the shredder without further consideration. In some cases, documents will be shredded right after the scanning. The originals that are not shredded are either sent to a client or saved with original documents in a fireproof file cabinet.

Profiling can take place at the time of scanning. Either the scanner will allow profiling and storage as the documents or scanned or the documents are scanned to a file and, at a separate station with computer, profiled. A version of the latter includes the lawyers or staff involved with those documents doing the profiling, which ensures a more meaningful and useful profile for later retrieval.

When a hard copy is mailed (such as a cover letter and pleading for a filing in a non-electronic court), only the copies needed for mailing are made. One complete package is scanned and profiled for the records.

> Every document coming into the office goes through the steps above. We batch-scan. The reasons are threefold. First, it is easier to do it on the computer than on the copier. Second, the documents get scanned right away and are in the system. As soon as they are used, they are profiled. Third, the profiling is generally done in conjunction with other work on the matter and thus is more complete.
>
> Not all documents are profiled into the master practice management database. Those massive documents from discovery associated with a case are profiled through the case management program.

> No paper passes by the mail counter to the office unless it has been scanned. Few papers do so pass, and generally they are originals being saved as such. We do not scan, for example, the can of cookies our office supplier occasionally sends us.

Profiling the documents does require upfront time. But this is time well spent. If it is a document on a new matter, a new matter needs to be created and profiled. Depending on who the contacts and clients are, those may or may not need to be profiled.

> The more information profiled, the more useful the information can be because it will be more easily reached. Profiling can be minimal to complete initially. If at the time of profiling there are unknowns, profile what you know and update later.

MAKING THE TRANSITION

Once the lawyer understands what the end system looks like, creating the bridge from where she is to that goal is much easier.

1. Acquire the needed equipment and software.
2. Immerse yourself and staff in the handling of documents paperlessly through the tools provided with PDF—word processing, and spreadsheets—individually and in combination.

> This makes an ideal time to systematically go through all of the equipment and software and update it.

3. Make sure that security and backup systems are in place and operating.
4. Install the equipment and software.

> Having a consultant to provide assistance, and in some cases even do the acquisition and setup, will generally be worth the time and effort. There is so much to learn about the different functionality of various brands and types of equipment and software. Even though as an attorney you are used to learning things, the curve can take too long to get this job done.

5. Continue to operate the office as before. Until the "full go" is announced, the office should continue to handle everything as before with paper files, etc. It is very important that there be no break that will leave a crack into which a client may fall.

> There is no magic day to start. It is a process over a period of time, not a light switch. We started in the middle of the year to use the paperless system. The next year we continued to make paper file folders but stopped filling them. Then we relied entirely on the paperless system.

6. Train everyone on the use of document management program and the document-handling procedures. Provide dummy files that use a dummy drive to open matters, add and remove documents, add e-mails, etc.
7. Initially load the document management software with as much information as possible. The first place to begin is adding all of the contacts and the calendar items to the system. Also load matters currently being handled.

> Don't worry about old and finished matters. There will be little need to add them to the system. As time goes on, if an old matter is revisited, then add it to the system. Over time the database will contain all of the matters you will be handling.

> The question then becomes, what do you do with all of the old paper files? At first we discussed scanning everything. When we realized we had millions of sheets of paper—the vast majority of which would never be used again—we abandoned that project. Then we talked about scanning all files for the year we started. That too was scratched because we knew as we tracked cases that about 80 percent of our matters were resolved within six months, and by the end of 12 months only a handful of cases remained. The solution was not to scan any old files until we needed to work on them. Very few of these older files got scanned.

> Over the years we began to reconsider the scanning of older files. The decision was to select those that had a connection to current clients and would be needed for reference, such as corporation formation, contract negotiations, etc. In those cases, we scanned the entire contents of a folder as one pdf. It left us with a huge file, but no different than if it had been given to us in a physical form. Finally, after several years, we found that those files we did not scan were never referenced. Boxes and boxes of files had been put in storage and never opened.

> After some checking we found that storing our file boxes in a bonded moving and storage company was cost-effective compared to a storage shed along the interstate highway. They were placed in a climate controlled space that was far more secure.

8. Begin the process of scanning and profiling every document that comes in the door as well as e-mails. Do not destroy the documents as described earlier. Rather, the system of filing should continue until you no longer use it.

> As a task comes up on a pre-conversion matter, add that matter to the system. You can add the documents in any number of ways. If they are already electronic, connect them to the document manager. If they are not electronic, scan the entire file as a single PDF or, if larger, as a series of PDF files, which you can then index with the document manager

9. Scan documents received prior to starting the system from on-going files only. In those cases, treat the documents as one would incoming mail, by scanning and profiling it.
10. In every task, use the document management system to store and organize the material. This includes documents, e-mails, notes, and calendar items.
11. Integrate the document management with all of the programs that are routinely used. Most document management systems provide such integration as part of the system.

> Replace (or at least move) the save icon in the ribbons and task bars with the icon for saving under the document management system. This avoids inadvertently saving a file in the wrong place and turns a longtime habit into the new system.

12. Check to see that profiling properly organizes documents. While the old system is in place, compare what has been electronically saved versus by paper. The former should be complete.
13. Continue for several months. Identify ways paper is being used and look for paperless alternatives. Make sure that everything in a matter is being profiled into the system for that matter.
14. Pick a date after which all new files are done exclusively on the system. When you are comfortable that the system works, no longer rely on a papered system for the new files.
15. Reach a level of comfort. There will come a point when the process is as smooth and automatic as earlier processes. Over time, the number of actual matters opened prior to the conversion will become fewer and fewer.
16. Convert completely to the new system. There will be a point where using the papered system is a waste.

> A key hint that this time has arrived is when you realize that during the day you never went to a paper file. If you are not there yet, look at where it is not complete and dedicate attention to changing that procedure.

17. Discontinue using the paper system. Welcome to the State of Paperlessness!

Moving forward within the State of Paperlessness

There is no standing still in this new state. As great as it is, it can be better. After the matter files reside digitally, the next place to consider converting is corporate minute books and other support material. Granted, these should not be destroyed, but for usefulness in operating the paperless office, scanning and placing them on the system is important.

In addition to matter files, create a "library" with a unique numbering and label system to store digital copies of such information. Add to the library using the digital tools, such as OneNote and PDF Portfolio, or simple folders to collect information regarding very special projects and items of recurring reference.

Finally, bring the paper from the desktop (the physical desktop and surrounding space), which is the third and uncharted "paper storage," into the paperless system. This includes those notebooks of quick reference, pages and slips of notes and reminders, directories, and regulations routinely referenced. Scan or re-create all of these digitally and store in a library as well. It is likely that as the pieces are reviewed, many will find their way to the trash or shredder.

The result is the panorama of uncluttered furniture, which is a wonderful view in the State of Paperlessness.

The process of moving to the state of paperlessness continues. Each day the lawyer is presented with paper. Each time he should ask these questions:

- *Can this document be stored digitally?* If it is a piece of paper, the answer is obviously in the affirmative. But there are some physical objects that defy being digitized (like the defective coffeemaker). At least for purposes of preparing the case and reference, a series of digital images, video or still, can replace the document.
- *Does it have to remain a physical document?* As described elsewhere, there are some documents that have to remain in physical form. Wills are an example. Fortunately there are few, but even those few can be processed digitally except when the original needs to be delivered.
- And finally, *does this document ever have to be a piece of paper?* Strive to have documents originate in digital form. This means encouraging transmittal of memoranda, letters, contracts, and the like by e-mail or other digital means.

Don't look back!

Regardless of the planning and marshaling of resources and complete dedication from all, there will be obstacles and events along the transition. Do not just assume the system is doing what is expected. Periodically check by calling up e-mails profiled or documents stored. Trying finding these by keywords and persons used in the profile.

Along the way, there will be those tasks that in the "old days" were quick and easy but now take longer. Those will be few, and in time fewer yet. Allow time for early missteps so you can go back if you need to. Make plenty of document backups as you progress until you are comfortable with the system.

Keep in mind that much of the paperless office consists of upfront work in terms of profiling and scanning. The time benefits come with use and show up later in the process. Also, there is a greater likelihood that the documents are actually filed and filed correctly.

Obstacles are not signals or even excuses to discontinue, but are just part of the learning experience. Initially, because it is new, the work will take some extra time. This is particularly the case in profiling files in process or building forms libraries. Allow for this extra time. Add an extra hour a day for a while. By adding some extra time each day in the early days, you will quickly be up and running. The point then is to focus not on immediate gratification but on ultimate satisfaction. There will be immediate benefits, but patience is required to see all of them.

SPECIAL DOCUMENTS

Handling faxes

Fax of the "old" medium can easily be brought into the digital world. Optimally, the lawyer should be using a digital fax that is part of the network. Various programs and equipment will receive a fax and send a digital file to the system, profiled and stored for later retrieval.

> Faxing, that great technological improvement in the '80s, is now passé. Our offices receive very few faxes now, and the vast majority of those are junk faxes direct "to the employees" from the "travel department."

Processing e-mails

E-mails are handled the same as paper mail—sorted between "keep" and "delete." The kept e-mails with their attachments are profiled and saved with the system. E-mails are profiled as they are sent. Depending on the management software, much of the profiling can be automatically generated by the names of the senders and recipients.

> Elsewhere, there is discussion on how to declutter the in-box to limit the number of e-mails that need to be profiled.

Calendar and deadlines

Calendaring, which includes deadlines as well as events, is entered into Outlook and profiled upon being made. The Outlook calendar, or other if used, should automatically synchronize with the laptop, tablet, PDA, and other remote units.

Audio and video recordings

Voice recordings and video constitute a major form of documents. These include voicemail, speeches, broadcasts, trials, or depositions. They can even be in the form of dictation specifically for recording.

Leave it in an audio format

The first option is to leave the information in the recorded format. Saved and stored media files like documents are at least equal to paper documents and usually superior. To make it searchable, give it a more descriptive file name, or make an Excel worksheet on which you list the audio file, identify key words and elements, and then insert a link. The original audio is always better.

Edit the audio

There are numerous programs from the simple to the complex that are available for editing audio. Why would you want to do that? First, there may only be a small portion of the audio or visual medium that is relevant. Why save 10 hours of useless audio when a minute would suffice?

The other reason to edit is that in the course of interviews and depositions, there are numerous pauses. They do not show up in the written transcript but on the screen. While a live witness can be forgiven for pauses, it is unacceptable when doing depositions. Get rid of the dead time.

Transcribe the document

The method of conversion to written form depends on the need. The lawyer can transcribe himself if there is little chance that the information will be useful in trial or litigation. When the lawyer is part of the conversation, he can do it more quickly because he knows the context, the terms, etc.

> You may transcribe what you want to hear, not what was said.
> So be careful.

There are a host of online services that will transcribe and return a .docx document. The quality of these varies immensely, and generally they are worth what is charged. Due to issues of confidentiality, the lawyer should be sure that whoever does it has the same appreciation for confidentiality and professionalism. Having a professional stenographer do it can provide that security.

When accuracy is important, hire a court reporter to transcribe the material and certify its accuracy. There are a number of online services, but control of confidentiality and knowing that you are dealing with people who understand your professional culture should not be sacrificed.

Handling the archived paper from prior practice

Seldom do practices start fresh as paperless; they almost always have a papered past. Whether to back-file older files is a question answered by need and cost.

> We made the decision to convert older files initially only if:
>
> - The matter was currently being handled in the office.
> - The matter was related to other matters being handled.
> - We received a request to review or otherwise look at the matter.
> - The matter provided necessary history for current clients.

As the foregoing shows, operating in a paperless office differs from the papered in two ways—all documents are scanned and everything is profiled. The lawyer wanting to practice in the State of Paperlessness must, in addition to a computer system readily available, have a quality scanner, a database program such as a practice management program, a system to approach the documents, and the discipline to stick to it.

> Creating the discipline to profile is the single most important task necessary to a successful practice in the State of Paperlessness.

The benefits of things being "online" are difficult to fully describe rather than experience. In one week, while preparing this book, I had four tasks requiring research in old, if not ancient, files. A Form 803 for Hart Scott Rodino notification required the collection of documents from dozens of different matters that I had worked on. An IP case required me to look through a number of files that went back 17 years to find notes regarding the development of the property. Litigation discovery demanded correspondence going back seven years from a dozen matters. In completing an application to practice in another state, I was pulling up files over 30 years old. I responded to a third-party document request for about 200 pages of documents. Finally, in a case seeking injunctive relief in an administrative case, I needed to pull out briefs and pleadings from cases 20 years ago, the last time the issue had been litigated.

All the information had been scanned into the system except for a few cases. In those cases, the box number and where that box was located were online. Rather than spending hours or others spending hours scrounging through old boxes, I went to the file online, scanned the contents, pulled what I needed, and proceeded accordingly.

All of these were handled in addition to other demands in a few days, almost always without leaving the desk.

Converting web views to digital documents for the future

The web is an enormous supply of information. Once found, it needs to be captured and saved within the realm of the document management system. There are a number of ways to do this:

- Save the url in the document system. Most of these programs provide this facility.
- Use www.tinyurl.com to reduce the longest web addresses to a couple of dozen characters.
- Use Quick Response code or QR. This matrix will take the user to the selected website. Many PDAs can snapshot the matrix and go immediately to the website. The following one jumps to www.yalelawoffice.com. QR can be generated at www. http://qrcode.kaywa.com/.

- Print the screen and save. If the website provides the ability to print, use that function; otherwise, use the Print in the browser menu. Not all websites allow printing, copying, or downloading the information. In those cases, saving the url may be all you can do.

> I have a subfolder in My Documents called PDF Dump where I initially save PDFs from the web and then profile them. If it is not a PDF, I print to PDF into the same folder. Doing this also captures the date as well as the URL.

- Print screen and paste in a PDF or Word document. When the Print Screen button is hit, it saves the contents in the Clipboard.
- Snapshot in PDF. If the document is a PDF, you can select the section you want and use the Snapshot function of PDF to capture it and then save in a Word or other document.

Outside processing for the extraordinary file

Some information comes in sizes, shapes, and volumes that do not flow easily in the standard office. These include X rays or other imaging, or blueprints, surveys, and drawings for buildings. These can be scanned offsite and the digital record saved. Today almost all of these originate in a digital format that can be profiled and stored.

In the case of massive volumes, the use of offsite services to scan, Bates stamp if necessary, and profile provides a means to balance the workload without a huge investment in equipment for a one-time project.

THE STATE OF PAPERLESSNESS NEEDS TO INCLUDE EVERYONE TO GET THE FULL BENEFIT.

Everyone has to be on board; without full participation within the firm, the full benefits will not come. For offices with more than one attorney or staff, everyone must "buy in" to the program. This obviously includes the support staff, who need to learn to send messages of phone calls, calendar reminders, and other communications by e-mail rather than writing them out on slips of paper, or to send typed drafts electronically rather than printing them out.

Every person in the firm shall participate fully in the paperless office.

This can be a generational thing, and there will be those who think it's a great idea but are unwilling to make the commitment to change their habits. After all, they reached the present stage in their practice without any of these new-fangled techniques. They need to understand the value to the firm as well as to themselves. The reality is that if left to use the old method, in time they will become isolated from the rest of the firm. Loss of complete communication will result, and those not making the change will find themselves being subsidized in a way that is unfortunate and unfair to those who made the change. In the digital world, they will not be able to deliver the kind of service that they should.

You are there!

CHAPTER 17

MANAGING YOUR ENTIRE LAW PRACTICE IN THE STATE OF PAPERLESSNESS

Managing a law practice no longer requires the use of paper. Its use can be removed or substantially reduced in almost all cases.

MANAGEMENT OF THE ENTIRE PRACTICE

The office in a State of Paperlessness is wherever a computer, PDA, or remote computer has access. While there are certainly physical access issues, management of the entire law practice is primarily the management of access to data. At the core of this level of management is a practice management system (PMS), which digitally *is* the practice. In non-law practices, these systems are sometimes referred to as Enterprise Resource Planning, or ERP, which brings together all aspects of the business from finance to sales to providing the product or service. That is what a comprehensive PMS system should provide.

> **To get the full benefits of practicing in the State of Paperlessness, the lawyer should have a fully functioning and integrated practice management system.**

These systems come with a wide range in power and sophistication (and price) and where they are based—individual computer, network, or the cloud. But all of them have the following characteristics:

- They encompass all of the management components of the office—information, events, business, billing, communication, and practice.
- They integrate with the core office programs—e-mail, contacts, calendar, word processing, spreadsheets, documents, case-specific programs, phone, and billing. In some cases the program provides the module itself or works with existing programs. For example, the PMS may have its own contact list that is synchronized with Outlook Contacts, or it relies entirely on the latter. Integration means information is entered once and is thereafter accessible by all functions and by all matters as needed.
- They provide single-location access to matter information. By identifying a matter, the program will identify all documents, contacts, e-mails, events, notes, phone calls, billing, etc., related to the matter.
- They are media-neutral in accessibility. Regardless of the medium such as .docx, .xls, .pdf, .jpg, or others, the system must handle them all.
- They organize matters by date opened, client, matter type, activity, attorney assignment, court, etc. Once the information is entered into the database, it can be accessed not only by matter but through the data submitted. The more powerful ones permit multiple factor keys—for example, Attorney, Matter Type.
- They capture billing data as tasks are done. By tracking documents, e-mails, phone calls, and other tasks by matter, the program produces a real-time trail of billable events. The programs also allow these billable moments be edited and completed either in real-time or afterwards.

These are sophisticated programs, but once properly installed, they operate consistently and easily. The secret is to find the system that fits the lawyer's practice. That means the size of the firm, the number of staff, the mobility of the lawyers, types of matters, and other factors. Having an expert come on board to help choose the system will benefit the lawyer for a long time. Also, having an expert install the system, train, and be available as a consultant will also ensure smoother results.

> Viewing the system as a sum of many parts and focusing on the parts and their relationship to others is better than trying to see the whole thing at once. I always had in mind a complete system but tried to focus on developing one part, such as document management or billing, at a time. Starting with a program that did everything but incorporating pieces one at a time was better than doing it all at once.

> The lawyer has enough to learn and new skills to develop to use the system. To spend precious time in gaining the equivalent of years of experience an expert can bring is not a good investment.

CALENDARING THE DIGITAL OFFICE BRINGS GREATER CONTROL OVER THE LAWYER'S TIME.

Calendars schedule the practice. They tell the lawyer and her staff when things are due, what tasks need to be done, and how a project rates in importance, and remind her of upcoming deadlines and events. The word "tell" means just that—events or reminders are displayed on the computer, iPad, or PDA with sound and sight to tell her something is due or will be due. These messages can be displays, text messages, e-mails, phone calls, or some or all of those. But it is more than just that; it provides a place to collect agenda, phone numbers, directions, itinerary, documents, websites, contacts, and other information relevant to the event. Upon opening the event, all relevant documents present themselves.

Dates and times define what the lawyer does and when she does it. They mean the difference between having a case or missing a statute of limitations. They mean being heard on the merits or sitting by silently. They mean showing up for a hearing or being in the office instead. They mean being fully prepared or sending out incomplete work.

Seeing the right side of a date does not come naturally. Identifying the trigger date and computing the operative date is as much merit law as is legal or factual research. That is because calendaring is legal and factual research coupled with legal analysis. What date counts in starting? Is it the day posted or received? Does the operative date come before or after? How are holidays, weekends, court closings, and emergencies considered? Does it matter that the court or a litigant triggered the event? How many days should be counted? Those are all legal questions based on facts.

It then should surprise no one that the largest basis for malpractice is missing deadlines.[1]

> For example, if a board conference call is scheduled for a particular time, in profiling the event, insert the agenda and other materials into the calendar item. When the call comes up, the system will remind you and put the materials needed on your desktop. No need to search.

The rule on calendar use is to put in everything as a matter of course and depend on it. There can be multiple calendars. These should appear merged on the lawyer's display, but each can have a different purpose with a different audience. Calendars for specific purposes include an event schedule, conference room calendar, personal calendar, work-flow calendar.

The good lawyer must:

- *analyze every document* initially for operative or triggering dates;
- *record those dates* in her calendar;
- *reread the rules* regarding the dates;
- *identify and record* intervening steps;
- *provide ample reminders* of when the dates occur to ensure preparation;
- *repeat reminders* in critical matters;
- *allow cushion* to prevent the last-minute disruption or emergency from causing a date to be missed;
- *follow up* in two ways—relook at dates to ensure that the work was done and, on following dates, to double-check that the deadlines were met;
- *compare dates* with administrative staff, co-counsel, other lawyers, or even opposing counsel to get agreement on unclear dates; and
- *distribute dates* to all concerned.

The standard for calendar software is provided in Outlook. It contains virtually all that is needed, and it readily integrates with multiplatform and multiuse networks, such as home computers, tablets, notebooks, and PDAs.

The calendar should:

- be kept up to date continuously;
- be backed up routinely and asynchronously to multiple sites;
- be accessible at all times; and
- provide for audio, text, and other reminders in advance of the event.

The lawyer should:

- use the calendar religiously;
- look at a week and month a time; and
- schedule time to work on matters, rather than wait for time to just open up.

The calendaring program automatically determines if there are conflicts with other events. The software will also remind the lawyer that the date chosen is a holiday, weekend, or other special day, such as the lawyer's anniversary or spouse's birthday.

With the meeting and invitation functions, the lawyer can set a meeting and send invitations to all of the participants with supporting material. It will automatically track those who have agreed to attend or sent regrets.

By integrating with the practice management software, these events provide additional detail to help audit billing input and also to detail time lines when addressing the progress of projects.

Scheduling the workflow

Planning how the lawyer approaches tasks contributes more to efficiency and productivity than the hardware and software. In the State of Paperlessness, the inefficiencies of handling paper in all of its forms no longer exist. When something was needed, the lawyer would ask for it or look for it herself. In the paperless office, there is almost no time between requiring and retrieving a document or other information. What is needed should be there already. If everything is profiled as it is received, then that should be the case.

After several years in this paperless mode, I still am amazed at how fast projects move along, and the reason is there is no interruption to get a file, search a binder, or flip through notes. Nor do I walk from room to room looking for the transcript some-one else was working on, or the box of exhibits which has been misplaced, or notes from the last time we worked on this matter.

It is not just that no time is spent on those activities, it is that the focus and thoughts are not broken. There is no time spent to restart the thinking, and thinking and concentration build to levels not present generally in the papered world. Know-ing this, when I start a project like a memorandum or a con-tract, I check to see that everything I need has been loaded.

Tasks come in multiple sizes. Going paperless also brings a lot of short but not mundane tasks, such as profiling documents and e-mails. A lot of time can be spent on those. But that pays off when those items are needed.

There are no killer apps to manage your time. It is a skill you must develop and discipline you must follow. There are, however, programs that will assist you

- Practice management software is the primary tool. The project management software should provide lists of open files that re-quire attention. You should routinely look at the list to be sure that nothing is overlooked and that all relevant deadlines are noted. Some matters are merely awaiting a decision or signature from the client. Others require work now.

This is why I used matter numbers rather than clients early on as the primary file of matters. I could look down a list of mat-ters and mark what was closed. The very number of an open file told me its age. Alphabetical lists provided no sense of timing or priority.

- The calendar program provides the next level of guidance. Reli-giously and routinely populating the calendar with such tasks and reminders can direct you in terms of what needs to be done. In addition to the regular calendar, you can establish a more detailed calendar in which daily tasks and goals are listed.

- Related to the calendar program is the task program. As tasks are created, note the deadlines along with previews of when they are due.

When creating a task file, also enter hyperlinks to the documents and places you need to reference to complete the task.

- E-mail can provide a reminder of tasks that need to be done. Use it sparingly, and generally only as a reminder that someone is owed something.
- The windows on the screen help to manage tasks. When a task is identified that needs to be completed that day, open or initially create a document for that matter and leave it on the desktop. Try to keep the desktop clean by completing each of these documents.
- The physical desktop and workspace can also assist in project management. Handwriting a sticky or placing a note on the keyboard to remind you of something you need for a project is good use of a little bit of paper. Routine lists, however, should be shifted to the electronic kind that are carried everywhere.
- Finally, synchronize the calendars automatically with laptops, tablets, and PDAs so that these reminders go wherever the lawyer goes.

Written calendars as a backup can help avoid missing deadlines.

With automatic synchronization of calendars, you should have certainty that what is in Outlook on the desktop is the same as what is in the calendar on the iPad and on the BlackBerry. The danger is that if one of these is wiped out or dates are inadvertently deleted, they all can be. This can happen too easily. To ensure that the calendars are preserved, you can take several steps:

- Maintain two separate calendars in different formats. For example, one could be in Outlook and the other on the tablet.
- Designate one calendar as the master. It is always correct. In the end, everything must conform to it.
- Manually synchronize the two calendars. Do not have this done automatically. Thus, if something is on one and not on the other, it can be replaced.

- When synchronizing the master calendar with other databases, require the program to send an alert on any changes to the Outlook calendar and allow review of the changes before they occur.
- Periodically save the calendar in an Excel spreadsheet or other media format as a backup to use if there is a major loss of data.
- Print the calendar to an Adobe PDF routinely. Using the Compare function of Adobe, the calendar can be compared to previous versions to look for changes and ensure that those changes were intended.
- Periodically compare your calendar with the one created by administrative staff or other lawyers.

CONFLICTS

A fully populated PMS system with names and contacts should allow you to quickly see if you have any conflicts. Being ignorant of a potential conflict is no excuse. Being able to do this requires ongoing work ahead of time.

- Make sure that all of the relationships of clients, subsidiaries, owners, officers, employees, and witnesses are properly noted and linked to matters and other individuals. Doing this as they arise is much faster than trying to catch up after a thousand matters reside in the data management system.
- When taking on a new case, gather all of the information possible, such as the names of the client's competitors and subsidiaries.

> Specifically ask your clients if they know of any person or company they would view as a conflict.

- Do the search several different ways, using all the names that you have.
- Search on the Internet to see if there are connections reported there that would show a potential conflict.

> Provide clients with a form which specifically asks for information that would lead to a more thorough conflict check.

PAPERLESS PRACTICE AND THE BILLABLE HOUR

At some point, the work provided by the lawyer needs turn to cash. Practicing in the State of Paperlessness provides opportunities to make what is a time-consuming task become more efficient.

With all of the documents, dates, notes, and other information being managed through the PSM, the activities for billing are captured. This occurs as they are being done, or, in retrospect, these details need to be identified for purposes of billing.

> I liked to have the system prepare me a monthly calendar showing the total billed hours for each day as well as for the month. Then I knew which days needed to be looked at. I could identify all of the activity done that day, including phone calls and document preparation. The detail was edited to show the total time spent.
>
> By doing this, I was able to make sure all of the billing detail was captured. Then it was a matter of printing out the bills and checking them.

> Today, tracking long-distance phone calls, copies, etc., is easy to do. Whether you want to "nickel and dime" clients is another issue. I for decades have refused to do so, but some continue. I recently reviewed a bill from outside counsel for over $10,000 in fees and seven cents for long distance!

There are other benefits of billing and the State of Paperlessness. The system can automatically prepare an engagement letter as part of opening the case. As part of that letter, include the following terms relating to the paperless practice:

- Make arrangements when entering into an agreement with the client that the client will accept bills by e-mail.
- Make arrangements to receive payment by wire transfers to the bank account or by credit/debit cards that are automatically credited to the firm account.

The problem with the paperless office is that it makes the use of hourly billing even more archaic. All of the efficiencies gained by the full use of those tools are not transferrable to the client when time is billed by the hour. There is even a perverse incentive in firms demanding that associates not use the tools so that there are more hours for the project.

The answer is to look at alternative billing mechanisms that recognize the higher productivity. If the hourly rate persists, then bill as high a rate as the market allows to cover the extra productivity.

In no event should inability to capture the full economics deter making the transition. It will free time for more work or allow for some needed rest. There are a number of processes that are not "legal" but are part of the legal process in most offices and generate a lot of paper. Here are some ideas to reduce the paper load.

EMPLOY OUT-OF-OFFICE SOLUTIONS.

- Send some of the back-office functions, such as bookkeeping and payroll, to an accounting firm.
- Large-scale scanning can be done by services dedicated to meet the needs of lawyers.
- When snail mail is required, a number of services will convert an e-mail into a document and sends via the U.S. Postal Service.
- Occasionally you will have a large volume of paper documents that need processing or work product that has to come out in a final printed form. The easiest way to handle that in the paperless state is to send them to outside copying services in the digital form. For example, a brief filed in the Supreme Court still needs to be printed in a booklet, and there are services that can do that.

> Companies include NEtGrams E-mail Bridge, Postal Shout, eSnailer.

Note

1.   Mark C.S. Bassingthwaighte & Reba J. Nance, *The Top Ten Causes of Malpractice—and How You Can Avoid Them*, ABA TECHSHOW 2006, *available at* http://apps.americanbar.org/lpm/lpt/articles/tch12062.pdf (last visited Oct. 11, 2011).

CHAPTER 18

BEING ETHICAL IN THE STATE OF PAPERLESSNESS

Abolishing paper has not abolished the requirement that lawyers practice in ethical and professional ways. In some ways, the speed of digital communication coupled with greater transparency have unmasked otherwise-hidden unethical and unprofessional conduct. Where the process of dictating, typing, editing, and mailing a letter slowed down, tempered, or even stopped outrageous language, the unthinking Send button speeds it.

The digital world is also unforgiving. In the old days, if a printed letter was sent to the wrong person, a quick call and the wrong recipient would return the envelope, sometimes unopened. Today a missent e-mail, even if deleted by the wrong recipient, remains in those servers to be recovered later. There is no real deletion. Lawyers who have litigated with e-discovery have uncovered e-mail unintended for the person on whose server it sat, and with surprising content.

In addition to the generally applicable ethical and professional obligations, in the State of Paperlessness there are some special ones generally applicable to the digital age.

PROTECTING THE CONFIDENCE

One of the greatest challenges to keeping confidentiality in the State of Paperlessness is not just that information can slip out easier, but also that the unintended release can be copied and distributed in seconds to thousands of locations. The risks of loss of confidential information are even greater than they were before the days of computers. Once gone, it is not retrievable and is available forever. Tracking down and retrieving digital data is nearly impossible.

Lawyers must recognize that any communication sent, e-mail or letter, will be Exhibit A in a lawsuit against him or his client. In the past, one advantage was that over time those letters got destroyed, lost, or buried in forgotten storage someplace. That is not the case today.

> A question to ask in addition to whether to send the document or not is, do you want to keep explaining this letter 5, 10, 20 years later? Or do you want this to go viral and be the topic of news articles, comics' routines, or discussed on cable news?

Chain e-mails are called "viral" because like disease they transmit quickly, replicate faster than you can stop them, and never really disappear.

> The Annenberg Public Policy Center has a fact-check site that catches viral and untrue stories, at www.factcheck.org.

This openness and longevity brings a new concern with what is in e-mails and documents. Besides avoiding the unnecessary personal insults, sarcasm, dark humor, and other no-no's, it is important to say only what needs to be said. The documents need to assume there is no context.

- *Start with the rules.* The ABA Model Rule says that a lawyer "shall not reveal information relating to the representation of a client without the client's informed consent."[1] The key here is reasonable expectation of privacy. The committee on the rules determined that when compared with other means of communication (phone, mail, etc.), the use of e-mail presented the same reasonable expectation of privacy.[2]

But we all know that there are different levels of expectation with the same technology. California has instructed that the attorney has to evaluate the technology within the context of its use. This is a case-by-case analysis, not a general one. The use of outside resources to store digital information, too, is permitted by the rules on confidentiality.[3]

E-mail from the lawyer to an employee's work e-mail or the employee opening personal e-mail on the employer server is not a reasonable expectation of privacy.

Different states have addressed the issue of e-mail confidentiality. It is a rapidly developing state. As a general rule, confidentiality applies when four basic elements are fulfilled:

- The holder of the privilege must be a client or prospective client of the attorney.
- An attorney acting as such at the time must be at the other end of the communication.
- The communications must be for the purpose of obtaining legal advice or counsel.
- The communications must be made in confidence (no strangers present).

The term "in confidence" is based upon the intent of the client, and the conversation will generally be deemed confidential where the client has a reasonable expectation of privacy and confidentiality. Because this "reasonable expectation of privacy" exists in e-mails, most states have taken the position that e-mail communications are entitled to confidentiality.

At the same time, attorneys are not guarantors of absolute privacy. In the same way that there is always the risk of someone physically and illegally entering the office and forcing open a file cabinet, so too is there a risk that someone will hack into an e-mail account and disclose the contents.

As a rule, my firm does not keep Social Security numbers or credit card numbers of clients. Where we have to have them, we use them in those documents but redact them when stored.

Finding Social Security numbers in older files, before the rules, and redacting them is a challenge. There is software, IdentityFinderwww.identityfinder.com, which will search your database and identify the numbers.

The most important part of security is having access to material limited. This can be done by one or a combination of several of the following:

- *Password.* An absolute that should be used at all times.
- *Equipment or location limited.* Access to data can be limited to specific machines or urls to avoid others from invading the system.
- *Encryption.*
- *Ability to remotely wipe portable data,* such as on PDAs, laptops, and tablets.

THE LAWYER SHOULD TREAT HIS COMPUTER AS A PIECE OF PROFESSIONAL GEAR, NOT A TOY OR ENTERTAINMENT DEVICE.

The computer can be used for all whole lot of things. It is one of the most powerful professional tools available to lawyers to deliver their work in a professional and efficient manner. It also has a lot of personal uses, such as e-mails to family regarding when dinner will be ready or other things of similar import, or as a means of communicating social and community events. It allows conduct unacceptable in the profession or even by society as a whole, some of which is actually illegal. On a computer anyone can gamble, solicit or procure sex, view or share pornography, participate in vicious hate postings, and a multitude of other activities.

Every lawyer meets societal standards for special occasions or professional events, such as a court appearances, weddings, or attending a house of worship. None sanely would appear in court wearing pajamas or clothes worn when emptying manure out of the horse barn, or the outfit worn playing several games of tennis on a hot, humid day. The reason is that those special clothes are part of the professional look. Appearance can contribute to a higher level of performance and affect how seriously others accept your comments and arguments.

Because so much communication is done through computers, the computers have become the "dress." They are a powerful tool used by the profession. They should be clean and professional. If a lawyer wants to use the computer to gamble, pursue sex, demean others, or play games, those activities should be reserved for a computer not used in the practice.

- Use of the computer for these purposes can easily and unexpectedly spill over into legitimate files and be displayed in the worst time and place. Congressman Anthony Weiner, thinking he was sexting to a woman, unwittingly posted it to his Twitter account. Within weeks he was out of office.[4]

- A lawyer's computer contains confidential client information that can be placed at risk. If the computer is used in criminal behavior, it creates a risk that that computer, and those confidential files, can be seized and, in the process, can compromise the integrity of clients' information.
- Display of the information can be embarrassing and untimely, such as part of a live use of the Internet.

Surprises can come in strange ways. Every time a website is searched for or visited, it leaves traces. Search history, viewing history, previous websites are all there to be shown when least expected or needed.

> In another presentation at a convention, an individual opened his browser to call up a website. As he did so, the history in the browser bar displayed a number of pornography websites he probably visited the night before.

Part of the discipline that makes a paperless law office successful and professional is to leave the professional equipment for the profession, not sideshows.

> As part of using your laptop for a presentation, make sure your history is cleared and the icons are removed unless they are needed for the presentation. Even innocent sites can be misunderstood. I generally will put anything I want presented on a thumb drive that has been cleared and use the computer supplied by the sponsor.

Even exposure of the content of home computers is at risk. A federal judge was being hounded by an unsuccessful litigant who illegally gained access to the judge's home computer through the wireless router. He got into the judge's personal computer and obtained documents indicating it had been used to access pornography sites.[5] Though clearly a criminal act was employed to get the material, which was later disclosed to be that of his sons, it was nonetheless damaging.

THE ABILITY TO QUICKLY AND SEAMLESSLY ALTER DOCUMENTS SHOULD NOT OVERLOOK THE OBLIGATION OF CANDOR.

The biggest danger, with the ease of making and modifying documents, is that documents can be altered almost without others knowing it. This alteration can occur during negotiations without disclosing the change. In the case of large documents, the removal of a "not" may not be noticed unless noted. The rules of ethics and professionalism require that the lawyer notify others of the changes made. This is easily done by using the Track Changes in Word, the visual edits in Adobe, or running a comparison of the documents in either program.

> Depending on who I am working with, I generally trust their indication of changes, but before a final signing I will run a comparison with the last version or versions that I knew were right.

A consumer of satellite TV sued his supplier for a refund of a late-payment penalty he alleged was illegal. In several court filings he attached a purported agreement. Language providing for settlement was copied onto the original consumer agreement for the satellite service. The language dropped into this preexisting agreement said that a settlement of $600,000 would be deemed accepted unless the provider rejected it within so many days. The modified agreement was submitted as an exhibit to several affidavits in the case. The consumer argued that the settlement was accepted and binding since it had not been rejected. The court rejected the claim.[6] The attorneys who drafted the change never notified the other side until just before a hearing on the motion. But it shows how easily even "boilerplate" can be altered.

> This demonstrates why protecting the original agreement is so important in this age of easy modification.

A TECHNICAL EMERGENCY ON THE LAWYER'S END IS NOT NECESSARILY EXCUSABLE NEGLECT TO THE COURT.

The challenge has always been to have things on time. Attorneys are notorious for waiting until the day after the deadline. The power of the paperless office allows more time to prepare documents with less time between completion of the lawyer's work and filing. Without all of the printing, copying, collating, binding, packaging, and delivery, those hours can apply to getting the job done or excuse more delay.

Waiting until the last moment becomes a serious problem when a digital disaster occurs and the deadline may be missed. In most cases there is always the option of seeking leave to file *instanter,* with an affidavit detailing the woes and vagaries of the electronic meltdown that led to the late filing. One lawyer sought a continuance because his motion was filed shortly after midnight and his brief was filed several hours later. His rationale was that he had been on the road and at the motel he could not scan his signature. After he got it done, he filed it. The court denied the motion. In doing so, the court noted that under ECF an actual signature was not needed in any event.[7]

But even if the court is inclined, in some cases, to extend the filing date, it has no authority to do so. For example, rules for filing motions for a new trial or altering judgments[8] are required on the specified date, and the court has no jurisdiction to change those. In Ohio, petitions for certiorari with the Ohio Supreme Court are due on a certain date, and the clerk has no authority to accept a late filing or a motion to that issue.[9]

> Note that the rules require that the filing of a motion or pleading be in a .pdf that has searchable text. That means the document should be generated by the Word or WordPerfect program and not printed, signed, and scanned as a digital image.[10]

MAKE SURE THAT THE SOURCE OF COPYING IS CORRECT AND RELEVANT.

Not taking care to copy and paste can have severe circumstances. A doctor filed a defamation claim against an investigator and another employee of the state medical board. In response to a subpoena duces tecum in another case involving the doctor, the agency's employee checked a computer database and mistakenly cut and pasted the status of another doctor whose name was adjacent to the plaintiff's name. As a result, the state medical board responded to the subpoena with a statement that the plaintiff doctor received disciplinary action regarding a medical license in the state of Rhode Island. However, he never held a medical license in Rhode Island.[11]

There can be all kinds of things in the clipboard. Cut and paste is certainly easy—easy to be wrong.

ACTUALLY, NOT VIRTUALLY, KNOW TO WHOM YOU ARE TALKING.

Today is the day of avatars. We all have other names. Some e-mail addresses, which may or may not correspond to our real name, are made-up names, user names—the list goes on and on. The john.smith@amazinggracecompany.xcom at work might be silvernight@theroundtable.xcom at home. In some ways, nicknames are common to describe other individuals or even ourselves. But what lawyer would choose to communicate to a client by sending an e-mail to walkingupthetreetoseeken@xaol.com if he could not verify who was on the other side? Do we really know who is at the other end of a conversation? Should we communicate confidential information without even knowing that it was our client and that no one else was present?

So it is when the lawyer uses the e-mail to tell Rhoda Frances Smith about issues with her pending divorce settlement and the e-mail provided is Toreadorsamiga@xaol.com. How does the lawyer really know who will get that e-mail? Does she know for sure that it won't be received by the spouse against whom counsel is being sought?

> One especially dangerous situation exists when there are a series of e-mails with multiple recipients and people are using Reply All. It is easy to assume that the rule of *noscitur a sociis* applies here. (The law Latin term means a word is known by the company it keeps.) But buried in the e-mails of six co-counsels could be one from a non-party, an expert, or even the judge's clerk. That avatar says nothing about who the addressee is, and there is no reason to believe it is in the same category as the other six. You have an obligation to know who is receiving an e-mail.

> Be careful not to include others in the e-mail that are not within the zone of confidentiality. The ease by which you can hit the Reply All button and send information to many who are not within the zone of protection poses a danger.

The commonplace boilerplate that says "This e-mail and any files transmitted with it are confidential and are intended solely for the addressee, etc." does no good because it also appears on notes to family members about picking them up after school or to the local deli ordering lunch. A broad statement on truly confidential e-mails, such as "CONFIDENTIAL: Attorney Client Communication," might help.

KNOW THAT THE RECIPIENT OF THE E-MAIL IS THE INTENDED RECIPIENT.

The danger that communication with clients presents, even if the e-mail is the correct address, is that the e-mail may be retrievable by other people who share the computer, or by an employer on whose computers the e-mail is received. As a result of these possibilities, it is important for clients to understand the risks associated with transmitting e-mail and how confidentiality can be lost. Depending on sensitivity, tighter measures may be required. Here are some things to consider.

> **The lawyer shall know the identity of the person who actually is the recipient of an e-mail.**

- *Use secured e-mail.* This can be done through mobileme.com even if you are not an iPhone or iPad user. Other packages are out there.
- *Create a special e-mail for the customer.* If the client is sharing the e-mail or does not have an account of his own, direct him on how he can create one with one of the free e-mail services, such as Gmail or Hotmail. Helping him choose a strong password is part of this effort.
- *On supersensitive material, do not e-mail.* Everything does not have to be e-mailed. Call the client and, after you are assured it is indeed a private conversation, tell him what needed to be conveyed. Or write it out on paper, seal it in an envelope, and give it to him so he can read it privately. Or discuss the matter in a face-to-face conference.
- *When sending long lists, create a distribution list and send it to a blind cc.* Do not send other people e-mail addresses from your own contact list.

IN A DIGITAL WORLD, THERE ARE NO "HIDDEN" OR "ERASED" WORDS OR FILES.

What appears digitally exceeds what would appear on paper. Behind every document is a whole lot of information that would not show up if the document were printed. The rule is to never put anything in the computer that you would not want to share with the world. A broad rule, but a necessary one.

In the paper days, there was always the first draft that would be thrown away, totally destroyed, and no longer available to the rest of the world. In that document you could vent, practice single syllables with Old English origins, and describe your opponent, the judge, co-counsel, or even your client any way wrath takes. It was said, it was written down, it was off the lawyer's chest, and then it was thrown away. The lawyer took a deep breath and wrote what the professional should write. No one was the wiser.

But in a digital world, there are a whole lot of risks. If the "paper" the lawyer vents on is the rough draft and that language was deleted, the deletions can still be there. If the "paper" was an e-mail and "Reply All" was struck instead of Delete, that simple stroke of the Send button will turn the smoking vent into a raging fire that consumes a lot, including maybe your license.

Hidden columns in spreadsheets can be trouble as well.

> The story goes that someone in personnel sent a spreadsheet with every employee's telephone and e-mail address. The problem was that there were hidden columns with other information, such as wages, bonuses, and the like. They were "hidden" only to those inept at working in Excel.

> If you do not know what a hidden column is, understand it. Generally, when you look at a spreadsheet, the letters of the columns go across in alphabetical order. If there is a gap, and the letters go A B C H I, for example, there are hidden columns. If you must have them, make them unavailable, not just hidden.

There is other metadata within documents. Depending on the native program and options chosen, the document can also show the source of the document, when and by whom it was reviewed, and when it was reviewed or saved. Different contexts mean different results if it is disclosed.

Documents have histories that can substantiate (or not) what you claim in terms of timing.

The hidden metadata can tell when a document is created. When timing is a key issue, the hidden data regarding the document's history can be very telling as to what was done and when.

> Finally, there is the document known as 5560, which is a "feature sheet" dated December 4, 1997. (Ex. 1059.) Armament presented this document as the most detailed 1997 document corroborating a June conception date, and Parsons testified that he created the sheet for a December 4, 1997, meeting with his patent counsel, Brad Hulbert. Defendants have expended considerable effort in an attempt to show that this document is a fraud. Computer searches and meta-data analyses have shown that the only discernible creation date on the document is March 21, 2000. There is, in other words, no digital record of the document having been created in 1997.[12]

This also goes for claims to the court for attorney's fees. Electronic documents that are dated contemporaneous with the event are more believable than a spreadsheet that was dated just before the motion and attached to equally dated support documents.

Don't operate a paperless office when under the influence of drink or drugs.

The digital or paperless office speeds up everything you do. Though many systems and programs have cross-checks for errors, from spell check to making sure you do not delete the wrong file, all of these can be overwritten by human intervention. There is nothing that checks to see if the human choice is correct. An authorized but even slightly inebriated operator brings serious risks to the operation of a computer for which there is little protection. It puts the practice at risk.

This admonition is not confined to illegal use of drugs but to legitimate use as well. A lawyer recovering from surgery and taking pain-killers, for example, needs to be especially careful, and watched. And generally being drunk at home or at the office is not illegal.

In the pen-on-pad writing world, a lawyer who is "buzzed" could draft a garbled memorandum. Under that scenario, that nonsensical brief had to pass through a secretary and possibly a paralegal or even another attorney before anyone else saw it. They provided a bulwark against it going anywhere. It is wadded up and thrown away, never to be seen. Today, the impaired lawyer can draft nonsense, libelous comments, or contradictory arguments extremely efficiently and disseminate them to the entire world in seconds, and no one stands in the way. And those comments are forever readable.

There are those who, in an incoherent state, do lousy, hurtful, and hateful things. Others are just plain silly, though the consequences can be almost as bad. It is not just doing lawyerly stuff amazingly badly; a lawyer in less than a full and sober state of mind can harm his clients and his practice.

Here are some of the mistakes that were revealed by individuals who admitted being drunk when they did them:

- Deleted files that should not have been deleted;
- Sent a mean-spirited or derogatory e-mail;
- Changed passwords to key sites and forgot the new passwords;
- Saved files in a strange and forgotten place;
- Removed all of the programs from the computer; and
- Formatted the disk.

LAWYERS ARE OBLIGATED TO PRESERVE DIGITAL FILES AS THEY WOULD PAPER DOCUMENTS.

When you can carry a warehouse full of file cabinets around in your briefcase, it is easy to forget how much material is there and what it means. Though those files fill less than a few cubic inches, you have the same obligation to store and keep them as if they were paper. That means protecting them against fire, storm, and theft. Protection of data can include the metadata embedded in the native file.

Sitting on a high bar stool sipping a mocha latte and working on a laptop while listening to music on your MP3 player can feel great. But just because portability allows you to work in such a place does not mean it is the best thing to do. It is not just the risk that the drink will be spilled onto the laptop and fry the keyboard, there are other risks as well. Cell phone conversations can be overheard, your computer screen seen, and if you are not using a secured broadband, password and e-mail information stolen.

> One great place to see what other attorneys are doing is on airplanes. For three hours you can read briefs and other documents the attorney is reading or writing by just looking at the screen she is so proudly displaying in front of you.

The lawyer shall be ever vigilant and recognize the source of
all risks to the lawyer's and the client's information and its confidentiality.

The ease of capturing, storing, maintaining, retrieving, and using
information makes it easy to ignore the most basic question: Should
you save the information in the first place?

Notes

1. ABA MODEL RULE 1.6.
2. ABA Standing Comm. on Ethics and Prof'l Responsibility, Formal Op. No. 99-413.
3. *See, e.g.*, State Bar of Cal.'s Proposed Formal Op. Interim 08-0002.
4. Monica Hesse, *Weiner and the modern e-ffair*, WASH. POST, June 7, 2011, *available at* http://www.washingtonpost.com/lifestyle/style/weiner-and-the-modern-e-ffair/2011/06/07/AGnnjPLH_story.html (last visited Oct. 10, 2011).
5. Scott Glover, *Ninth Circuit's chief judge posted sexually explicit matter on his website*, L.A. TIMES, June 11, 2008, *available at* http://www.latimes.com/news/local/la-me-kozinski12-2008jun12,0,6220192.story (last visited Oct. 10, 2011).
6. Mattingly v. Hughes Elecs. Corp., 147 Md. App. 624, 810 A.2d 498, Nov. 4, 2002.
7. Graves v. Deutsche Bank Securities, Inc., 2011 U.S. Dist. LEXIS 27336, March 4, 2011.
8. U.S.C.S. FED. R. CIV. P. R. 6(b)(2).
9. Ohio Sup. Ct. Prac. 2.2(A)(b).
10. AZ Holding, L.L.C. v. Frederick, 2009 U.S. Dist. LEXIS 110546.
11. Farber v. Bobear, 56 So. 3d 1061, 2011 La. App. LEXIS 40 (La. App. 4th Cir. 2011).
12. Armament Systems & Procedures, Inc. v. IQ Hong Kong, *not reported* in F. Supp. 2d, 2007 WL 2154237, E.D. Wis., July 24, 2007.

CHAPTER 19

MAINTAINING SANITY IN THE STATE OF PAPERLESSNESS

In the practice of law, both in the State of Paperlessness and outside, a darkness looms, pulling many lawyers into its prison of frustration, lack of self-confidence, anger, and self-abandonment. It is a darkness found throughout the population, lawyer and non-lawyer alike, but it has a particularly strong presence among highly educated professionals in the legal field. It dims or turns out the light in the lawyer's life. The light that made her want to be an attorney, the light that guided her to represent her clients, the light that came from her community, her family and herself, dims and darkens. Different lawyers experience it differently. For some it is a dullness or dimness; for others it is almost total darkness. For some it is a gloomy and lonely ride along a muddy river in a dark fog that leads to nowhere special; for others it is a bumpy ride leading to calamity for the lawyer, her practice, those she loves or those who love her. For some it results in death. Male lawyers commit suicide at twice the rate of the general population.[1] This career, family, and life destroyer has a name: depression.

Depression affects lots of lawyers. In a CLE seminar, pick any four lawyers. Odds are that of those four lawyers, one suffers from depression. In the typical courtroom with several lawyers and a judge, statistically one of them could be suffering from depression.[2]

Long before computers existed or even the potential of a State of Paperlessness, lawyers suffered from depression. Some move along seemingly unscathed. Others experience the disease and its destructive results publicly. The difference is more luck than anything, but the lucky ones are those who have the support and concern of staff and colleagues around them to help them avoid the misjudgments that bring them before disciplinary boards, civil lawsuits, criminal charges, or the morgue.

Are you one of those lawyers? Do any of the lawyers in your practice or circle of colleagues fit that pattern? While actual diagnosis requires a professional evaluation, there are many symptoms which suggest that depression is present.

- Do things seem distant? Different people have described this in different ways. Some speak of going through the day as an observer, not feeling anything. Others have a sense of loneliness, even in a crowd. Withdrawing into oneself is natural.
- Is there a preoccupation with death? The individual sees her funeral and contemplates the feelings of others over her death. Or views that death is inevitable and imminent and cares nothing about taking care of herself or her health. To her, it makes no difference.
- Are the moods extreme? Either the individual is overly angry over nothing or unreasonably calm when anger would be appropriate. Boisterous laughing overstates a joke or comment.
- Does the lawyer think or speak of violence to others? This goes beyond saying in an guarded moment that he wishes someone were dead. Instead he dwells upon ways to bring death or destruction to another, enemy or not.
- Does darkness hang over the lawyer? No matter what the season, the event, or the context, the lawyer feels like she is living in a dark fog.
- Do things that originally brought pleasure no longer interest the lawyer? It could be the loss of that love of watching sports, or sexual intimacy with a partner, or shopping, or going to parties, or a number of other interests that are now ignored.
- Feeling of worthlessness. Does the lawyer feel like he has no value to his clients, or the firm, or his family or himself?
- Is the lawyer making poor decisions? Are you watching a great lawyer miss deadlines, fail to file cases, fail to clean up briefs or contracts before submission, or agree to take on terrible cases?
- Has the lawyer just been charged or accused of DUI, contempt of court, domestic violence, or other antisocial behavior?

- Is the lawyer getting too little sleep (restless) or too much (will not get out of bed)? A serious deviation from about eight hours suggests reason for concern.
- Is the lawyer gaining or losing weight without explanation? While disease can explain this, so can depression. A person who has lost interest in life can often lose her appetite. Similarly, a person trying to find pleasure in the midst of misery may seek to satisfy herself by eating and thus weight gain.
- Is the lawyer unduly tearful? This is more than crying at weddings or funerals. It is crying for anything and nothing, like shaving in the morning.
- Does the lawyer ignore his appearance and personal hygiene?

The presence of any one or more of those symptoms suggests the lawyer is suffering from depression. The more symptoms there are and the stronger they are, the greater the probability. Such a person needs to seek help.

WHY IS DEPRESSION SO PREVALENT AMONG LAWYERS?

While research shows a significant increase in depression and depression-related events among lawyers, we still don't know why lawyers are more susceptible. Having some idea can help prevent or mitigate its effects. Those who have studied the problem have come up with some reasons:

- Decisional fatigue. Research is showing that the more decisions a person makes during the day, the greater the impact on his or her ability to think. As the day wears on, decisions become more difficult and sometimes desperate.[3] Lawyers are required to make decisions all the time. Doing this over longer days and for longer periods without rest demands more and more the brain. One of the results is depression.

Practicing in the State of Paperlessness can speed up the work, resulting in more decisions and more work done per day. Continuing at the higher pace for the same length of time in the papered world can result in even greater fatigue.

- The practice of law involves conflict. There is a correlation between emotional defense to assault and resulting depression. Lawyers are actively, almost daily, in assault either as the assaulter or the assaulted. They are assaulted by other attorneys, their clients, judges, colleagues, and family. The brain begins to process information symptomatic of assault differently to protect the person from the impact. The result can be depressive symptoms.
- Depression is "contagious." Symptomatic depressed lawyers and judges inflict venom and dysfunction upon others in the profession, which in some cases brings out depression in those individuals.

> In the State of Paperlessness this becomes even more prevalent, as communication increasingly is via e-mail and not face-to-face. Without having to judge the impact of words, verbal assaults increase in number and intensity.

- The social contact often involves dealing with others who are depressed. With statistics showing one in four lawyers depressed, the odds are that the lawyer is dealing with a depressed person during the course of business. That may include a judge whose manifestation is uncontrollable anger, which in turns spreads the disease throughout the profession. Clients often come to the lawyer in difficult times. Common client issues include death in the family, bankruptcy, foreclosure, criminal charges, or difficult family situations—all of which create situational depression which the lawyer has to confront.
- Lawyers are trained to see the glass less empty—or even no glass. Lawyers are expected to see the "big picture"—to know where things can go wrong and prevent them from happening. Not turning that off can result in seeing what is wrong with life, the family, the job, the house, the career—ever increasing their sense of worthlessness.
- Lawyers push themselves too much. Some lawyers take on the burdens of their clients and the world and shove all they have into the fray, only weakening themselves.
- Lawyers get captivated by interaction with the computer. It does what the lawyer asks, unlike human interaction. It can become a comfort zone. A Pennsylvania lawyer was suspended from the practice because he had a game addiction that kept him from

his work. The court found that he "reacted to the pressures of practice as well as the pressures of a troubled home life by retreating into a world of computer and video games even when he was employed by others."[4]

TREATMENT FOR DEPRESSION

The great news in depression is that in most cases it is easily treated and even cured. Sometimes the treatment is counseling. A recent development in psychotherapy is cognitive behavioral therapy. It places an emphasis on how a person thinks about feeling and doing things. It recognizes that thought patterns can affect how a person responds emotionally and mentally to stimuli. By identifying the underlying thoughts, the person can be retrained to view the situation differently, freeing her from the depression.

Depression can come from many sources. It may be a chemical imbalance in the body or a response to events long in the past. Both of those require professionals to find the cause and prescribe treatment. Even if the reason for the depression can be determined (loss of a loved one, for example), professional treatment can help speed recovery.

The following are other things lawyers can do to lessen the symptoms of depression or avoid them altogether.

- Take a break during the day, and don't push too much too often.

One dreary, rainy Friday afternoon I defended a client in a preliminary injunction hearing in federal court. The opposing counsel arrived late due to delayed flights. Very early his arguments rambled from one unfocused and confused point to another. The judge was a good judge and helped direct with some questions, then thanked the lawyer. Although we won the case, it was more on the merits than his performance, but it certainly did not hurt.

I knew the attorney. I had cases with and against him over the years. I respected his talents. A few weeks later we were talking on the phone on another matter and I asked him how things were going. He nearly broke down as he explained the 80- and 90-hour work weeks piling up one after the other. The day of the hearing, the forced pause by the plane delay and the exhaustion had caught up.

While it sounds great to carry so much, it is really dangerous.

- If you or someone who cares about you thinks depression is an issue, check into special bar association programs. Most state and many local bar associations have "lawyers helping lawyers" programs where you can anonymously talk with individuals trained to spot depression and direct treatment.
- Learn to do nothing. The brain can be overworked. You need to take breaks during the day, weekly breaks, and periodic breaks from work, including breaks from the BlackBerry and the iPad, and to think about nothing.
- Focus on things other than the practice of law to balance mind and spirit. This could be sports, the arts, or religious or charitable activities. Anything other than the strain of making legal decisions.
- Actually seek professional help. Seek professional help when you first suspect you may be depressed. Depending on the seriousness, even the emergency room should be considered.
- Learn to find something good and redeeming in every event or situation. When something is said or written that hurts, interpret it with a more positive spin. Don't dwell on how bad it can be.
- Get plenty of sleep. Sleep deprivation is a serious problem. The stresses of family, social, and work life make the days too short, and the easy answer is to take away from sleep. Symptoms of lack of sleep are constant drowsiness; falling asleep whenever at rest, such as in a plane, car, or a pew in church; always looking for opportunities for naps.
- Have a buddy to talk to. Don't take this journey alone. Friendships developed and nurtured through life become lifesavers during difficult times. Talk through the issues with a friend.
- Step away from the e-mail and iPhone. Actually talk to opposing counsel or your client. Meet them for lunch or coffee. Spend time with your family.

Most important is your ability to develop relationships. One of the greatest joys of practicing law for me has been meeting people and having them get to know me. They add so much to my life. You hear their stories, share their struggles. You find you are not alone, and that other lawyers also have the awful client or a case heard by a difficult judge. It makes a great stew of life. There is some sugar. There is some salt. Both enrich life with delicious flavor. This does not come in an e-mail.

The same goes for clients. Lousy clients sometimes bring fantastic cases, but the really great cases are the ones with great clients, win or lose. Meeting and getting to know the client as a person energizes you; it demands something more for this person. It is not an abstract concept, but is truly being an important and positive part of someone's life. That does not come in an e-mail.

I have long considered myself a very, very lucky man to have literally fallen into the particular focus in my practice because I have the opportunity to meet thousands of wonderful people coast-to-coast and border-to-border. Through that I gain of sense of who people are and where they're going. I have learned how great this country really is because of its people. I've come to celebrate their weddings and the birth of their children. I mourn at their deaths and rejoice in their lives.

Psychologists and psychiatrists have long studied the stunting in life that occurs without human contact. In the State of Paperlessness, much of what people did, digits do today. Fewer people means less human interaction in the practice. It is still there, but it requires greater lawyer effort to find and foster it.

Notes

1. Lawyers with Depression, Depression Statistics in General and in Lawyers, http://www.lawyerswithdepression.com/depressionstatistics.asp (last visited Aug. 31, 2011).

2. *Id.*

3. *Do You Suffer From Decisional Fatigue?* N.Y. TIMES, Aug. 17, 2011, *available at* http://www.nytimes.com/2011/08/21/magazine/do-you-suffer-from-decision-fatigue.html?_r=1 (last visited Aug. 31, 2011), based on JOHN TIERNEY & ROY F. BAUMEISTER, WILLPOWER: REDISCOVERING THE GREATEST HUMAN STRENGTH.

4. Office of Disciplinary Counsel v. Eshelman, 167 D.B. 2009, Pa. S. Ct. 2011.

CHAPTER 20

GROWING PROFESSIONALLY IN THE STATE OF PAPERLESSNESS

Practicing law in the State of Paperlessness is not a destination; it is a path to places not yet experienced. Along that path the lawyer will acquire new skills, find new and better ways to use the technology and equipment, and become a better lawyer.

BEING THE BEST IN THE STATE OF PAPERLESSNESS REQUIRES
CONSTANTLY LOOKING FOR NEW AND BETTER WAYS TO WORK.

Always look for ways to improve performance. Manual taasks provide the easiest place to begin the process. If it can be automated, it probably should be.

> An example is keeping your calendar updated on all the computers you use and your tablet or PDA. Tools such as MobileMe, Google Calendar, and even software with your PDA synchronize automatically. With those tools your calendar is on your tablet, in the cloud, in your Outlook. Most airline, hotel, and other reservation systems give you the option to have a calendar entry automatically prepared. More and more events advertised on the web or in e-mail give you the same opportunity.

CONSTANTLY LOOK FOR NEW TOOLS, NEW WAYS TO USE OLD TOOLS

The practice of law is called a practice because the lawyer is constantly learning new things and more about old things. He uses it over and over again and, through practice, gets better and better. So it is in making the most of the State of Paperlessness.

You should constantly strive to make better use of the tools you have and the benefits of their many built-in features. Understanding what those features are and how they can work is a combination of just trying them out and learning from others who have used them or read about them. Besides the official manuals that software companies provide users, there are many blogs and other websites that constantly discuss different features. They can be a great source to see how these tools work.

- *When new software comes out, check out its benefits.* In particular, look at the comparisons. Odds are that you will find you already have a lot of tools you never used.
- *Take CLE classes on technology.* There are a lot of highly skilled lawyers who understand the tools of the paperless office very well and can explain them clearly. These presentations are by fellow lawyers who have learned how to use the tools to make their practice better and have an opportunity to share those tips with other lawyers. The annual ABA Technology and the Law conference is a great place to see what tools other lawyers are using, visit the booths, and talk with vendors about new and exciting technology.
- *Read new technology articles in general circulation periodicals to see what new tools are available.*
- *Do not be afraid to try to accomplish old tasks in new ways.* Surprise yourself.

CHAPTER 21

RECOGNIZING WHEN YOU HAVE ARRIVED IN THE STATE OF PAPERLESSNESS

You know when you have arrived in the State of Paperlessness when you:

- no longer carry pens and paper as a matter of course;
- have a sense of amazement at the amount of work you completed in a day;
- can leave the office and really leave it behind without lugging books and folders;
- can carry the requirements for a hearing or meeting in the palm of your hand or find it in "the cloud";
- can't remember the last time you wrote on a legal pad;
- haven't looked at a paper case file in months; and,
- in an office supply store, walk past shelf after shelf of stuff used only in the papered world.

I realized it had come together when I drafted a major post-hearing brief. Typically, when finished, I had the ritual of cleaning my desk of the piles of notebooks, exhibit folders, transcripts, highlighted and annotated cases and statutes, pages of notes, and stacks of drafts redlined during previous edits. This time, none of that existed. I closed some windows on my computer and closed a single reference book. The desk was already clean. And what would have been weeks of work with long days took only a few days.

The extremely powerful computers in the world today outdo old computers in massive ways. It is said that more computing power resides in the typical PDA than was used to put astronauts on the moon. Recently a computer has become a "Jeopardy" champ. But with all of this power, they do not have the power to think. They can manipulate data, sort it, and all kinds of things, but they cannot think; you can, and that is what you bring to the mix.

Before the computer and Internet revolution and disruption, the lawyer sat at her desk, listened to the person describe his situation, and wrote notes on a long legal pad. Depending on the complexity of the issue or the attorney's expertise, she might have had to go to the bookcase, pull down a statute or two here and some cases there, read them, and make some notes. There may have been some investigation into facts—a visit to the courthouse to see the cases that had been filed or to where the deeds were filed or to city hall to read the zoning issue. All of that depended on the issue.

Then the two would face off again. In the meantime, the lawyer had thought about the case, weighing the options, the risks, and the rewards. It was not just facts but emotions—sizing up the client for what he could handle in terms of litigation emotionally, physically, and financially.

Now she lays out the issues and the options and gives her advice. She asks questions, seeks clarification, and explains what she hears. The client replies, answers, and corrects through this thinking progress. Together they think and arrive at a solution.

Come forward to the twenty-first century. The same characters fulfill the same role. Notes are taken on an iPad. When questions arise, she turns to the Internet to look at the court docket, examine a record, and look up the law.

Then it is the same as before. She lays out the possible paths and makes sure the client understands. She thinks it through and communicates her thoughts. The client considers those and responds. They think it through and a plan is made.

The scene is now a courtroom. Standing at a table is the lawyer, and beside her sits a frightened woman charged with a crime she did not commit. Her family, in tears and terror, sit a few feet behind.

Across the aisle is another table where a prosecutor with the power of the state sits with a representative of the police or sheriff. In front of both of them sits a powerful judge who is going to make a decision that will decide the direction of this woman's life and her family.

In the old days, the lawyer had books in front of her, papers with notes. Today she has a laptop computer. But what will make the difference is not the paper or the computer but the thinking—the ability to communicate, and the courage to stand up for her client. This courage to argue before a powerful judge against the state's attorney does not come from paper or computers, but from herself.

A paperless lawyer without courage is no lawyer at all.

A paperless lawyer who does not think is not a lawyer.

Being a lawyer means making choices or helping the client make choices, wise ones. Wisdom for these choices comes not just from knowing what displays on the computer or prints out on the paper or shows up in a law book; it comes with experience, principles, goals, foresight, thought, and courage.

Being paperless does not create wisdom.

The pride is not in practicing law in the State of Paperlessness, it is in practicing law with compassion, courage, and wisdom. Those come from the heart of the lawyer—the person, not a computer. The State of Paperlessness simply aids in doing it better.

INDEX